D0536743

IT HAPPENED TO ME

Series Editor: Arlene Hirschfelder

Books in the It Happened to Me series are designed for inquisitive teens digging for answers about certain illnesses, social issues, or lifestyle interests. Whether you are deep into your teen years or just entering them, these books are gold mines of up-to-date information, riveting teen views, and great visuals to help you figure out stuff. Besides special boxes highlighting singular facts, each book is enhanced with the latest reading lists, websites, and an index. Perfect for browsing, there are loads of expert information by acclaimed writers to help parents, guardians, and librarians understand teen illness, tough situations, and lifestyle choices.

1. *Epilepsy: The Ultimate Teen Guide,* by Kathlyn Gay and Sean McGarrahan, 2002.
2. *Stress Relief: The Ultimate Teen Guide,* by Mark Powell, 2002.
3. *Learning Disabilities: The Ultimate Teen Guide,* by Penny Hutchins Paquette and Cheryl Gerson Tuttle, 2003.
4. *Making Sexual Decisions: The Ultimate Teen Guide,* by L. Kris Gowen, 2003.
5. *Asthma: The Ultimate Teen Guide,* by Penny Hutchins Paquette, 2003.
6. *Cultural Diversity—Conflicts and Challenges: The Ultimate Teen Guide,* by Kathlyn Gay, 2003.
7. *Diabetes: The Ultimate Teen Guide,* by Katherine J. Moran, 2004.
8. *When Will I Stop Hurting? Teens, Loss, and Grief: The Ultimate Teen Guide to Dealing with Grief,* by Ed Myers, 2004.
9. *Volunteering: The Ultimate Teen Guide,* by Kathlyn Gay, 2004.
10. *Organ Transplants—A Survival Guide for the Entire Family: The Ultimate Teen Guide,* by Tina P. Schwartz, 2005.
11. *Medications: The Ultimate Teen Guide,* by Cheryl Gerson Tuttle, 2005.
12. *Image and Identity—Becoming the Person You Are: The Ultimate Teen Guide,* by L. Kris Gowen and Molly C. McKenna, 2005.
13. *Apprenticeship: The Ultimate Teen Guide,* by Penny Hutchins Paquette, 2005.
14. *Cystic Fibrosis: The Ultimate Teen Guide,* by Melanie Ann Apel, 2006.
15. *Religion and Spirituality in America: The Ultimate Teen Guide,* by Kathlyn Gay, 2006.
16. *Gender Identity: The Ultimate Teen Guide,* by Cynthia L. Winfield, 2007.

17. *Physical Disabilities: The Ultimate Teen Guide,* by Denise Thornton, 2007.
18. *Money—Getting It, Using It, and Avoiding the Traps: The Ultimate Teen Guide,* by Robin F. Brancato, 2007.
19. *Self-Advocacy: The Ultimate Teen Guide,* by Cheryl Gerson Tuttle and JoAnn Augeri Silva, 2007.
20. *Adopted: The Ultimate Teen Guide,* by Suzanne Buckingham Slade, 2007.
21. *The Military and Teens: The Ultimate Teen Guide,* by Kathlyn Gay, 2008.
22. *Animals and Teens: The Ultimate Teen Guide,* by Gail Green, 2009.
23. *Reaching Your Goals: The Ultimate Teen Guide,* by Anne Courtright, 2009.
24. *Juvenile Arthritis: The Ultimate Teen Guide,* by Kelly Rouba, 2009.
25. *Obsessive-Compulsive Disorder: The Ultimate Teen Guide,* by Natalie Rompella, 2009.
26. *Body Image and Appearance: The Ultimate Teen Guide,* by Kathlyn Gay, 2009.
27. *Writing and Publishing: The Ultimate Teen Guide,* by Tina P. Schwartz, 2010.
28. *Food Choices: The Ultimate Teen Guide,* by Robin F. Brancato, 2010.
29. *Immigration: The Ultimate Teen Guide,* by Tatyana Kleyn, 2011.
30. *Living with Cancer: The Ultimate Teen Guide,* by Denise Thornton, 2011.
31. *Living Green: The Ultimate Teen Guide,* by Kathlyn Gay, 2012.
32. *Social Networking: The Ultimate Teen Guide,* by Jenna Obee, 2012.
33. *Sports: The Ultimate Teen Guide,* by Gail Fay, 2013.
34. *Adopted: The Ultimate Teen Guide, Revised Edition,* by Suzanne Buckingham Slade, 2013.
35. *Bigotry and Intolerance: The Ultimate Teen Guide,* by Kathlyn Gay, 2013.
36. *Substance Abuse: The Ultimate Teen Guide,* by Sheri Bestor, 2013.
37. *LGBTQ Families: The Ultimate Teen Guide,* by Eva Apelqvist, 2013.

LGBTQ FAMILIES

THE ULTIMATE TEEN GUIDE

EVA APELQVIST

IT HAPPENED TO ME, NO. 37

THE SCARECROW PRESS, INC.
Lanham • Toronto • Plymouth, UK
2013

Published by Scarecrow Press, Inc.
A wholly owned subsidiary of The Rowman & Littlefield Publishing Group, Inc.
4501 Forbes Boulevard, Suite 200, Lanham, Maryland 20706
www.rowman.com

10 Thornbury Road, Plymouth PL6 7PP, United Kingdom

British Library Cataloguing in Publication Information Available

Library of Congress Cataloging-in-Publication Data

Apelqvist, Eva.
  LGBTQ families : the ultimate teen guide / Eva Apelqvist.
    pages cm. — (It happened to me ; 37)
  Includes bibliographical references and index.
  ISBN 978-0-8108-8536-3 (cloth : alk. paper) — ISBN 978-0-8108-8537-0 (ebook)
  1. Gays—Family relationships—Juvenile literature. 2. Sexual minorities—Family
relationships—Juvenile literature. 3. Children of gay parents—Juvenile literature.
  4. Families—Juvenile literature. I. Title.
  HQ76.25.A64 2013
  306.874086'64—dc23   2013015488

♾™ The paper used in this publication meets the minimum requirements of American
National Standard for Information Sciences—Permanence of Paper for Printed Library
Materials, ANSI/NISO Z39.48-1992. Printed in the United States of America.

Contents

Introduction   vii

1 What Is a Family?   1
2 The Kids Are All Right   19
3 The *T* in LGBTQ: A Discussion about Sex and Gender   39
4 Love and Marriage . . . Amendments   57
5 Other Legal Issues   69
6 Bullying   83
7 Media, Popular Culture, and LGBTQ Families   99
8 Religion, Politics, and Corporations   115
9 Activism   135
10 It's a Small World after All   153
11 Celebrating Family and Community   169

Glossary: Words Matter   183
Resources   187
Index   195
About the Author   199

Introduction

As a young professional in Santa Barbara, California, I worked in an office where gay jokes were the norm. Not wanting to be a wet blanket, I usually ignored them. But one day when I was feeling crabby and exhausted, my boss told a particularly tasteless gay joke in a big meeting and I snapped. I told her that my best friend was a lesbian and that I found these jokes insulting (killing any dreams of a promotion for the next one hundred years or so). After an awkward silence and a bit of hemming and hawing, the meeting went on. Later, during a break, I found myself in a bathroom stall next to a coworker. Timidly she whispered from the stall next to mine, "Thank you. I'm gay."

This event became an important reminder to me that we should not wait to speak up until we can no longer stand it, but do it when we first meet with injustice and offensive behavior. When I was presented with the opportunity to write this book, it became a chance for me to reevaluate my role as a straight ally and better learn where I fit into the LGBTQ (lesbian, gay, bisexual, transgender/transsexual, and queer) rights movement. I will allow the book to answer this question.

Even though injustice is a red thread throughout the pages, as it must be at this time in history, this book is not primarily about injustice—it is about what it's like to have LGBTQ parents. And here I encountered my first conundrum—the difficulty of keeping issues relevant to children with LGBTQ parents separate from those of the parents themselves and other LGBTQ persons. The more research I did for this book, the more I realized what should have been obvious from the very start—that children with LGBTQ parents are affected by *all* issues LGBTQ. Any injustice and prejudice shown toward the parents affect the children. All laws that exclude LGBTQ persons from rights other people have also affect their children and partners. Therefore, I have allowed the book to stray where it must. When I explore bullying in schools, for example, I look not only at the children of LGBTQ persons being harassed, but also at young LGBTQ persons themselves and what the schools are doing or not doing to protect these children and young adults.

My next conundrum had to do with words. When it comes to words, LGBTQ issues are a fast growing wilderness constantly expanding and changing. After thoroughly researching LGBTQ-friendly vocabulary, I have tried to be as "correct" as possible, but the truth is there is no *one* right way. LGBTQ persons refer to themselves in many different ways and identify with various subgroups too numerous to mention. Even words that seem obvious, such as the definition of *gender* and *sex* and *sexuality* and *sexual orientation* are up for grabs. My intent here has been to introduce this exciting, evolving vocabulary and hope that my readers come away with an open mind and a sensitivity to people's right to self-determine what they want to be called.

As I propose in this book that we adopt a more flexible view on sex, sexuality, and gender, I also propose, in exploring LGBTQ issues in other countries, that we transcend international borders when considering our human family and that we extend our concern and our curiosity to all those sharing this earth.

Lastly, the absurdity of this book is not lost on me. When conducting interviews, I heard myself asking questions like, "What is it like to grow up with a gay dad?" It seems like a deeply irrelevant question, like "What is it like to grow up with a blue-eyed mother?" Or rather, it *should* be an irrelevant question, but it isn't. Blue-eyed people are not under attack but LGBTQ persons are, which is one of the main reasons why it is relevant to know what it is like to grow up with a gay dad. In a perfect world, this book would not be needed. And it is my hope that it will soon be dated and that the topic of LGBTQ will become boring and mainstream.

My interviews with LGBTQ persons and children and grandchildren of LGBTQ persons have been sprinkled throughout the book in no particular order. It is my hope that my readers will be as intrigued with these interesting, insightful, and brave families as I am.

1

WHAT IS A FAMILY?

In August 2011, David Gregory, the host of NBC's *Meet the Press*, interviewed a smiling, well-groomed woman on his show. He asked her if she believed that a gay couple with adopted children could be called a family. The woman hemmed and hawed, then she said, "You know, all of these kinds of questions really aren't about what people are concerned about right now [*sic*]."[1]

Gregory's interview would probably not have drawn much attention were it not for the fact that his interview subject was Minnesota Congresswoman Michele Bachmann. At the time, Bachmann was a Republican contender for the presidency and had long insisted that gay marriage was indeed a defining issue for the presidential campaign, so her dismissing comment claiming that this was not important was strange indeed.

LGBTQ persons and their families are slowly becoming more visible in our society—more mainstream. However, the interview with Bachmann indicates that not everybody agrees on what it means to be a family.

According to *Merriam-Webster's Collegiate Dictionary* a family is "a group of individuals living under one roof" and "the basic unit in society traditionally consisting of two parents rearing their children; *also* any of various social units differing from but regarded as equivalent to the traditional family." And to make sure we leave no gray areas, here is a definition for the word *group*, also from *Merriam-Webster's*: "two or more figures forming a complete unit in a composition."[2]

Sex and Gender

While the words *sex* and *gender* tend to be used in a very similar way, there is actually an important linguistic difference between the two. *Sex* is a biological term and refers to the physical and hormonal characteristics that make us male or female. *Gender* is a sociological term that refers to the degree to which we express femininity or masculinity.

Any two or more individuals living under one roof and choosing to see themselves as a family *are* a family.

By definition the word *family* has nothing to do with sexual orientation, sex, or gender. In fact, it contains a whole world of possibilities. More and more people are starting to embrace the idea that any two or more individuals living under one roof and choosing to see themselves as a family *are* a family.

The reason why this dictionary exploration is necessary is that the teens and adults interviewed for this book—perhaps from a family like yours—have families that are often not included in our common definition of family. They are also often refused the legal rights and social status that other families take for granted and are often the victims of harassment, prejudice, and discrimination, simply because of how we, in society, have chosen to define family.

Abbie E. Goldberg, author of *Lesbian and Gay Parents and Their Children*, describes family in the following way in her book: "Family is not a static institution but one that is constantly being reworked, reshaped, reimagined, and reenacted in complex and dynamic ways." Goldberg feels that families with LGBTQ parents should not just be accepted, but recognized for being beneficial for the rest of society in that they help challenge stale assumptions about family—for example, that marriages should be heterosexual and patriarchal. Being faced with this new way of looking at life forces us to stretch and create new healthy approaches to family, Goldberg believes. And the fact that LGBTQ parents are often not biologically related to their children makes them more prone to finding creative means to challenging traditions and norms, something that Goldberg feels we can all learn from.[3]

According to Goldberg, one important thing to keep in mind when discussing specific research findings regarding LGBTQ families is that many families are closeted. This, she believes, might be especially true for minorities, people living in geographically remote areas, and transgender persons.

Goldberg's caution about a slanted research base was very much evident in the group of people interviewed for this book. While the interview subjects came from varied socioeconomic backgrounds, had different sexual orientation, and had varying degrees of gender conformance, most came from white, upper-middle-class families in larger metropolitan, LGBTQ-friendly communities. So it is important to keep in mind that these teens and adults who chose to speak about their families tend to represent a certain privileged subgroup of LGBTQ families. Together with other research findings, however, these voices add an important dimension to the book. And even though these families tend to live in LGBTQ-friendly communities, they are still struggling with many of the issues related to society's prejudice against their families.

As in Goldberg's book, in order to add retrospection and a perspective of maturity, not only teens but also adults were interviewed.

A Few Words about Trans

While the concept of family should be an inclusive one, the idea of lumping very different groups of people together in one initialism, such as LGBTQ, is worth thinking about. These different groups of people might not even be dealing with the same issues and might prefer to be viewed as separate entities.

Casey's Family

Casey, who was seventeen at the time of the 2012 interview, grew up in Ohio. In her high school all juniors had to give a speech to the entire high school about something close at heart. Casey's speech was about growing up with two moms. This is how Casey began her speech:

You know those stickers, the ones usually on minivans? I'm sure you do—with the mom, the dad, Johnny and Suzy and Spot, the dog? Whether you think they're kind of cute or kind of creepy, you have to admit, they say a lot about how we picture family.

The back of my family's car has never featured cartoon versions of each of us. I mean, people would be really confused. Why are there three cartoon chicks on the back of that PT Cruiser? The answer: my moms. I have two, no dad, just two moms. One I call Kima, which means "Spirit Mother." Kima is the non-biological mom, the proverbial other mother. The one I call "Mom" is my mother by blood.[4]

Casey had two moms from the time she was born and has never known any other way of being a family. As a young child she didn't think much about it. Her friends never wondered or commented . . . until second grade. That seemed to be the year when everybody suddenly started noticing that Casey's family was different, she said. And being right at that age when kids are struggling with understanding the basic facts of life, such as reproduction, some kids had a particularly difficult time understanding Casey's family.

"There was this one little boy Kyle," Casey said. "He actually became my friend later. But he was really preoccupied with how I could exist. And even though I knew that I had a dad, who wasn't really my dad, just a sperm donor, I wasn't very good at articulating it at that point."

For a few years, things did not get much more complicated for Casey than her inability to articulate how she came to be (and how many second graders with heterosexual parents know how they were conceived?). But a few years later, something disturbing happened. In her high school speech and again during our interview, Casey told the story of going to leadership camp at the age of eleven. Casey was really excited to hang out with the other kids at camp, especially one particularly cool kid named Clay, a true leader it seemed, warm and accepting. Casey felt safe and happy with the kids in the group until one day when the leader left the room and the conversation landed on gay and lesbian issues. Out of the blue, Clay, ever the leader, stated that if he had a son and he found out that his son was gay, he would never talk to him again. From there the conversation escalated. Casey didn't know what to do. She was bewildered and felt horrible. It seemed to her as though most of the kids in the room agreed with Clay, that being gay was definitely not okay.

"The environment I had felt so comfortable in, so happy in, had become a mess of toxicity," Casey said in her high school speech. "The people who had previously been so welcoming to me would never be willing to come to terms with the thing most vital to my existence—my family."

After that incident, Casey began lying about her family. When people asked what her dad did, she told them that he was a therapist and that her mom was a psychologist, then added that they were in practice together. It made her feel horrible to refer to her Kima as her "dad," but the alternative, to have people say hateful things about her family, was worse.

Still, Casey considers herself lucky. She went to a private school with a zero tolerance policy when it comes to bullying. "If someone bullies, they're out of there," she said. All of her friends were accepting of her family. In fact, for her junior year speech they had been told to write about something deeply personal, and Casey's friends wondered if Casey wasn't taking the easy way out writing about her family. "You can't just write about your parents," they told her. "That's so boring." Secretly, Casey was pleased with her friends' reaction. It told her that they were so used to her having two moms that it was a boring topic to them.

Growing up, Casey and her moms belonged to a supportive church, where all people and families were affirmed, she said, no matter their constellation. Casey also knew many other kids with same-sex parents. "My parents were set on me being best friends with other kids with two moms. I can easily think of nine people from my childhood who were in the same situation," she said.

Despite having an excellent support system with her friends, her church, and her school, and despite living in an accepting community and having learned to be proud of her family and who she is, Casey said that to this day she isn't necessarily quick to share information about her moms with people she doesn't know well. It is more difficult with new people, before she knows them, she said. "I tend not to say anything to people in places like camp. It just complicates things."

A junior in high school at the time of the interview, Casey pursued many other interests. Between taking her ACTs and SATs and visiting colleges, among other things, she also played field hockey and took voice lessons. For her personal speech at school, she might have talked about a number of things that had nothing to do with being the daughter of two moms. She might have, for example, discussed going to a private school where she felt like she belonged to an entirely different socioeconomic class from most of her schoolmates. Sometimes it bothered her to park next to a Mercedes convertible in the school parking lot, she said. But mostly she was happy to be able to attend a good school because the public schools in her area were not that good. So while having two moms is far from the only thing that makes Casey who she is today, she feels that it has defined her in a number of ways. "Not necessarily because I want it to be that way," she said. "But it puts me in a certain social group. It may not be the first thing that defines me, but it's pretty high on my list and I'm fine with that."

Then there's the often-brought-up topic of not having a dad. Whenever there is a discussion about having two moms, Casey said, it comes up. In her school speech Casey said that as a young child, she was sometimes jealous of kids who had a dad and felt she was missing out. She wanted one too. When she got older and more content with her own family, however, this was no longer an issue, though she is still curious about her sperm donor, the man responsible for half her DNA. All Casey knew about him was that he was tall and blond and lived in California. Casey said that as soon as she turned eighteen and it would be legal, she planned to, maybe even for her senior project, find him and any potential half siblings she might have. You're allowed to donate enough sperm for twenty children, she said, which means she could potentially have nineteen half siblings. She would like to make a documentary about finding her half siblings.

While Casey very much wanted to know her own genetic makeup in order to learn more about herself, she has long since stopped wishing for a dad. "Now I realize how great it is to just have two parents who love each other," she said.[5]

L Is for *Lesbian*

As we have already seen, it is virtually impossible to discuss LGBTQ issues without struggling with word choices. For example, when you rattle off the puzzling group of letters—LGBTQ—people raise their eyebrows. "Huh?" Some people even refer to this word conundrum as alphabet soup.

Let's first clarify the words that make up the long and cumbersome initialism LGBTQ while keeping in mind that these definitions are very fluid and often vary from user to user:

L is for *lesbian*—Lesbian can be used as a noun to refer to a woman who feels same-sex attraction toward other women. It can also be used as an adjective to refer to that same-sex attraction.

G is for *gay*—Gay is usually used as an adjective and may be used to describe a homosexual male. The word *gay*, perhaps even more than the word lesbian, is also sometimes used in a derogatory manner and has seen something of a comeback lately, especially in schools where students sometimes describe things that are not cool as "so gay." This, of course, can be particularly hurtful to students with gay parents and students who identify as LGBTQ themselves. The word *gay* is also sometimes used to refer to any LGBTQ person, both by people in general and by the LGBTQ community itself.

B is for *bisexual*—This word is mostly used as an adjective (though sometimes as a noun) to describe the sexual orientation of someone with sexual and emotional attractions toward both males and females. Bisexual persons may also refer to themselves as bi, pansexual (meaning they are attracted to someone regardless of gender), omnisexual, or polysexual.[6]

T is for *trans* (transgender or transsexual)—Transgender sometimes refers to a person whose self-identified gender does not match the sex assigned at birth. According to *Merriam-Webster's* this means "having personal characteristics . . . that transcend traditional gender boundaries and corresponding sexual norms." Transsexual on the other hand, usually refers to someone who strongly identifies as the opposite sex from the one assigned to them and often undergoes surgery and/or hormone therapy in order to look and act more like that sex. Transsexual persons may not consider themselves a part of the LGBTQ umbrella at all. They might simple identify as their new gender: male or female. It should be added here that the issue of trans is too complicated to explain in a few short paragraphs. It deserves our attention, however, because many people see themselves on a spectrum, not all male and not all female, and sometimes neither, and in order for us to understand this issue, it might mean that we have to abandon some of our black-and-white thinking. (Chapter 3 treats the issue of trans in more depth.)

Q is for either *queer* or *questioning*—Questioning is an adjective used to describe someone who is unsure of or exploring his or her sexual orientation and/or gender identity.

Sometimes, perhaps more often in the younger generation, Q stands for *queer*. Queer can be defined in several ways: "a) attracted to people of many genders; b) self-identity label for people who feel they do not fit cultural sexual orientation and/or gender identity norms; c) sometimes used as an umbrella term for all people with non-heterosexual sexual orientations; d) historically, a pejorative term—its use today is met with disfavor by some and worn proudly by others."[7] *Merriam-Webster's* usage note to the word *queer* is interesting enough to put it here almost in its entirety: "Over the past two decades, an important change has occurred in the use of queer. . . . The older, strongly pejorative use has certainly not vanished, but a use by some gay people and some academics as a neutral or even positive term has established itself. This development is most noticeable in the adjective but is reflected in the corresponding noun as well.

The newer use is sometimes taken to be offensive, esp. by older gay men who fostered the acceptance of *gay* in these uses and still have a strong preference for it."[8]

So, while it is worth keeping in mind that the term *queer* might indeed be hurtful to people who have, for example, been the victims of bullies using that term, and that far from all LGBTQ persons consider themselves queer, a large part of the LGBTQ population uses the word *queer* more and more, especially the younger generation. Children of LGBTQ parents can now be seen proudly wearing T-shirts referring to themselves as Queer Spawn.

Sometimes the letter *I* is added to the initialism (LGBTQI), referring to the word *intersex*, meaning a person who might have (sometimes underdeveloped) both male and female genitalia. The word *intersex* is preferred to the old word *hermaphrodite*, which intersex persons consider dated and offensive.

Another letter combination sometimes used is LGBTQIDK, where the last three letters simply refers to "I don't know" and like the Q in questioning intends to cover people not sure of their sexual orientation or gender but also future groups and identities not currently covered.

A comment to an article about LGBTQ-friendly symbols on *PrideSource*, a Michigan-based LGBT-focused online magazine, well illustrates the confusion with the labeling. A bewildered "Charles" wrote,

> This may be a bit off topic, but it strikes me as odd that people would find the rainbow flag passé but readily accept the awkward label 'LGBT.' I suppose it's a tad better than some earlier versions that were thrown around in the early to mid-90s (like L.G.B.T.T.S.—i.e. Lesbian Gay Bisexual Transgender Two Spirit). I just think it's too broad a spectrum of sexual identities to be forced together in one breath, and it is also, IMHO, ridiculously oppressively PC. Queer is probably the closest thing to a word applicable to all of the communities covered under LGBT, but I realize that's a problematic term for many. Any suggestions?[9]

No suggestions were made following Charles's comments, though his sentiment is echoed all over the Web where many feel it is problematic to refer to such diverse groups of people with one long cumbersome string of letters.

Transgender and transsexual, for example, have nothing to do with sexual orientation (transgender and transsexual persons may identify as heterosexual, gay, lesbian, or other). Yet, Goldberg writes in her book *Lesbian and Gay Parents and Their Children* that she believes it makes a lot of sense to include trans persons when discussing issues concerning sexual minorities. According to Goldberg, trans persons (and families with a trans parent) tend to be just as marginalized and stigmatized—some will argue even more—and face many of the same challenges that families with gay, lesbian, and bisexual parents do.[10]

A Few Words about Bisexual

While transgender and transsexual persons probably get the brunt of discrimination in the LGBTQ community because they might be visibly different, bisexual individuals are certainly among the most misunderstood. As we do with sex and gender—expect things to be either female or male, feminine or masculine—we do with sexuality: we expect people to be either homosexual or heterosexual. But in an article on the National Gay and Lesbian Task Force website, Director Sean Cahill explains bisexuality in a way that is easy to understand. Bisexual persons, Cahill says, "describe themselves as being emotionally, sexually and/or romantically attracted to both women and men and feel capable of loving and forming relationships with either. To most bisexuals, the gender of the person they find attractive is substantially less important than who the person is."[11]

Cahill also shows research indicating that people's sexuality is much more fluid than how we usually perceive it. In a study quoted on the website, 2.3 percent of men and 1.3 percent of women age 18–44 said that they identified as homosexual; 1.8 percent of the men and 2.8 percent of women in the study identified as bisexual; and a full 3.9 percent of men and 3.8 percent of women identified as "other." But, significantly, a much larger percentage of both men and women answered yes to the question of whether they were attracted to both genders—12.9 percent of the women and 5.9 percent of the men.[12]

Contrary to what people tend to believe, bisexuality has nothing to do with promiscuity. Being bisexual only means that you are attracted to people of both sexes. It has nothing to do with "past or current sexual activity."[13]

Thus, bisexual persons might be married to an opposite-sex partner, in which case they have no legal obstacles regarding marriage or other issues as described in this book. Or, a bisexual person may be in a relationship with a same-sex partner, in which case they have all the same legal obstacles that the gay and lesbian population has.

Being Defined by Your Family

In this book, families with one or more lesbian, gay, bisexual, transgender, or questioning/queer parent are sometimes referred to as LGBTQ families. It is worth noting, however, that families with heterosexual parents are not usually referred to as heterosexual families. In most contexts, unless someone chooses this label for him- or herself, sexual orientation or gender identification should not be the way a family is defined from the outside looking in.

Zach Wahls, the young man who became famous when he spoke passionately in support of gay marriage in the Iowa House of Representatives in 2011, talks in his book *My Two Moms* about not allowing the fact that you have LGBTQ parents to define you, or at least not letting it be the only thing that defines you. Having two moms, Wahls indicates in his book, is pretty far down the list of things that most defines who he is today. He is also an Eagle Scout, a college student, the son of a woman who struggles with muscular dystrophy, a devout Unitarian Universalist, and an obviously accomplished writer and public speaker.

Wahls also rejects the stereotyping trap that he often encounters when being introduced as someone from an LGBTQ family. "I might be like the kid with two moms," he wrote in his book. "But not all kids with two moms are like me."[14]

Monica Canfield-Lenfest, a daughter of a trans woman, says in her *Kids of Trans Resource Guide*, published by People with Lesbian, Gay, Bisexual, or Transgender Parents (COLAGE), that she struggles with the fact that having a trans parent infringes on her identity. "Everything about you is not determined exclusively by them," she writes, referring to her parent. "You will continue to learn, grow, and develop your own identity. While people may be really focused on your parent's identity, you can remind them that you are your own person, an individual with a unique set of experiences and interests."[15]

Kaley, age twenty-one, however, has a slightly different point of view. Kaley feels that growing up with two moms had indeed defined her, and she embraces how it has influenced her and the direction her background has given her life. Working toward a women, gender, and sexuality studies major in college, Kaley said that while she isn't particularly religious, "I feel blessed to have grown up with two moms. I have gotten a completely different view of the world by growing up in a marginalized community. I love my moms so much and I'm so grateful they adopted me. I am sure I would never have had the same opportunities [had I not grown up with two moms]. Even the essays I write now [in college] include my moms."[16]

Regardless of family constellation, all people are, of course, complex human beings with endless defining characteristics, something that is good to remember.

Then and Now—a Short LGBTQ History Lesson

"I don't know where it all came from. It probably started a couple of thousand years ago when it was decided that being gay was not okay," said Thomas, age fourteen.[17]

Perhaps Thomas is right. What we do know is that homosexuality, just like heterosexuality, dates back as far as mankind and is referred to in the very first human cave depictions and later, in the first human writing. A history of more recent developments regarding LGBTQ persons and their families, however, might begin with, rather randomly (though definitely an important event), the Stonewall riots in New York in June of 1969. On that day, instead of allowing themselves to be arrested or quietly slipping into the night, LGBTQ persons of all walks of life began fighting back when police raided the bar, the Stonewall Inn, in New York City, where many LGBTQ persons liked to congregate.

During the raid, the police, while looking for violations of alcohol laws, used homophobic slurs on bar patrons (though the word *homophobia* was not yet used at that time) and attempted to arrest several men dressed as women—something that was illegal in New York at that time. The bar patrons fought back, riots broke out, and the incident marked a beginning of sorts in the LGBTQ movement, stating to the rest of the world that LGBTQ persons would no longer allow themselves to be abused and trampled. One of the people interviewed in the PBS documentary *Stonewall Uprising* said that watching other people refuse to get arrested was revelatory and new to him. "I'm not alone," he thought. "There are other people that feel exactly the same way." Another man interviewed said, "This was the Rosa Parks moment, when the gay people stood up and said no."[18]

In 1972 something else happened to throw fuel on the LGBTQ rights fire. A young gay man, Morty Manford, was badly beaten at a gay protest rally and the police stood silently watching. Manford's mother, Jeanne Manford, wrote a letter to the editor in the *New York Post* after the incident, publicly affirming her love for her gay son. Nothing revolutionary there, it seems, but at the time Manford's letter stirred up quite the controversy, which led to a number of speaking engagements for her, as well as appearances on television and radio shows. But the most important thing to come out of all this was that Manford became the cofounder of what is now Parents, Families and Friends of Lesbians and Gays (PFLAG), one of the most well-known and widespread organizations in support of LGBTQ persons in this country.[19]

Even the briefest of LGBTQ history requires mentioning Dr. Robert Spitzer, whose formerly serious reputation took a nosedive somewhere in the early days of the new millennium.

What Dr. Spitzer was first known for, and what gained him respect in 1974 among colleagues as well as in the LGBTQ community, was changing the American Psychiatric Association's (APA) holy script, *Diagnostic and Statistical Manual of Mental Disorders* (*DSM*), removing homosexuality from its list of mental disorders. In the manual, homosexuality had earlier been referred to as a "sociopathic personality disturbance." Spitzer accomplished this feat after having discussions with protesters who were becoming more active after the Stonewall riots. This change in the manual was a major victory for the LGBTQ community.[20]

In 1999, however, Spitzer was approached by ex-gay protesters; that is, people who had gone through "treatment" for being gay and now considered themselves "cured." Through these conversations, Dr. Spitzer became interested in learning whether a person could change his or her sexual orientation. He gathered some interview subjects from the ex-gay movement and conducted interviews with them. He fairly quickly concluded that "the majority of participants gave reports of change from a predominantly or exclusively homosexual orientation before therapy to a predominantly or exclusively heterosexual orientation in the past year."[21]

From Spitzer's previous work with the APA manual he had gained much respect, and his research therefore seemed unbiased. People felt that he should be taken seriously. Now, many years later, however, Spitzer himself admits that his study was seriously flawed. In conducting his study he simply asked people if they had changed their sexual orientation and then accepted their answers as the truth. He did not factor in, for example, that people sometimes lie, both to others and to themselves, and that just because somebody says something that doesn't necessarily make it true. In addition, the study never went through the scrutiny of the customary peer-review process that academic papers usually have to undergo. "Dr. Spitzer in no way implied in the study that being gay was a choice, or that it was possible for anyone who wanted to change to do so in therapy. But that didn't stop socially conservative groups from citing the paper in support of just those points," a 2012 *New York Times* article said.[22]

Dr. Spitzer had misgivings about his study fairly early, and about having published it, but the straw that broke the camel's back came when he was visited by a man who had undergone "reparative therapy" and had been described as a success story by the ex-gay community because he had been cured of his homosexuality. This man did, in fact, look cured to the rest of the world, but he also entertained thoughts of suicide and suffered a badly damaged self-image. The meeting with the man shook Dr. Spitzer up, and in 2012 he drafted a letter to the *Archives of Sexual Behavior*, the magazine that originally published his 1999 study about reparative therapy and the possibility of curing homosexuality, publicly refuting his earlier findings. He concluded, "I believe I owe the gay community an apology."[23]

It remains to be seen if Spitzer's recantation of his own research will have as positive an effect on LGBTQ issues as his original study had a negative one.

From the Closet to the Courtroom

In his book *From the Closet to the Courtroom: Five LGBT Rights Lawsuits That Have Changed Our Nation*, Carlos A. Ball discusses five major cornerstones of LGBT legal history:

1. *Baehr v. Lewin* (1993) became the first in an ever-increasing string of lawsuits questioning the constitutionality of not allowing same-sex marriages.
2. *Nabozny v. Podlesny* (1996) determined that school officials have a responsibility to protect gay students from bullying.
3. In *Romer v. Evans* (1996) the state of Colorado's attempts at "making it illegal to protect sexual minorities against discrimination based on sexual orientation" was stopped and deemed unconstitutional.
4. *Braschi v. Stahl Associates* (1998) established that two men in a committed relationship can constitute a family.
5. *Lawrence v. Texas* (2003) affirmed the dignity of LGBTQ persons, stating that private and consensual gay sex could not be criminalized by the government.[24]

While all aspects of LGBTQ history are important, the most nagging issue to teens interviewed in this book is the question of why their parents are not allowed to get married. It might also be the issue at the forefront right now that has the most direct consequences for LGBTQ families. (The unique history of same-sex marriage is explored in more depth in chapter 4.)

Maggie Gallagher, president of National Organization for Marriage, an organization that vehemently opposes same-sex marriage, has long blamed Europe for influencing the United States in promoting gay rights—and same-sex marriage in particular. Gallagher might be right in this. In 2012, at the time of this writing, only eleven countries in the world had legalized gay marriage, eight of them European. (See chapter 4 for a complete list of countries, and states in this country, with legalized same-sex marriage.)

Another event in recent LGBTQ history worth mentioning is the creation in the 1990s of COLAGE. It is, among many other feats, the publishers of the Kids of Trans guide. COLAGE is, according to its website, "a national movement of children, youth, and adults with one or more lesbian, gay, bisexual, transgender and/or queer (LGBTQ) parent/s. We build community and work toward social justice through youth empowerment, leadership development, education, and advocacy."[25] More than anything, COLAGE connects with children who have LGBTQ parents and helps them meet other families like theirs.

What Being a Teenager Has to Do with It

In a 2003 Gallup Poll, 51 percent of American teens responded that they felt that same-sex couples should be able to adopt children. (Forty-six percent said they did not believe that they should be allowed to.[26]) But we know that despite these numbers, and despite the fact that a majority of their peers support them, at least in theory, teens in LGBTQ families experience a reality that is far from accepting and free of homophobia and fear. While perhaps lessening in both strength and occurrence, there are still loud, powerful voices out there telling teens with LGBTQ parents that their families are wrong, such as these:

> "Don't misunderstand. I am not here bashing people who are homosexuals, who are lesbians, who are bisexual, who are transgender. We need to have profound compassion for people who are dealing with the very real issue of sexual dysfunction in their life and sexual identity disorders."—*Senator Michele Bachmann, on homosexuality as a mental disorder, speaking at EdWatch National Education Conference, November 6, 2004*

> "We fight gay marriage—and win."—*Maggie Gallagher, President of National Organization for Marriage, www.nationformarriage.org*

> "The feminist agenda is not about equal rights for women. It is about a socialist, anti-family political movement that encourages women to leave their husbands, kill their children, practice witchcraft, destroy capitalism and become lesbians."—*TV preacher Pat Robertson speaking at the 1992 National Republican Convention*

While comments like these are hurtful and offensive to all members of the LGBTQ community and their friends and families, there are indications that dealing with homophobia and transphobia, as well as hostility toward your family, might be especially difficult for teenagers. Public discourse, creating an atmosphere where ostracizing and bullying by peers is okay and even sanctioned, can be more traumatic and have more dire consequences during the teen years than during any other time in life.

In an article about the brain in *National Geographic*, David Dobbs talks about teens' vital needs for social acceptance and peer interactions. Dobbs describes how the neural hormone oxytocin "makes social connections in particular more rewarding. The neural networks and dynamics associated with general reward and social interactions overlap heavily. Engage one, and you often engage the other. Engage them during adolescence, and you light a fire."[27]

Not only do teens prefer each other's company (more than people of any other age group do) to the company of an older or younger person, but according to Dobbs there are other, even more powerful reasons for teens to need social

Fitting in with our peers is more important during our teen years than any other time in our lives.

relationships to go smoothly. Peer relationships, he said, are an investment in the future for teens. Dobbs uses the example of socially adept rats and monkeys and discusses how getting to know peers and building the right relationships gets them the best nesting areas, the best food, the most sex with the fittest mates, and so on. Humans are even more dependent on these social interactions than rats and monkey, according to Dobbs. While, yes, we are brought to life by our parents, Dobbs said, we still are mostly dependent on our peers for our future survival. "This supremely human characteristic makes peer relations not a sideshow but the main show. *Some brain-scan studies, in fact, suggest that our brains react to peer exclusion much as they respond to threats to physical health or food supply. At a neural level, in other words, we perceive social rejection as a threat to existence* (my italics)."[28]

While teens with LGBTQ parents seem to feel a great deal of guilt when they lie about having two mothers or two fathers, or make up a parent they don't have to their peers, this is very understandable in light of Dobbs's article, which shows that teens will do almost anything for social acceptance.

Children of LGBTQ Parents—a Not Insignificant Group

So how many children in this country actually have LGBTQ parents?

A lot, it turns out. According to a 2011 study by the Williams Institute, approximately 3.5 percent of adults in the United States identify as LGBT and 0.3 percent identify as transgender or transsexual. That's almost nine million Americans based on current population numbers. It is estimated that approximately two million children are currently being raised in LGBTQ households, and as LGBTQ persons are gaining better access to reproductive services, there are reasons to believe that LGBTQ families will grow, thrive, and become a force to reckon with.[29]

Notes

1. David Gregory, "Bachmann, Branstad, Murphy, Robinson, Martin, Todd," *Meet the Press*, NBC, August 14, 2011, www.msnbc.msn.com/id/44136028/ns/meet_the_press-transcripts/t/meet-press-transcript-august/ (accessed August 20, 2012).
2. *Merriam-Webster's Collegiate Dictionary*, 11th ed., s.v. "family" and "group."
3. Abbie E. Goldberg, *Lesbian and Gay Parents and Their Children: Research on the Family Life Cycle* (Washington, D.C.: American Psychological Association, 2010), 49, 186.
4. Casey Elliott Lange, "Everything Is Political," *Prodigy and Partner*, March 1, 2012 (presented at Columbus Academy, Columbus, Ohio, February 2012), outlookcolumbus.com/2012/03/prodigy-and-partner-march-2012/ (accessed April 15, 2012).
5. Casey, in-person interview by author, April 27, 2012.

6. LGBT Ministries, "Basic Definitions: Sexual Orientation and Gender Identity," Unitarian Universalist Association of Congregations, www.uua.org/lgbtq/identity/index.shtml (accessed May 12, 2012).
7. LGBT Ministries, "Sexual Orientation and Gender Identity 101," Unitarian Universalist Association of Congregations, www.uua.org/lgbtq/identity/index.shtml (accessed October 9, 2012).
8. *Merriam-Webster's Collegiate Dictionary*, 11th ed., s.v. "queer."
9. Charles, "A 'Rainbow' of Possibilities," *PrideSource*, June 4, 2009, www.pridesource.com/article.html?article=35356 (accessed October 3, 2012).
10. Goldberg, *Lesbian and Gay Parents*, 5.
11. Sean Cahill, "Bisexuality: Dispelling the Myths," National Gay and Lesbian Task Force, http://uwvw.ngltf.org/downloads/reports/BisexualityDispellingtheMyths.pdf (accessed September 19, 2012).
12. Cahill, "Bisexuality."
13. Cahill, "Bisexuality."
14. Zach Wahls, with Bruce Littlefield, *My Two Moms: Lessons of Love, Strength, and What Makes a Family* (New York: Gotham Books, 2012), 69.
15. Monica Canfield-Lenfest, *Kids of Trans Resource Guide*, COLAGE, www.colage.org/resources/kot/ (accessed August 10, 2012), 21.
16. Kaley, Skype interview by author, October 30, 2012.
17. Thomas, in-person interview by author, June 6, 2012.
18. Kate Davis and David Heilbroner, dir., *Stonewall Uprising: A Documentary from American Experience* (Monroe, Mich.: Q-Ball Productions, 2010).
19. Tom Owens, "One Mother's Voice: PFLAG Cofounder Recalls Group's Beginnings," PFLAG, July 14, 2005, community.pflag.org/page.aspx?pid=288 (accessed November 6, 2012).
20. The paragraph regarding the *Diagnostic and Statistical Manual* comes from *Wikipedia*; for the rest of the information in this section, see note 21. *Wikipedia*, s.v. "Diagnostic and Statistical Manual of Mental Disorders," http://en.wikipedia.org/wiki/Diagnostic_and_Statistical_Manual_of_Mental_Disorders (accessed June 27, 2012).
21. Benedict Carey, "Psychiatry Giant Sorry for Backing Gay 'Cure,'" *New York Times*, May 19, 2012, 1, 3.
22. Carey, "Psychiatry Giant Sorry," 1, 3.
23. Carey, "Psychiatry Giant Sorry," 1, 3.
24. Carlos A. Ball, *From the Closet to the Courtroom: Five LGBT Rights Lawsuits That Have Changed Our Nation* (Boston, Mass.: Beacon Press, 2010), 2–3.
25. COLAGE, "About," www.colage.org/about/ (accessed June 27, 2012).
26. Heather Mason Kiefer, "Teens Split on Gay Adoption Issue," Gallup, 2003, www.gallup.com/poll/9760/Teens-Split-Gay-Adoption-Issue.aspx (accessed June 26, 2012).
27. David Dobbs, "Beautiful Brains," *National Geographic* 220, no. 4 (October, 2011): 55.
28. Dobbs, "Beautiful Brains," 55.
29. Zack Ford, "Study Shows There Are at Least 9 Million LGBT Americans," Think Progress, April 7, 2011, thinkprogress.org/lgbt/2011/04/07/177334/study-shows-there-are-at-least-9-million-lgbt-americans/ (accessed August 20, 2012).

THE KIDS ARE ALL RIGHT

While Zach Wahls, the young man speaking in support of gay marriage in the Iowa House of Representatives in 2011, quickly rose to the status of poster child for successful children of LGBTQ persons, it is counterproductive to look at Wahls and talk about what a great success he is. Yes, he is a pleasant-looking, well-spoken, and intelligent young man, but praising Wahls means in some ways that we believe him to be an unlikely success. As if we are wondering, "How could a lesbian couple possibly raise such a great person?" Wahls is, of course, far from the only well-adjusted child with LGBTQ parents. There are children like him everywhere, in every state and in every town. And while not all children of LGBTQ parents are well-adjusted and grow up to be productive members of society, the same is true for children with heterosexual parents. The truth is that you would not be able to tell from talking to someone that he or she has LGBTQ parents. So, what then is all this about?

What's Best for the Kids

Interestingly, while many studies show how much better children with married parents fare compared to children with single or divorced parents, these same studies are conspicuously absent in the same-sex marriage debate. Journalist Lisa Belkin brings up this fact in a 2009 *New York Times* article. She writes,

> We demand that public policy—on health care, or education, or stimulus money—consider the needs of children as surely as it does the needs of doctors, teachers and businesses. (I am not saying that public policy makers always respond, mind you, but "what about the children?" is certainly a rallying cry.) We devour research on how to build our children's self-esteem, to keep them from being bullied and to expand their intellects.
>
> It is striking, then, how comparatively rarely children are mentioned as an argument in favor to gay marriage. The issue is framed as a debate

over equality and justice, of personal freedom and the relation of church and state, not about what is good for kids.[1]

Indeed, if what we aim for is what is best for the kids, and we show in studies, time and again, that the most stable setting in which to raise children is within a marriage, then why not use that fact to argue that everybody should be allowed to marry?

What Science Says

So what *is* good for the kids?

In an infamous 2012 speech in New Hampshire, former U.S. Senator and then presidential hopeful Rick Santorum said that it was better to have a father in prison than to grow up with two lesbian mothers.[2]

We don't have to search very hard to find that sentiment echoed other places as well, in the higher ranks of a number of churches and among many politicians, even among the board of the Boy Scouts of America.

Research, however, shows another picture. It turns out that it's not actually better to have a parent in prison than having lesbian mothers.

During the past few years, several scientific studies focusing on the health and well-being of children with lesbian mothers have been conducted (lesbians being the largest and most visible of LGBTQ parent groups for the simple reason that it is comparatively easy for lesbian couples to have children). In their article "Quality of Life of Adolescents Raised from Birth by Lesbian Mothers: The U.S. National Longitudinal Family Study" (the longest running U.S. study on this topic), researchers compared the overall quality of life of teens raised by lesbian mothers with that of teens raised by heterosexual mothers. The study also tried to determine if certain things affected the children's health, such as if they had been victims of stigmatization and if their parents were still together. While studies often focus on problem behaviors or the absence thereof, this study emphasized and tried to establish the "positive psychological adjustment" of the children involved. The study found that children of lesbian mothers "function as well as, or sometimes better than, those reared by opposite-sex parents."[3]

Researchers also looked at whether it was important for children to know their sperm donor, but found that it did not seem to matter to the children's well-being whether or not they did. In fact, the study found no difference in the quality of life in children with known as opposed to unknown sperm donors. Perhaps the most surprising thing in this study was the fact that it found no negative effects of children being stigmatized due to their family. This last point can perhaps be explained by the intentionality of many lesbian mothers. These mothers, the study authors suggest, might have prepared their children so well from a young age about living in an LGBTQ family that the children learned methods of coping with stigma and discrimination. Another finding that might need explanation was that children in this study whose parents were separated seemed to be doing just as well as those whose parents were still together, which runs contrary to some other studies that claim that children do best when their parents stay together. But the study authors attributed this phenomenon to the fact that in these lesbian parent households almost seventy-five percent of the parents who separated continued to share custody of the children (the same number for heterosexual couples was lower, at sixty-five percent).[4]

The study authors conclude, "This finding supports earlier evidence that adolescents reared by lesbian mothers from birth do not manifest more adjustment difficulties (e.g., depression, anxiety, and disruptive behavior) than those reared by heterosexual parents."[5]

Richard Green is a psychologist, lawyer, and author, and a sexologist specializing in homosexuality and transsexualism. He was also the founding president of the International Academy of Sex Research and has often been called as an expert witness in court cases involving LGBTQ persons and issues. In one court case, Green was asked by an attorney to determine what effects living in a homosexual household and seeing two same-sex parents having a loving relationship would have on children. Green replied that children who grow up with homosexual parents tend to be accepting of homosexuality in others and be overall less prejudiced than children in general. He drew parallels with children growing up in racially integrated neighborhoods being more likely to be open to other races. Children who relate to children of other religions, Green said, are more likely to be tolerant of people of diverse religious backgrounds. Green believes that the same is true for homosexuality. It is not good for children, he believes, to grow up in a social vacuum. It can, of course, be jarring for children who grow up with same-sex parents to see the stark difference between their own families and the ones they see on television or read about in books—the cultural standard. But Green feels that these children can transcend the norm. In the end, the only difference Green sees between children of same-sex parents and children of heterosexual parents is that those with same-sex parents show a greater tolerance of homosexuality in others.[6] In other words, one of the world's foremost researchers in sexology concludes that growing up in an LGBTQ family can be a positive and growth-inducing experience making for more well-rounded and tolerant human beings.

The American Academy of Child and Adolescent Psychiatry conveys this message as well in their *Facts for Families* publications. While children in LGBTQ families might indeed face discrimination, teasing, and bullying, *Facts for Families* states, "Research has shown that in contrast to common beliefs, children of lesbian, gay, or transgender parents:

1. Are not more likely to be gay than children with heterosexual parents.
2. Are not more likely to be sexually abused.
3. Do not show differences in whether they think of themselves as male or female (gender identity).
4. Do not show differences in their male and female behavior (gender role behavior)."[7]

It can be argued that all of the preceding points, except for the second one, should be rather irrelevant, though it is clear from today's media debate that this is not so.

Not just Richard Green, but many scholars and researchers feel that children with LGBTQ parents are not only doing fine, but that gay parents might bring something to parenting that heterosexual parents are actually unable to provide.

Clark University professor and author of *Lesbian and Gay Parents and Their Children*, Abbie Goldberg, has been especially prominent in showing different aspects of LGBTQ parenting. In an article in *LiveScience*, journalist Stephanie Pappas interviews Goldberg. Gay parents, Goldberg says in the interview, "tend to be more motivated, more committed than heterosexual parents on average, because they chose to be parents."[8] The point is not, of course, that heterosexual couples are never intentional about their families—they certainly can be—but that lesbian women usually don't have children by accident. Goldberg also echoes Green's findings that children with LGBTQ parents tend to be more tolerant. "The only consistent places you find differences between how kids of gay parents and kids of straight parents turn out are in issues of tolerance and open-mindedness,"[9] she said in the interview. In a study Goldberg conducted for the *American Journal of Orthopsychiatry*, she also found that "these individuals feel like their perspectives on family, on gender, on sexuality have largely been enhanced by growing up with gay parents."[10]

In Pappas's article, Goldberg talks about the fact that children raised by LGBTQ parents have fewer gender stereotypes than people in general. She believes that this has to do with the fact that lesbians "tend to have more egalitarian relationships than straight couples."[11] (In her book *Lesbian and Gay Parents*, Goldberg actually shows the other side of this coin as well—how some same-sex couples suffer many of the same inequalities in the division of household duties as heterosexual couples do, though in general, same-sex couples seem to challenge gender roles more than heterosexual couples do.[12])

In another interview, this one in the *New York Times*, Goldberg talks about some other aspects of children with LGBTQ parents. For example, girls raised by lesbian mothers, she found, have a slightly higher number of sexual partners than other girls, and boys raised by lesbian mothers have a slightly lower number of sexual partners than other boys their age. Girls raised by lesbian mothers

Same-Sex Marriage and the Well-Being of the Children: A Dutch-American Study

A 2008 cross-cultural study comparing the welfare of children in planned lesbian families in the Netherlands with the welfare of children in planned lesbian families in the United States showed some interesting results. In 2001, the Netherlands became the first country in the world to legalize same-sex marriage. At the time of this writing in 2013, no longitudinal studies have been published exploring the direct result between the welfare of the children and their parents' right to marry, but this particular study still gives us an idea of how life changed for these families when the political stigma was lifted. The study, *Children in Planned Lesbian Families: A Cross-Cultural Comparison between the United States and the Netherlands*,[15] explores whether there is a difference in the children's well-being in the two countries, bearing in mind that one (the Netherlands) has a state-sanctioned right to marry and the other one (the United States) does not (though while not recognized on a federal level in March of 2013, some states in this country have legalized same-sex marriage).

The study found that "children (boys and girls) in the American sample were significantly less open to peers about living in a lesbian family than children in the Dutch sample." The study also showed that there were significantly higher levels of "anxious/depression, social problems, thought problems, rule-breaking behavior, aggressive behavior, and sex problems," among the American children in the study than among the Dutch children.[16]

While negative effects of homophobia could be detected in the children in both countries, the researchers believed that because the culture of the Netherlands and the northern European countries has a less strict division between male-female roles (something the researchers determined using a number of variables), the citizens of these countries are also more prone to being accepting of lesbian and gay persons and couples. They also believe that socioeconomic class has a great deal to do with acceptance of gay and lesbian families, though when comparing children from the two different countries, most families in the study were from the same socioeconomic class. (The Netherlands is known for having a very large, well-educated middle class.)

The conclusion of the study was that "cross-national differences in the acceptance of homosexuality and same-sex parenthood have consequences for the well-being of children growing up in lesbian families, with greater acceptance of lesbian and gay people and same-sex parenting associated with more openness and fewer experiences of homophobia."[17] In other words: it matters to LGBTQ families if society around them is homophobic and negative toward their families. On the other hand, if society is accepting, the children are happier and healthier.

The preceding study examined only planned lesbian families, so no conclusions can be drawn regarding children with gay or transgender parents, though an educated guess might be that the difference in well-being between the children in the two countries would be even greater if we looked at these other, often more stigmatized groups.

are also more likely to go on to a higher education and to get professional jobs traditionally viewed as male dominated. And adult children of LGBTQ parents are more likely to seek out jobs having to do with social justice. According to the *New York Times* article, Goldberg's study subjects also tended to socialize more with gays and lesbians than did children from non-LGBTQ families. The major disadvantage of growing up with LGBTQ parents, according to Goldberg, comes from society. "More acceptance of gay and lesbian families, not less, would help solve the problem," she said in Belkin's interview.[13]

And finally, in her own book, *Lesbian and Gay Parents and Their Children*, Goldberg explains in greater depth these same teens' view on sexuality. She found that children with LGBTQ parents have a more open mind about sexuality in general and about potentially exploring same-sex attractions. Even if the young people interviewed had never had a same-sex attraction, it was not a given to them that they would be in a heterosexual relationship as adults.

Overall, Goldberg said about her study subjects, "participants often held the view that there was more than one acceptable sexual identity and expressed discomfort with sexual binaries and labels. [Having LGBTQ parents] influenced their ability and willingness to think deeply about their own sexuality and to understand it in more complex and nuanced ways."[14]

The Netherlands was the first country in the world to legalize same-sex marriage.

A Controversial Study

As we have already seen, studies about the welfare of the children with LGBTQ parents abound. Researchers on both sides of the fence—those supporting all families and those who believe that only heterosexual couples should be able to have children—get their funding from somewhere, that is, from some organization or even private person with a purpose and a goal. And where the funding comes from may well influence the results of the research. There is a reason why political candidates are so eager to point out their adversary's funding sources. If the tobacco industry gives a lot of money to one candidate, is it likely that that candidate will support anti-tobacco legislation? Probably not. And if a candidate gets money from the National Rifle Association, you can be pretty sure that a handgun ban will not be on his or her agenda.

In 2012, Mark Regnerus, associate professor at the University of Texas in Austin, published his controversial "New Family Structures Study," which quickly came under fire. The study examined the current life of three thousand adults who grew up with LGBTQ parents, comparing them to adults who grew up with married, heterosexual parents. It found that people with LGBTQ parents were wanting in many areas of life. While many of the questions in the study did not produce statistically significant differences among the two groups, the study claimed to establish major differences in a few categories: when compared to adults with heterosexual parents, the adult children of gay couples were two to four times more likely to be on public assistance, more than twice as likely to be unemployed, and more than twice as likely to have contemplated suicide.

Regnerus admitted in a *Fox News* interview that the study failed to take into consideration the fact that LGBTQ families more often live in poverty due to legal inequities (such as not having the legal benefits that come with marriage or even domestic partnership in some states) and that society's stigmatizing and ostracizing of LGBTQ families—especially those who have now grown to adulthood and grew up under worse circumstances than LGBTQ families do now—would contribute to the hardship of these persons as adults. He also said, somewhat surprisingly in light of these conclusions, that he believed that same-sex parents could do a good job of raising children.

While a small group of people have come out in defense of this study, a much larger group has railed against it. It was expected, of course, for the LGBTQ community to take offense, but a large number of researchers have also rejected the study and one author asked to audit the study even called it "bullshit." The biggest, most glaring problem with the study is the fact that all the adults with LGBTQ parents except two (of thousands of adults) came from single-parent households. These study objects were compared to people who had grown up with two married parents in the home.[18]

In response to the controversy, Regnerus wrote, "It is certainly accurate to affirm that sexual orientation or parental sexual behavior need have nothing to do with the ability to be a good, effective parent." He rejected the suggestion that being funded by the Witherspoon Institute and the Bradley Foundation, organizations very much opposed to same-sex marriage and invested in the promotion of right-wing Christian causes, had in any way influenced the result of his study.[19]

A Planned Parenthood

In a same-sex monogamous sexual relationship there can be no accidental preg-nancies, no surprise bundles of joy dropping through the chimney. In plain speak, children with gay or lesbian parents often know that they were not a mistake. (Though children with LGBTQ parents might, of course, have been conceived before their same-sex parents' relationship began.) And we might assume that it is likely that parents who really wish for and plan for a child would also be more intentional about parenting. In the book *Are There Closets in Heaven?* that she wrote with her father, Carol Curoe talks about how much thought and planning went into her and her partner's decision to have children. Curoe and her partner took a class offered by an organization called Chrysalis to learn if having a child was the right decision for the two of them. In fact, they attended the class twice. They also spent a lot of time debating whether having a child was a selfish deci-sion. While this is something many other parents do as well, LGBTQ parents are more likely to be forced to ask themselves this question as it takes considerably more planning for them to conceive. In the end, this usually means that the chil-dren of such couples (or single parents) are fiercely wanted and welcome.[20]

Extended Family

While it may not be the goal of an LGBTQ couple, their extended family, which might have been slow in warming up to the fact that their son or daughter is in a same-sex relationship, often come around when a baby arrives on the scene. For Casey, seventeen, this was very much the case. One of Casey's mothers' parents had not been particularly excited about their daughter's same-sex relationship, but as soon as Casey arrived on the scene, they put their prejudice aside and em-braced their new grandchild.[21]

In Carol Curoe's family, getting pregnant definitely sped up the acceptance process. Curoe's father, Robert Curoe, who had struggled to accept that his daughter was a lesbian, not only embraced the fact that he would be a grandfather but even wrote a letter to friends and family telling them that his daughter was pregnant through insemination.[22]

Pressure to Be Perfect?

Studies about children with LGBTQ parents abound, and LGBTQ parents turn themselves inside out to prove that they are worthy of parenting, but should

Sometimes it is difficult for parents to accept their son's or daughter's same-sex relationship, but they often come around when their child has his or her own children.

LGBTQ parents really have to be so very perfect? Should they have to be *better* than other parents? Should children with LGBTQ parents have to show that they are *better* adjusted than those with heterosexual parents? Children of LGBTQ parents have the same drug problems, the same early pregnancy statistics, the same statistics regarding SAT or ACT scores. In light of the fact that a larger number of children from LGBTQ families grow up in poverty, the numbers should be allowed to reflect this. But media scrutiny of LGBTQ families does not usually allow for this inequality. These families are often expected to be better, to prove themselves. But what makes us believe that gender identity or sexual orientation has anything at all to do with good parenting? Or bad parenting for that matter.

John Grohol, PsyD, is the CEO of Psych Central, a mental health social networking site on the World Wide Web. He finds it curious that some people believe that someone's sexual orientation should in any way determine how good a parent a person would be. "It's a ridiculous assumption to begin with," he said on his blog. "Why not suggest that people who have a certain religious perspective make the best parents, or only those who were raised in a house with more than 2 children themselves?"[23]

Do LGBTQ Parents Have LGBTQ Kids?

If my parent is transgender, does that mean that I will become transgender or gay? This is a question that Monica Canfield-Lenfest, author of *Kids of Trans Guide*, gets fairly often from children with trans parents. Her reply: "It is very unlikely that you will become transgender just because your parent is. Or gay for that matter. Many gender normative parents raise transgender children and many heterosexual parents raise homosexual children."[24]

That said, it is not, of course, unheard of for gay or lesbian parents to have gay or lesbian children. Thomas, age fourteen (interviewed in chapter 7), was raised by lesbian mothers and he himself is gay. The unique thing in Thomas's situation is not that he is a gay kid with lesbian moms but the fact that he felt free to come out at a very young age because he had great emotional support at home. This is also what research indicates—that children of gay and lesbian parents that identify as gay or lesbian themselves are more likely to come out early than other gay and lesbian children or young adults who might not be sure of their family's reaction.

As early as in 1974, sexologist Richard Green testified in an Ohio court case, *Hall v. Hall*, regarding the appropriateness of a lesbian mother raising a child. According to Green this case has been characterized as "the beginning of the use of experts [in court] on homosexuality." (Since then Green has served as such an expert many times.) The answer that Green gave, when the attorney asked him whether homosexuality in the parents would lead to homosexuality in the children, has been widely quoted since then:

> It is an erroneous view to say that because the parents are homosexual the children will be. If that were the case homosexuality would have died out long ago. Almost all, if not all, homosexuals have had heterosexual mothers and fathers. So if it is merely parent role modeling, how do we explain that ten percent or more of the population is homosexual? It has to be something beyond that. Frankly, I don't know of any theory which has been advanced which has suggested that having homosexual parents in and of itself is going to be a significant contributor to a homosexual orientation.[25]

Why it should matter whether LGBTQ parents have LGBTQ children is, of course, a question worth debating, but there is no doubt that at this time for a large group of people it *does* matter.

"It is what it is," writes trans woman Jennifer Finney Boylan in her book *She's Not There*. While Boylan talks about being transsexual in particular—and transsexuality comes with its own set of challenges—the comment is indeed relevant to other LGBTQ persons and families as well. "Whether I 'really' am a woman, or whether I 'had a choice' or not, or whether *anything*, no longer matters," she writes. "Having an opinion about transsexuality is about as useful as having an opinion on blindness. You can think whatever you like about it, but in the end, your friend is still blind, and surely deserves to see. Whether one thinks transsexuals are heroes or lunatics will not help to bring these people solace. All we can do in the face of this enormous, infinite anguish is to have compassion."[26]

Keeping Secrets

"I'm not gay, but I know what it feels like to be in the closet," Zach Wahls wrote in his book *My Two Moms*.[27]

Ruth, age twenty, interviewed in Judith Snow's book *How It Feels to Have a Gay or Lesbian Parent*, said something very similar. "Around the seventh grade I just realized that having a gay parent is a lot like being gay yourself. You have no control over it."[28]

To a child or a teen with LGBTQ parents, even the innocent question "What do your mom and dad do?" can cause a great deal of anxiety. For Wahls, who moved from Wisconsin to Ohio in the fourth grade and who already felt awkward because of having to wear a heel lift in his shoe, the question sent him scrambling for an answer. Back in Wisconsin everybody knew that he had two moms, but suddenly in these new surroundings, things were different. So he lied. He said his mom was a doctor, which was true enough, and that his dad was a lawyer, which *could* be true as his sperm donor had indeed been studying to become a lawyer. But in the back of his mind Wahls felt that he was selling his nonbiological mom down the river and it made him feel terrible.[29]

While Patrick, age seventeen (interviewed in chapter 11), did not feel that he necessarily kept his two moms a secret, he said that he didn't tend to tell people because it didn't come up that often. "What am I going to say?" he said. "By the way . . ."[30]

In *Our House*, a documentary about children with LGBTQ parents, Daniel, age thirteen, talks about how frustrating it is for him to have to come out all the time to his friends at school about having two dads. "It annoys me to have to keep talking about it," he said. "I want everybody to be in one big room and then I won't have to tell them anymore. I'll be free for the rest of my life not having to answer them anymore."[31]

Cindy, who is now an adult but who grew up with a gay dad in the Midwest, said that even though she was in an accepting community, she still didn't go out of her way to tell people that her dad was gay. If it came up, she would, she said.

Mostly she doesn't tell people even now, she said, because there is simply no reason to.[32]

In her essay "Getting Closer," Laura Zee writes about growing up with a gay dad. "My parents didn't tell me not to talk about my dad to other people. They didn't need to. It was understood that his secret was something we kept in the family."[33]

The sentiment seems to be the same among many children with LGBTQ parents. Even children who live in more supportive communities, while not going out of their way to hide their families, don't volunteer information about them. Then again, it might be worth keeping in mind that children of heterosexual parents don't tend to volunteer information about their parents' sexual orientation either.

When Parents Come Out

Goldberg writes in her book *Lesbian and Gay Parents and Their Children* that the most important emotions she noted among children when their parents came out to them as LGBTQ were worry, shame, shock, disbelief, anger, guilt, or enhanced closeness.

The most important element to a successful family transition when a family member comes out seems to have to do with the age of the child. According to Goldberg, children who learned in early childhood of their lesbian mother's sexual orientation tended to maintain higher self-esteem than those who learned about it during adolescence. Goldberg felt that this was due to the fact that adolescence is already such a difficult age, fraught with psychological, biological, and social changes. She also brought up the oft-repeated importance of peer acceptance, which during adolescence is at an all-time high.[34]

Abigail Garner is the author of *Families Like Mine: Children of Gay Parents Tell It Like It Is*. She was five years old when her dad came out to the family. "Homophobia is taught," Garner wrote on her website, "and at five, I had not learned it. What I knew was that my dad loved another human being who made him happy and who just happened to also be a man. My experience would have been very different if my dad had told me when I was thirteen or so after I had joined with my peers in making fun of gay and lesbian people and telling anti-gay jokes."[35]

Casey, age seventeen, had no coming-out experience with her parents as she was born to two lesbian mothers. She does believe, however, that it might be especially difficult to have your parents come out to you during your teen years. "I think thirteen would be the hardest age [to have your parents come out to you]," she said. "Seventh grade is already a hard time. A lot of my friends whose parents went through divorces [at that time] had a hard time with it."[36]

Andrew, age eighteen (interviewed in chapter 7), was in preschool when his parents got a divorce and his mom moved to Connecticut. Not long after that his dad moved in with Bob. Andrew was so young that, just like for Casey, the coming out part never happened. Dad and Bob were as natural to him as dad and anybody (other than his mom) would have been. He was struggling with the fact that his parents had gone through a divorce, he said, not that his dad was gay.[37]

Even adults may struggle when their parents come out, as in the case of Australian psychotherapist Stephen Gunther, who was an adult when his father began the process of changing gender. His father was, Gunther wrote in *Australian Humanities Review*, "a staunch fundamentalist Christian, patriarchal 65 year old." The process was entirely unexpected and very shocking for Gunther. Nothing helped him prepare for it, he said. There was no manual where he could learn what it was like to have a parent come out as transgender. "I am a very flexible, broad-minded person," he wrote. "But all my tolerance and intellectual acceptance does not help me come to terms with the intense emotional experience I have. Sadness, confusion, hurt, and—I have very painfully had to admit to myself—dislike. I don't like what my father has become, not primarily because of the new person there, or even of the different gender, but because of her barely masked anger at me as a reminder of the years she was suppressed as a shadow of my father."[38]

While anger toward the adult coming out certainly exists, relief that the person you love is finally able to be who he or she needs to be seems common as well, especially after some time has passed. Carol Curoe tells the LGBTQ person's side of the story in her book *Are There Closets in Heaven?* After Curoe started to admit to herself that she was a lesbian, she witnessed a number of friends come out and then get cut off from their families who did not accept that they were homosexual. Watching her friends become alienated from their families frightened her and made her even more hesitant to come out to her own family. But Curoe was lucky. While not exactly jumping up and down with excitement that she was a lesbian, her family was committed to her and was not ready to cut her off. When her father, Robert Curoe, was having a difficult time dealing with her coming out, Curoe sent him information to keep him educated on homosexuality. This, in the end, was how Robert Curoe became an LGBTQ advocate himself.[39]

JamieAnn, a sixty-five-year-old TransWoman (interviewed in chapter 3; JamieAnn prefers to capitalize "TransWoman") who began her process of becoming a woman more than ten years ago but didn't come out to her children and grandchildren until four years later, feels that coming out is something you keep doing for the rest of your life. "It happens almost every day," she said. When looking for an overnight apartment for when she came to babysit her young grandchild in a neighboring town, she felt compelled to tell the landlords that she was a TransWoman. "I always feel like I have to identify myself. I wasn't sure if I would pass [for a woman]. I wanted people to know about my identity up front."[40]

After JamieAnn came out to her adult son and daughter, she and her wife were concerned that the neighbors might wonder who the strange woman moving in and out of the house was and decided to come out in the neighborhood as well. Together JamieAnn and her wife wrote a letter to neighbors, close friends, and relatives, about twenty-five letters in all, telling them of Jim's transformation to JamieAnn. "I can count on one hand the letters we got back," JamieAnn said. Of those who wrote back though, people showed amazing support. JamieAnn was also happily surprised by a neighbor, whom she had always considered "a manly man," who came over and gave her a hug, telling her how much he and his wife supported JamieAnn and her wife.

While mourning the losses of the friendships of people who could not deal with the fact that Jim was now JamieAnn, JamieAnn felt that in the process, she learned much about people. "[Before] I was always in the closet," she said. "I was always on the defense. But you can be so freaking wrong about people. Then they turn out to be the most generous, understanding people in the world. There is no way to know."

JamieAnn also talked about the fact that every time she comes out, she also outs her wife, her family, her children, their children. "Me coming out affects everybody," she said. And she feels the same way about her transition from man to woman. "It's not just my transition, but everybody else's that I come in contact with. Everyone is affected in some way."

Missing Out on a Mom or a Dad

It is very likely that children growing up with two moms or two dads will wonder what it would be like to have a parent of the other gender. In Snow's book, *How It Feels to Have a Gay or Lesbian Parent*, Stacey, age eighteen, said, "I was real close to my grandparents so I had some male role modeling, but I don't know what it's like to live with a male figure and I worry a little about that."[41]

In his book *My Two Moms*, Wahls talks about the importance for all families, not just those with LGBTQ parents, of having a network of friends to rely on. Many of these family friends helped Wahls, not only by simply being male, but also by coming to the rescue when it came to other issues. "Our parents don't know everything," Wahls writes. "And sometimes we have to count on the friendship of others to learn more." He talks about how, for example, one of his mother's friends helped him learn about financial investments. Wahls feels that it wasn't who taught him all those different things that mattered, like shaving or throwing a baseball around or balancing his checkbook or driving a stick shift. The main thing is that you learn them, and that you have people around that can help you and that you can call on for advice. It is very important, Wahls says in his book, to have a large network of people around no matter what, and not only people with the same belief systems or the same skills. "My moms might not have been able to show me how to shave," he writes. "But they sure weren't able to teach my sister how to use makeup, either. And guess what? We both turned out just fine."[42]

The Kids Are All Right

Despite the unlikely relationship between Julianne Moore's character (a lesbian mom) and one of her children's sperm donor in the movie *The Kids Are All Right*, the title of this movie is especially relevant. Even with a messy affair threatening the children's relationship with their parents as well as the sperm donor's relationship with one of the children, the kids, in the end, are exactly that—all right! They are resilient and proof that there is no standard for how "family" should look in order to be "right."

The movie is fiction, of course, but it asks that important question again—why should LGBTQ families have different standards than other families? They have the same messy lives other families do. But as we have seen, there is sometimes pressure for LGBTQ families to prove themselves to the world. Their children seem to be scrutinized in a different way than other children. The teens interviewed for this book said they felt no pressure to represent their families in a good light, yet almost all of them did. They said they had a warm relationship with their parents and felt that their parents gave them the love and support they needed. What these teens might not realize, however, is that this is not necessarily the norm. Teens don't tend to speak with such affection of their parents, nor do they tend to express that they feel supported by them. This anomaly could stem from a number of reasons: An LGBTQ hostile world makes teens automatically and even subconsciously represent their families in a positive light as there is already so much negativity aimed at them. Also, the teens who agreed to be interviewed for this book were, as previously noted, a self-selected group and might well have a better relationship with their parents than do average teens. Another possibility is that an LGBTQ-hostile world actually *makes* the members of LGBTQ families closer and more loyal to each other.

There is also the succinct possibility that children of LGBTQ parents choose not to share, even with their parents, some of the difficulties that they may have, because they know how badly their parents will feel if they knew how difficult their children's lives were. In an e-mail interview, Zach Wahls said, "The reality is that, I think, some LGBTQ parents are unaware of the challenges that their children endure. It doesn't help any that, as children, we want to make our parents proud, so we're willing to pretend that things are easier than they are, that we aren't being harassed or bullied or anything like that. Further, no parent wants to think that he or she is making his/her child's life more difficult, but, again, the reality is that there are still huge swaths of this country where growing up with an LGBTQ parent(s) is very, very hard."[43]

Social Stigma

In her book *Lesbian and Gay Parents*, Goldberg says that one reason some people believe LGBTQ persons should not have children is because the children might be ostracized and bullied because of their parents.[44] Richard Green addresses this very issue in his book as well. Sometimes courts refer to the 1984 Supreme Court case *Palmore v. Sidoti* regarding this issue, he writes. The case deals with an interracial custody battle regarding whether or not the children would suffer too much social stigma when their European American mother married an African American man. The court determined that the prejudice of society could not be considered when deciding custody for the children.[45] In other words, Green is saying that LGBTQ families should not be punished for other people's prejudice.

Through all this conflicting research that tries to determine just how difficult growing up with LGBTQ parents is, it is important to remember that the teen years are a struggle for everyone. Most people feel alienated during the teen years. Some people are a racial minority in the area where they live and feel ostracized for that, some people have a parent in prison, some people are differently abled than others. The only reason why we even consider this children-of-LGBTQ-parents issue at all is because media, politics, and religion force us to. Nobody would suggest a study regarding the suitability for parents in wheelchairs to have children, or parents with a foreign accent, or, thirty years after the *Palmore v. Sidoti* case, the appropriateness of biracial parenting.

Notes

1. Lisa Belkin, "What's Good for the Kids," *New York Times*, November 8, 2009, www.nytimes.com/2009/11/08/magazine/08fob-wwln-t.html?_r=0 (accessed March 18, 2013).
2. Michael A. Memoli and Mark Z. Barabak, "Santorum Dwells on Gay Marriage," *Los Angeles Times*, January 7, 2012, articles.latimes.com/2012/jan/07/nation/la-na-campaign-20120107 (accessed October 10, 2012).
3. Loes van Gelderen, MSc, Henny M. W. Bos, PhD, Nanette Gartrell, MD, Jo Hermanns, PhD, and Ellen C. Perrin, MD, "Quality of Life of Adolescents Raised from Birth by Lesbian Mothers: The U.S. National Longitudinal Family Study," *Journal of Developmental and Behavioral Pediatrics* 33, no. 1 (January 2012), 1, 5, 6.

4. van Gelderen et al., "Quality of Life," 1, 5, 6.
5. van Gelderen et al., "Quality of Life," 1, 5, 6.
6. Richard Green, *Sexual Science and the Law* (Cambridge, Mass.: Harvard University Press, 1992), 29.
7. American Academy of Child and Adolescent Psychiatry, "Children with Lesbian, Gay, Bisexual and Transgender Parents," *Facts for Families*, no. 92 (August 2011).
8. Stephanie Pappas, "Why Gay Parents May Be the Best Parents," *LiveScience*, January 15, 2012, www.livescience.com/17913-advantages-gay-parents.html (accessed November 6, 2012).
9. Pappas, "Why Gay Parents May Be the Best Parents."
10. Pappas, "Why Gay Parents May Be the Best Parents."
11. Pappas, "Why Gay Parents May Be the Best Parents."
12. Abbie E. Goldberg, *Lesbian and Gay Parents and Their Children: Research on the Family Life Cycle* (Washington, D.C.: American Psychological Association, 2010), 11.
13. Belkin, "What's Good for the Kids."
14. Goldberg, *Lesbian and Gay Parents*, 133, 167.
15. Henny M. W. Bos, PhD, Frank van Balen, PhD, Nanette K. Gartrell, MD, Heidi Peyser, MA, and Theo G. M. Sandfort, PhD, "Children in Planned Lesbian Families: A Cross-Cultural Comparison between the United States and the Netherlands," *American Journal of Orthopsychiatry* 78, no. 2 (2008), 211–19.
16. Bos et al., "Children in Planned Lesbian Families," 214.
17. Bos et al., "Children in Planned Lesbian Families," 218.
18. Peter Montgomery, "Auditor Calls 'Gay Parenting' Study 'Bullshit,'" *Religion Dispatches Magazine*, July 27, 2012, www.religiondispatches.org/dispatches/petermontgomery/6228/auditor_calls_%E2%80%98gay_parenting%E2%80%99_study_%E2%80%98bullshit%E2%80%99 (accessed October 8, 2012).
19. "U. of Texas Backs Professor in Battle with Gay Blogger," *Fox News.com*, September 3, 2012, www.foxnews.com/us/2012/09/03/u-texas-backs-professor-in-battle-with-gay-blogger/ (accessed October 8, 2012).
20. Carol Curoe and Robert Curoe, *Are There Closets in Heaven? A Catholic Father and Lesbian Daughter Share Their Story* (Minneapolis, Minn.: Syren Book Company, 2007), 95–96.
21. Casey, in-person interview by author, April 27, 2012.
22. Curoe and Curoe, *Are There Closets in Heaven?* 112.
23. John M. Grohol, PsyD, "Children of Gay Parents," Psychcentral.com, November 9, 2009, psychcentral.com/blog/archives/2009/11/09/children-of-gay-parents/ (accessed August 2012).
24. Monica Canfield-Lenfest, *Kids of Trans Resource Guide*, COLAGE, www.colage.org/resources/kot/ (accessed August 10, 2012).
25. *Hall v. Hall*, No. 55900, Ohio C.P. Court Domestic Relations Div. (Licking County, October 31, 1974).
26. Jennifer Finney Boylan, *She's Not There: A Life in Two Genders* (New York: Random House, 2003), 248.
27. Zach Wahls, with Bruce Littlefield, *My Two Moms: Lessons of Love, Strength, and What Makes a Family* (New York: Gotham Books, 2012), 47.
28. Judith Snow, *How It Feels to Have a Gay or Lesbian Parent* (Binghamton, N.Y.: Harrington Park Press, 2004), 22.
29. Wahls, *My Two Moms*, 47.

30. Patrick, in-person interview by author, May 30, 2012.
31. Quoted in Meema Spadola, dir., *Our House: A Very Real Documentary about Kids of Gay and Lesbian Parents* (Brooklyn, N.Y.: First Run/Ikarus Films, 2000).
32. Cindy, telephone interview by author, May 23, 2012.
33. Laura Zee, "Getting Closer," in *Out of the Ordinary: Essays on Growing Up with Gay, Lesbian, and Transgender Parents*, ed. Noelle Howey and Ellen Samuels (New York: St. Martin's Press, 2000), 164.
34. Goldberg, *Lesbian and Gay Parents*, 145.
35. Abigail Garner, "FAQs about LGBT Families," Families Like Mine, familieslikemine.com/about-lgbt-families/faqs-about-lgbt-families/ (accessed July 16, 2012).
36. Casey, in-person interview by author, April 24, 2012.
37. Andrew, telephone interview by author, May 25, 2012.
38. Stephen Gunther, "My Transsexual Father," *Australian Humanities Review* (August 1997), 1.
39. Curoe and Curoe, *Are There Closets in Heaven?* 79, 104.
40. JamieAnn, Skype interview by author, August 15, 2012. The quotes from JamieAnn in the rest of this section all come from this interview.
41. Snow, *How It Feels to Have a Gay or Lesbian Parent*, 44.
42. Wahls, *My Two Moms*, 64–65.
43. Zach Wahls, e-mail interview by author, September 12, 2012.
44. Goldberg, *Lesbian and Gay Parents*, 126.
45. Green, *Sexual Science and the Law*, 48.

THE *T* IN LGBTQ: A DISCUSSION ABOUT SEX AND GENDER

What Do *Transgender* and *Transsexual* Mean?

"*Transgendered* is the preferred term for the whole range of people with gender issues," Jennifer Finley Boylan writes in her book *She's Not There*. She continues,

> *Transsexuals*—persons who feel that their body and spirit do not match—are a particular kind of transgendered person. At any rate, a transsexual is not a cross-dresser, for whom the issue is clothes. ("Transvestite" is now considered a pejorative term for "cross-dressers"; in any case, I am neither of these and would be grateful if you could appreciate this distinction.)
>
> Most of us have no personal experience with transsexuality, and lack even a basic language for talking about it. If you find this strange, or embarrassing, or even wonderful, you should know that your reaction is not atypical.[1]

While this short section from Boylan's book might not clarify the complicated issue of sex and gender, it does show us one person's view on her own sex/gender journey and it illustrates how very difficult finding the right words is.

Transsexual, as we remember from chapter 1, is someone who changes his or her biological sex from male to female or female to male. After the transition he or she is likely to think of him- or herself as either male or female, not trans and not LGBTQ (though they might indeed identify as LGBTQ as well, or trans). *Transgender*, on the other hand, can contain an array of gender expression that may not have to do with the person's biological sex.

Monica Canfield-Lenfest is the adult daughter of a trans woman and the author of the COLAGE publication *Kids of Trans Resource Guide*. Canfield-Lenfest wrote the guide to help other children and teens who were dealing with what for her had been a bewildering experience—her father becoming a woman when Canfield-Lenfest was only seventeen and knew absolutely nothing about what it meant to be trans. In her guide, Canfield-Lenfest talks about why she believes that it is so difficult for most people to accept when someone challenges what we consider "normal" gender behavior.

"Just like other people, we learn 'normal' ways of being male or female and are rewarded when we fit into these categories," she writes. "We are taught that a mother is a woman and a father is a man, that a man in a dress is some kind of joke and a woman with a beard belongs in the circus. Our trans parents' identities directly conflict with these messages."[2]

But our inability to understand and accept gender nonconforming behavior does not only have to do with confusion and wanting people to fit into the neat categories we assign them, according to Canfield-Lenfest. She believes that society's unwillingness to embrace trans persons also has to do with gender inequality. Since we treat men and women differently, it is confusing for us to know how to treat someone when we can't determine his or her sex/gender.

Canfield-Lenfest suggests that as a society, we move away from the gender binary system we now rely on—a system where a person with a male anatomy acts in what we deem to be an appropriately masculine manner and a person born with a female anatomy acts in a socially acceptable feminine manner. As with all prejudices and preconceived notions, this might not be a change that we can make overnight, but opening our minds to a wider range of gender and sexuality expression is a worthy goal, Canfield-Lenfest feels.

Children and teens growing up with transgender parents are certainly challenged to rethink the binary system of male-female and decide for themselves what gender means. "My father's a woman who races cars in her free time," says Jonathan F., age twenty-four, interviewed in the *Kids of Trans Resource Guide*. "And she constantly embarrasses men by knowing far more about high-performance engines and independent suspension than they do."[3]

JamieAnn, a sixty-five-year-old TransWoman interviewed later in this chapter, feels very much both male and female. When she first began her transition, she had a difficult time acknowledging the male part of her that she was, after all, trying to move away from, but it is now easier for her to accept that many of her positive characteristics are traits typically thought of as male. The entire concept of changing from male to female or from female to male is problematic, she believes. "Passing," or being able to be recognized as the sex you transition to, is important to many trans persons. Yet, JamieAnn asks whether this should even be

When we treat men and women differently, it might be especially difficult to deal with someone whose sex we are unsure of.

a goal. Isn't that just playing right into the binary system that many trans persons have been victims of all their lives? she wonders. On the other hand, because she knows the reality of living as a trans, "for many people it's a matter of emotional and physical safety," she said. Inevitably, JamieAnn believes, in the end, you are just trading one sort of privilege for another.[4]

Nothing to Do with Sexuality

People with trans parents already know this, but for the rest of society it is some-times difficult to remember that transsexual simply refers to the sex of the person. It tells us nothing whatsoever about sexual *preference*. In order to understand the difference it is helpful to look at Abbie Goldberg's explanation of "sexual identity" in her book *Lesbian and Gay Parents and Their Children*:

> *Sexual identity* has three components: gender identity, gendered role behavior, and sexual orientation. . . . *Gender identity* refers to one's self-identification as male or female—that is, one's sense of oneself as being either male or female. *Gendered role behavior* refers to the extent to which one's behaviors, activities, attitudes, conduct, occupations, and so on are culturally regarded as feminine or masculine, and therefore whether they are seen as appropriate or typical for the male or female societal role. *Sexual orientation* refers to whether an individual is more strongly sexually attracted to members of his or her own sex, the opposite sex, or both sexes (homosexual, heterosexual, and bisexual, respectively).[5]

A female-to-male (FTM) trans person might, for example, start out in a hetero-sexual marriage (married to a man) and thus be considered heterosexual. Then, if he, after he transitions from woman to a man, stays in the marriage, he is now considered gay as is his spouse. While in most states, even those that don't allow same-sex marriage, it is legal to stay married to your spouse after transitioning, this does not mean that the rest of society is accepting.

Having a Mom Become a Dad or a Dad Become a Mom— and How This Might Affect a Family

While children of trans parents deal with many of the same issues as children with gay, lesbian, and bisexual parents—such as divorce, stigmatization, and bul-lying because of their family, not to mention legal and financial prejudice—they also face issues that are unique to their situation. One such issue, according to Canfield-Lenfest, is a parent changing his or her sex while the children still live at home. This might mean that after a parent has gone through the transition process, the child might find him- or herself with no dad and two moms, or no mom and two dads.

Even under the best of circumstances, having a mother or father transition brings a dramatic change to the family. According to Noelle Howey, co-editor of the essay collection *Out of the Ordinary*, it was rather traumatic to have her father change into a woman. "I was terrified," she writes in her essay "Sexual Healing."

> I feared that if I paid attention to my father's transformation, I wouldn't be able to stem the inevitable tide of fierce emotions. Like many children of divorce, I saw my dad at lunch every weekend. He was still somewhat closeted, so he looked like a man. But each Saturday he would appear just a little more girlish. Maybe he would be wearing pedal pushers, or open toed sandals. Sometimes his long fingernails were polished. Often now, he would sit with his legs crossed instead of wide apart, or gently dab the corners of his lips with a napkin instead of rubbing vigorously. His voice started to get a little squeakier and giggly, as though he had been sucking on a helium balloon. I tried to ignore the changes, but each one sent a visceral shock through my body. Watching my father week after week was like watching a film progress one frame at a time.[6]

Things got even more difficult after Howey's father had surgery and made the last changes into fully becoming a woman. "In the aftermath of the surgery," Howey writes, "I fell into a deep clinical depression. Finally, I was grieving the death of a man I barely knew and didn't like but still loved. Moreover, I was lamenting the permanent loss of white-bread normalcy. The surgery made everything final: he was a woman, my parents weren't ever going to reunite, and no one would ever look at us like a standard middle-American family again."[7]

Boylan writes about her children's reaction to her transition as well. Her children were quite a bit younger, not yet teenagers, when she transitioned, and this might have made it easier for them to accept these changes—with the added note that Boylan, of course, is the one writing the book, not her now grown children. Boylan writes about talking to her children about the fact that she was starting to look more and more like a girl. One son commented and said yes, he had noticed and some of his friends even thought his dad was a girl. Boylan went on to explain that while she had looked like a man on the outside for most of her life, on the inside, she felt like a woman. She explained to her son that she was now taking medicine in order to look more on the outside like she felt on the inside. This made perfect sense to the young child. Some time later, when the word *Daddy* started to seem ill fitting, her son pondered what to call her. He quickly rejected Boylan's suggestion, Jenny, which is how she had thought of herself as a young child. Instead he came up with the wonderful word *Maddy*, a great compromise when the word *Daddy* no longer felt right.[8]

Australian psychotherapist Stephen Gunther was an adult when his father first came out as transgender. Gunther considers himself an open-minded person and

The Changes

Not everybody changes his or her sex the same way or goes through the same process. There are a number of factors involved in deciding the extent to which someone wants to transition—emotional, financial, and practical factors. These are some of the steps that someone changing his or her birth sex *might* choose to take. One of the first, most obvious changes might involve clothing—men starting to wear women's clothes and women wearing what we more traditionally think of as men's clothing—though it is often true that many FTM trans have been dressing in men's clothing for as long as they can remember. Someone might then consider what to do about his or her hair; men might grow their hair out, for example, and women might use makeup to add sideburns. People changing from male to female might choose to have their hair removed, on arms, legs, upper body, and in their armpits, as well as on their face. Then there is the issue with voice. While women's voices get lower from taking the hormone testosterone, men's voices will not gain a higher pitch when they take the female hormone estrogen. So male-to-female (MTF) trans persons might use the help of a voice coach to find the right pitch. Nonsurgical breast enhancement is available for MTF trans, such as padded bras or false breasts like those used for women who have had mastectomies. FTM transsexuals often start out by binding their chest in order to make their breasts less visible. Some FTM transsexuals "pack" their underwear to make it look as if they have a penis. (In the 2011 movie *Tomboy*, the main character, Laure, makes a fake penis of play dough, which he puts in his swim trunks to look more like a boy.)

When it comes to more invasive and permanent solutions, people might use silicone to enhance their breasts, or have a double mastectomy to remove them. After months of therapy, someone (over eighteen years old) going through a sex change might be eligible for hormone treatment. FTM trans persons will then take the male hormone testosterone, which brings many physical as well as emotional changes such as growth of facial hair, increased muscle mass, cessation of menstruation, redistribution of body fat, increased sexual drive, thinning of hair, and more.

A MTF person going through hormone treatment will be given the female hormone estrogen. Among other changes, this will lead to loss of body hair, increase in breast tissue, decrease of muscle mass, decreased sexual drive, and redistribution of body fat. (In addition to the obvious emotional trauma of having a parent transform right in front of your eyes, one thing that complicates the process is hormones. The hormone treatments that some trans persons undergo dwarf in intensity the hormone-related mood swings of other major life changes such as adolescence and menopause. This in itself could be enough to wreak havoc in a family.)

There are also a number of medical procedures that someone going through a sex transformation may or may not choose to have: a nose job, face-lifts, surgery to change the shape of the forehead or the angle of the lower jaw and/or the Adam's apple, cheek implants, or voice surgery.

The main medical procedure, however, is the sexual reassignment surgery, which includes a number of different operations including the removal of sex organs and the creation of new genitals. This operation can be both difficult and very expensive, though people ready to transition tend to welcome the changes that help them become more fully who they feel they are.

There are also legal changes to consider, such as updating documents like your driver's license, passport, and birth certificate to reflect a new name and sex.

All in all, many of these changes are physically and emotionally daunting, as well as expensive. From the beginning to the end—therapy, surgery, and legal changes—the full transition usually takes more than three years. Added to these difficulties is the fact that the person transitioning is under the constant scrutiny of his or her surroundings. If your parent or someone you know is going through these changes, it is good to remember that this is certainly not a whim, but something he or she must do to feel complete. It is also worth thinking about the fact that whether or not people have surgery and/or hormone treatment, people choose to express their gender identity in different ways. Sometimes families wonder, "Why does he need to wear a skirt?" The truth is, this is probably exactly what this person needs to do to feel on the outside like she feels on the inside.[9]

he is also, of course, a therapist. But it was still difficult for him to deal with his sixty-five-year-old father's changing into a woman. "He started having umpteen minor operations—to raise the voice, reduce the nose, remove all unwanted facial hair," Gunther wrote in an article for the *Australian Humanities Review*. "My well known and beloved father was disappearing, and in his place was a person I knew less and less. Whilst accepting his decision, I nevertheless tried to dialogue: why not try therapy; what if you regret this; look at the other transsexuals. But, his mind was made up, and this was his path to freedom."[10]

Gunther wrote that he still feels trepidation whenever he mentions to people that he has a transgender father. "There is usually a mixture of intense interest, sympathy, and incredulousness. Almost like I was fathered by a Martian. A part of me cowers in fear at the way others might react, although in fact I always find great support and warmth in the response. A slightly devilish part of me delights in watching the effect on people. There is no familiar niche to place this piece of information, no set response, no social context."[11]

Canfield-Lenfest points out in her *Kids of Trans Resource Guide* that it is important for everybody to remember that this transition is not about the children or teens, but something the parent needs to do for him- or herself. "They still love you. They just need to be who they are," says Robert H., age twenty-five, quoted in the guide.

As mentioned earlier, many children struggle when their parents come out as trans. "It's really hard to deal with sometimes. It gets overwhelming. I remember how my life was before I found out about my father's transition and I remember how perfect it was and how happy I was," says Emma, age fourteen, quoted in the *Kids of Trans Resource Guide*.

Those feelings should be respected, says Canfield-Lenfest. She encourages children and teens to remember that they are indeed the children in this situation and that they need to make sure they get their own needs met—sometimes that means asking for what you need. It might be things like space or time or distance or support from family or a professional. And sometimes it might be things we don't even know that we need.

According to the children of trans parents interviewed in the *Kids of Trans Resource Guide*, there is a positive side of this having-a-transgender-parent coin as well. Many of the now adult children in the guide said, much like the children of gay and lesbian parents, that they had come out of this experience with a greater understanding and tolerance of differences. They felt they could overcome difficulties and that when their parent transitioned and became happier with whom he or she was, they could have a closer and more genuine relationship. Colleen, age forty-four, is quoted in the guide: "I love Lily . . . wish I met her a few years sooner. She is the best Dad ever![12]

Injustice at Every Turn: A Report of the National Transgender Discrimination Survey

A 2011 survey presented by the National Center for Transgender Equality and the National Gay and Lesbian Task Force established some very sad truths about the injustices that the transgender population faces each and every day. In its sample of 6,450 trans persons around the fifty states as well as the District of Columbia, Puerto Rice, Guam, and the U.S. Virgin Islands, the study established some difficult facts, including the following:

- Discrimination was pervasive toward the entire trans community, but it was by far the worst if you were a trans person of color.
- Trans persons responding to the survey tended to live in extreme poverty at much higher rates than the population in general (trans persons were more than four times as likely as the population in general to have an annual income of ten thousand dollars or less).
- Forty-one percent of those who responded to the survey had attempted suicide (that number for the general population is 1.6 percent).
- Trans persons responding to the survey were more than twice as likely as others to be unemployed.
- Reports of harassment, physical assault, and sexual violence against trans persons were alarmingly high compared to those of the general population.
- A large percent of all trans persons in the survey said they had been denied a home or an apartment due to being transgender, though American Indian transgender persons seemed to be rejected in the largest numbers.
- More than half of all trans persons lost their families when they transitioned. Only 43 percent maintained some family bonds. In its consecutive summary the report concluded, "Transgender and gender non-conforming people face injustices at every turn: in childhood homes, in school systems

that promise to shelter and educate, in harsh and exclusionary workplaces, at the grocery store, the hotel front desk, in doctors' offices and emergency room, before judges and at the hands of landlords, police officers, health care workers and other service providers."

- Yet, and here is a very telling part of the survey, 78 percent of those who responded to the survey said that despite being mistreated at work and discriminated against, they still felt more comfortable in the workplace after transitioning than they did before.[13]

What about the Children?

Again, we must ask the most important question, What about the children? What does science say about children growing up with transgender parents? As we have seen, it is easy to get lost in the heated media debate of just how well children of LGBTQ families are faring, the debate often motivated by religious and political fervor. Psychiatrist, lawyer, and author Richard Green, however, approaches the issue of transgender parents from a strictly scientific point of view in his book *Sexual Science and the Law*. In his book, Green discusses a Colorado court case from 1978 in which he testified regarding transsexual parents' influence on their children: "The conclusions so far do not show any significant difference between the children being raised in homosexual or even transsexual settings compared to the children being raised in the traditional heterosexual settings." According to Green, there are a number of angles to consider when you look at how the children are faring, among them, the age and the sex of the children, the gender of the parents, and the political religious climate of the area where they live.[14]

In her book *Lesbian and Gay Parents*, Goldberg has also established the fact that children with trans parents have no more gender identity conflicts than the population as a whole.[15] (And it should be noted that "gender identity conflicts" might have nothing at all to do with the emotional health of a certain individual, but rather how we in society choose to categorize sex and gender. A gender nonconforming person might not have a conflict at all were it not for the rest of society's eagerness to fit that person into a role he or she has rejected.)

Blogger Diane Wilson writes on her website about this very issue—that no matter how hard it is, it is what must be done: "'Differently gendered.' Catchy, perhaps, but it would be more direct to say that I'm a transsexual. It's been an interesting life, but the only thing I can compare it to is pretending *not* to be transsexual. Stopping the pretense and being true to myself has been a much better way to live."[16]

Canfield-Lenfest—like blogger Wilson and Boylan with her "it is what it is" comment—also emphasizes that this is simply something that has to happen. Your parents, Canfield-Lenfest says, have to do what they have to do in order to be fully themselves; the world just has to allow it.

JamieAnn's Family

JamieAnn is not the daughter of an LGBTQ person. She is a sixty-five-year-old woman with short, wispy blond hair and a loud and ready laugh. She was born with male genitalia, and although it never felt right, she lived as a male for most of her life. Now referring to herself as a TransWoman, JamieAnn is married to the same woman she married as a man more than forty years ago. She hopes that her story will help people understand the concept of transgender better and also gain a better understanding about what gender nonconforming people go through when prevented from being who they really are.

"I knew when I was three that I was different and that I wasn't being treated the way I felt," JamieAnn said in our interview. Jim, as JamieAnn was then called, acted on his feelings by dressing like a girl and wearing his mom's shoes, something that can be seen as typical child behavior. But when it was time to start school Jim's dad said he couldn't go to school looking like a girl, and Jim had to cut off his red curls. Being a child in great need of love and affirmation, Jim wanted nothing more than to please his dad, so cutting his hair didn't even feel like that big a sacrifice. "Sitting in the barber's chair watching the curls fall to the floor, I decided that I would be the best little boy I could be," JamieAnn said.

Jim was fortunate to have inherited his father's athletic prowess and he excelled at sports, which made getting through school easier. "I carried on the charade," JamieAnn said. And Jim felt that while people admired him for his athletic ability, it wasn't really "him" they admired; it was the person he pretended to be. "I never felt accepted and I never felt affirmed because I was another person inside that scab of a boy."

Jim got married to his high school sweetheart at age twenty-one, and they had their first child that same year. He went to college and graduate school, and by the age of twenty-five, had a PhD in geology. Even though graduate school was a bit better—he was able to socialize with people with the same academic interests—having male friends was extremely difficult. "I had to try so hard to be a friend. I always felt fragile, never secure."

It was getting increasingly more difficult for Jim to live the life he had set up for himself. "I managed to get into my forties," JamieAnn said. "But I felt I had no control of my life." Jim acted out with sexual indiscretions, alcohol, and marking his body. (JamieAnn is completely covered in tattoos on her upper arms, her entire torso and her legs down to her mid-calves.) He felt extremely fragile. "I could not control the person buried inside. If I let JamieAnn out I thought I would lose everything, my wife, my kids, my job, my parents, so I sucked it up." At one point Jim even tried, unsuccessfully, to kill himself.

But there came a time when Jim could no longer continue the way things were. If he couldn't live with his true identity he would die. It was as simple as that. Without consulting anyone, and without the help of a doctor or a therapist, he started taking contraband estrogen. That is how many trans persons do it, JamieAnn said, because they simply don't have the money or access to the help they should have. "I was scared to death," she said. But at this point Jim was resigned to whatever might happen. In retrospect, JamieAnn is not proud of the fact that she did not consult her wife before beginning therapy, but at the time Jim knew that he would not allow himself to be talked out of it.

A few months into the estrogen treatment, Jim told his wife how he felt and what he needed to do. But even after that very difficult moment, Jim's trials were far from over. Four days after the conversation with his wife, his sister died (JamieAnn's sister's name was Ann, the name she added as a second name when she became a woman), and Jim and his wife did not speak of gender again for an entire year. JamieAnn thinks of that year as a year of darkness, or rather, she barely remembers it at all, that is how sad and difficult it was to be forced into hiding again after the mustering of courage and the initial rush of coming out. But Jim and his wife moved on. Jim understood that without counseling they would not make it, and here began a rocky and difficult road toward healing and JamieAnn's ability to finally become the person she had always been on the inside.

The coming-out process is still ongoing, JamieAnn said. For the following four years, while she was presenting increasingly more often as JamieAnn, her wife was struggling. She was adamant that they not share JamieAnn's transition with their adult children and young grandchildren. JamieAnn was well aware of and deeply sympathetic to the difficulties her transition brought her wife. "She lost her husband," she said. (Even after sorting through the gender and sexual identity vocabulary, while not always sure of the right word to use or even how to think of her own sexuality, JamieAnn now knows that she is pansexual. This means that the gender/sex of the person she loves is simply inconsequential.)

It took four years before JamieAnn's wife was ready for their adult children, forty-one and thirty-eight at the time, to find out. JamieAnn and her wife set up an appointment with the children and their spouses and told them to be there alone, without their children. They later found out that their son had been worried, wondering if one of his parents was seriously ill. But their daughter told him she was sure it had to do with gender. She had figured it out on her own.

When they met with their children, and JamieAnn (who was there as Jim) told them who she really was, the two in-laws and their daughter immediately embraced JamieAnn in a gesture of support. Their son was more hesitant. "What he finally said was, 'But Dad, you're the one I go hiking with, and play golf with.' It was a poignant statement that suggested that he believed that now he lost all that," JamieAnn said.

For their daughter, learning about Jim's unhappiness with his gender role explained a lot of things, things about Jim's failings as a father. JamieAnn coming out was an affirmation that there was something deeper behind her father's behavior, something that had nothing to do with her.

In a gesture of goodwill, and needing her family to love and affirm her, JamieAnn suggested that they could still call her Dad, something she is not so sure of anymore.

Shortly after JamieAnn came out to her children, her daughter called and invited her to her home. She had also invited one of her friends and her sister-in-law. For the first time when seeing her daughter and her daughter-in-law, JamieAnn went as a woman. She had taken time and care to dress just right, while staying somewhat conservative. "I looked cute," she said, "in jeans and a black top." The evening went wonderfully, and JamieAnn's daughter-in-law later confessed that she had been a little worried about meeting JamieAnn, expecting "some garish presentation of a guy in a dress." JamieAnn totally gets this. "It is the image that media has given us," she said. "We're always the butt of the joke." But she found their acceptance surprising and pleasing and her daughter and daughter-in-law helped alleviate many of her fears.

JamieAnn's son was not yet ready to face this new reality. "I don't want to talk about this, and about you," he said. Every time JamieAnn went to her son's house she had to present as Jim. For a while it was quite the ordeal. She had to carry an extra set of clothes in the back of the car, crawl back there before going to her son's house and change out of skirts or dresses, take off her wig and be Jim.

But about a month and a half after the evening at her daughter's home, the phone call from her son came. He was ready to meet JamieAnn. "He came over and brought lunch," she said. "We had a three-hour visit but didn't delve into any history. And he asked no questions, but that was fine. He was just like he always is. There seemed to be no animosity, no fear, and no feeling that he wished things were different."

There was still one more hurdle to jump through for JamieAnn and her wife before JamieAnn could present fully twenty-four-seven and not ever again have to hide who she was. The grandchildren!

Yet again she had to wait for everybody to be ready. "My kids didn't want me to come out to [the grandchildren]," JamieAnn said. "They wanted to do it." When told about her grandfather, JamieAnn's granddaughter, an unusually thoughtful sixteen-year-old at the time, immediately wondered, "What does this mean for Papa?" JamieAnn's grandson, then thirteen, cried and said, "It would be easier if Papa was gay!"

At the time for our interview, three years later, JamieAnn and her wife had just returned from a camping trip to Wyoming with their two children and their families. Many years earlier, when JamieAnn's father was seventy, she (as Jim of course) hiked up a peak with her father. Now JamieAnn hiked with her son and her grandson. She left her wig behind. "It was just one more thing to fuss with," she said. "I'm sure I must have looked like a gender queer person out there on the trail."

Both of JamieAnn's older grandchildren expressed interest in LGBTQ concerns after JamieAnn came out. Her granddaughter has written both creative writing and nonfiction pieces on LGBTQ issues, and her grandson expressed an interest in volunteering with Minnesota United, fighting the marriage amendment on the ballot in the fall of 2012. (The amendment was voted down in November 2012, in a historical first popular vote rejecting anti-same-sex marriage measures.) Both of the older grandchildren vehemently objected to their other grandmother when she said hostile things about JamieAnn and her wife.

JamieAnn also has another grandchild. He, however, never had to adjust to any changes as he was only five months old when JamieAnn came out (and four years old at the time of this writing), and this is the only reality he has ever known. He calls JamieAnn Gran and JamieAnn's wife Grandma. In fact, he pulls the two words together into one fabulous word, Grandmagran. He is entirely at ease with his grandma, and in its extension, all her wigs. "When he stays with us, he always comes into our bedroom in the morning," JamieAnn said. "Gran, get your hair, he says." JamieAnn and her wife have not tried to revise history. They embrace their past as a part of who they are today. They have pictures of Jim around the house and JamieAnn said she is waiting for the day when her grandson will start asking questions about why his grandma looks like a boy in the pictures.

JamieAnn does not identify as gender queer, she said, but as female. And lately she feels as if she can allow herself to reclaim some of the male characteristics that she actually likes about herself. This is sometimes difficult for Trans-Women, she said. "TransWomen in particular tend to want to be one hundred percent women because it is important for them not to be outed. For me," she said, "I'm happy to claim whatever male aspects of my life I *can* claim, some days more and some days less."

Overall while, admittedly, there are still things to work out within the family dynamics, JamieAnn feels that she and her wife, the kids, and the grandkids have come a long way, and she credits therapy with that success. "The grandkids are super," she said about their acceptance. "We are a fabulous family."

But JamieAnn emphasized that she feels that she comes from a privileged position and that her experience is unlike that of many, perhaps most, trans persons. Being white means that she does not have to deal with racial prejudice and that she is not denied social privileges based on race. She is educated, she said, she is able, and she is a Christian. According to JamieAnn, it is important to pay attention to what we have. Being a woman, she is particularly aware of male privilege in our society, she said, though there certainly is such a thing as female privilege as well, even if it looks different. Perhaps the most important female privilege she has noticed is having access to close female relationships, something she calls "deeply fundamental." JamieAnn is enormously grateful to be able to be a part of the loving, emotionally supportive community that women build. She talks about something she calls "gender privilege," which she said, "is not something cis gender persons ever think about." (*Cis gender* refers to people who are born with the genitalia that reflects the idea they have about their own sex—the majority of people are cis gender, or at least so we believe. The concept of cis gender, however, is controversial and only makes sense if we subscribe to the binary male-female.) In fact, JamieAnn said, "It is a cis gender privilege *not to* have to think about gender."[17]

Notes

1. Jennifer Finney Boylan, *She's Not There: A Life in Two Genders* (New York: Random House, 2003), 172–73.
2. Monica Canfield-Lenfest, *Kids of Trans Resource Guide*, COLAGE, www.colage.org/resources/kot/ (accessed August 10, 2012), 3, 5, 23.
3. Canfield-Lenfest, *Kids of Trans Resource Guide*, 5.
4. JamieAnn, Skype interview by author, August 15, 2012.
5. Abbie E. Goldberg, *Lesbian and Gay Parents and Their Children: Research on the Family Life Cycle* (Washington, D.C.: American Psychological Association, 2010), 127, 186.
6. Noelle Howey, "Sexual Healing," in *Out of the Ordinary: Essays on Growing Up with Gay, Lesbian, and Transgender Parents*, ed. Noelle Howey and Ellen Samuels (New York: St. Martin's Press, 2000), 43.
7. Howey, "Sexual Healing," 47.
8. Boylan, *She's Not There*, 157–59.
9. Cynthia L. Winfield, *Gender Identity: The Ultimate Teen Guide* (Lanham, Md.: Scarecrow Press, 2007), 105–26.

10. Stephen Gunther, "My Transsexual Father," *Australian Humanities Review*, August 1997, 1, 2.
11. Gunther, "My Transsexual Father," 1, 2.
12. Canfield-Lenfest, *Kids of Trans Resource Guide*, 11–25.
13. Jaime M. Grant, PhD, Lisa A. Mottet, JD, Justin Tanis, DMin, Jack Harrison, Jody L. Herman, PhD, and Mara Keisling, *Injustice at Every Turn: A Report of the National Transgender Discrimination Survey*, Washington, D.C.: National Center for Transgender Equality, National Gay and Lesbian Task Force, 2011.
14. Richard Green, *Sexual Science and the Law* (Cambridge, Mass.: Harvard University Press, 1992), 43.
15. Goldberg, *Lesbian and Gay Parents*, 128.
16. Diane Wilson, "Differently Gendered," Firelily Designs, www.firelily.com/gender/ (accessed October 12, 2012).
17. JamieAnn, Skype interviews by author, August 15 and September 30, 2012.

LOVE AND MARRIAGE ...AMENDMENTS

Love and Marriage

A discussion of LGBTQ rights must necessarily begin with marriage. Something so fundamental to how we in our culture organize our lives and our families—by legally joining our lives with that of someone we love and, in its extension, acquiring the legal and emotional protection for our children, which often comes with marriage—is not available to a large part of the population; nine million LGBTQ persons to be exact.

"Marriage equity is, to my mind, the distillation of America," Andrew Sullivan writes in a *Newsweek* article, reflecting on his own same-sex marriage. He continues, "If you're a heterosexual reading this, have you ever considered for a millisecond that your right to pursue happiness did not include your right to marry the person you love?" Sullivan goes on to talk about the fact that this fundamental right to marry is the reason why the U.S. Supreme Court has gone out of its way to make sure it is protected for prisoners on death row, soldiers at war, even noncitizens. In fact, you can be divorced ten times over, Sullivan reminds us, you can be a deadbeat dad or a felon, yet your right to marry is still protected. In his article, Sullivan quotes a 1959 passage by Hannah Arendt: "The right to marry whoever one wishes is an elementary human right. . . . Even political rights, like the right to vote, and nearly all other rights enumerated in the Constitution, are secondary to the inalienable human rights to 'life, liberty and the pursuit of happiness' proclaimed in the Declaration of Independence, and to this category the right to home and marriage unquestionably belongs."[1]

Still, this right to marry is not available to everyone. When Zach Wahls first learned that not everybody is allowed to marry, he was a young child watching television on the couch in his living room. On the TV screen a politician talked about marriage as being between a man and a woman only. Wahls was confused. He had been there for his moms' wedding. He had even walked down the aisle

In 2012, nine states and Washington, DC, had legalized same-sex marriage.

with them. He asked his moms what the man meant, if it was true that marriage was really only for a man and a woman. His moms confirmed to their bewildered child that yes, it was true; their marriage wasn't actually legal, just symbolic.

When Zach Wahls was fourteen, his biological mother, Terry, was very sick with multiple sclerosis (MS), a debilitating disease that affects the central nervous system. She was quickly becoming weaker and weaker. Wahls knew that MS could lead to coma and death, and as if having to worry about his mother's health was not enough for a fourteen-year-old, he also constantly worried about what would happen to him and his sister if their mother died or became incapacitated. Wahls's mother was married to Jackie, her partner of ten years, and someone Wahls and

> ## Same-Sex Marriage in the United States
>
> As of 2012, the following states in the United States had legalized same-sex marriage: Connecticut (2008), Iowa (2009), Maine (2012), Maryland (2012), Massachusetts (2004; Massachusetts was the first state in this country to legalize same-sex marriage), New Hampshire (2010), New York (2011), Vermont (2009), Washington, DC (2009), Washington (2012), and two west coast Native American tribes, the Coquille Tribe of Oregon (2009) and the Suquamish Tribe of Washington (2011).
>
> The state of California has a unique same-sex marriage history. In June of 2008, it became the second state in the union to grant same-sex marriage licenses. In November of 2008, due to the passage of Proposition 8, which said that "only marriage between a man and a woman is valid or recognized in California," same-sex marriage licenses were no longer issued. Marriages performed before Proposition 8, in California or elsewhere, are still recognized by the state of California. The 1996 Defense of Marriage Act states, however, that the federal government does not recognize same-sex marriages, no matter where they have been entered.

his sister had grown up with as their other mother, but in Iowa at that time, that marriage was not legally valid. Jackie had no legal custody rights to the children.

In addition to the children's fear of losing their mother, the two women's lack of a legal bond brought other complications as well. When Wahls's biological mother, Terry, was in horrible pain with MS-related "zingers," his other mom, Jackie, brought her to the hospital. Terry almost died after being given morphine for pain. In combination with her other strong medications, the morphine was too much for her system. The doctors were not legally bound to consider anything Jackie told them. Jackie was not only Terry's wife but also a nurse, and she knew that the doctors should not give Terry morphine, but because the two were not legally married, she was not included in the discussion.[2]

Kaley, age twenty-one (interviewed in chapter 10), said that while she was not aware of any legal problems due to her moms' inability to marry when she was growing up, she learned much later that there were indeed issues. Some time back, when she was speaking on a panel with one of her moms, her mom said that when Kaley was little and adopted from Peru, only one of her moms was able to be on her birth certificate. Later, her other mom got a court order for

> ## ❗ Civil Unions
>
> Civil unions are a close kin to marriage. They are available in some states and some countries and vary in their similarities to marriage in degree and number of rights. There is much controversy regarding the usefulness and legitimacy of civil unions. Many opponents of same-sex marriage feel that civil unions are just another way for same-sex couples to be married, that it is just another name for marriage. Same-sex proponents, on the other hand, often complain that civil unions don't offer the same legal rights and protections that marriage does. In addition, marriage in and of itself, some believe, holds certain symbolism not attached to civil unions and should be available to everybody.
>
> Some states have created their own alternatives to marriage. California offers the option of a domestic partnership, which addresses many (though not all) of the legal areas that marriage and civil unions do.

legal guardianship, which she always carried with her in case she would ever need to prove that she too was Kaley's mother.[3]

A Short History of Same-Sex Marriage

There is quite a bit of evidence that way back in history, in certain places and during certain times, same-sex marriages were not only accepted but even celebrated. But in recent history, in most parts of the world, LGBTQ persons have been closeted, and marriage has been nothing but a pie in the sky. In the late 1980s, however, the AIDS epidemic brought to light some new and soon very overwhelming problems for LGBTQ persons, gay men in particular, who were partnered but did not have legal ties. Many gay men with partners in the hospital suddenly found that they didn't have visitation rights and could not see their loved ones, even as they were dying. In addition, if their partner died, they had no right to the inheritance, even if they had lived together most of their lives. In some cases, they lost not only a beloved partner but also their home and their children.

This wave of deaths and the problems it brought to light made the LGBTQ community increasingly more active. They became more verbal and started demanding equal rights. "The marriage exclusion is offensive," says Nan D. Hunter, director of the Lesbian and Gay Rights Project of the American Civil Liberties Union, in a not atypical 1989 article in the *New York Times*. "It carries a strong symbolic as well as a legal message that lesbian and gay Americans are relegated to second-class status."[4]

Not surprisingly, increased gay-rights activism in the 1980s led to counter-attacks by gay-rights opponents. Gary L. Bauer, President Ronald Reagan's domestic affairs adviser and later the head of the Family Research Council, an active and media-savvy conservative Christian group located in Washington, says in the same *New York Times* article, "We see same-sex marriage as a major battleground in the 1990's." He went on to state that same-sex marriage would "undermine deeply held and broadly accepted ideas of normalcy."[5]

But same-sex marriage activists would not let themselves be silenced. In 1993, the first lawsuit questioning the constitutionality of not allowing same-sex couples to marry took place in Hawaii: *Baehr v. Lewin*.

"The same-sex marriage cases, of which *Baehr* was the first important one," Carlos A. Ball writes in his book *From the Closet to the Courtroom*,

> have done more to increase the visibility of LGBT people than any other strategy pursued by the LGBT rights movement in the last twenty years. The lawsuits have forced the country as a whole to grapple with the question of whether it is legally and morally defensible to deny an entire group of individuals access to the hundreds of rights and benefits that our society allocates through the institution of marriage. As a result of *Baehr*, and of the same-sex marriage cases that followed, it has become much more difficult for Americans to continue to pretend that LGBT people either do not exist or that their needs and aspirations are not worth considering.[6]

In 1996, Bill Clinton signed into law the Defense of Marriage Act (DOMA), which ruled that marriage was an act between one man and one woman. (Clinton has, since that time, shown increasing discomfort with his decision to sign DOMA into law and has asked that it be repealed. It is believed that he signed in order to assuage an aggressive Republican contingency right before the election, not wanting to hand it an issue—not signing—that could lose him the election.)

Until DOMA passed, the federal government had more or less stayed out of the marriage business; whatever an individual state decided was also recognized on a federal level. Since DOMA, however, federal law now prohibits same-sex marriages performed in an individual state from being recognized at a federal level. In addition, because of DOMA, neither California's domestic partnership nor civil unions in other U.S. states are, in May of 2013, recognized by the federal government.

First Gay Marriage?

According to a 2012 article in the Minneapolis-St. Paul daily paper, the *Pioneer Press*, Minnesota might be able to claim the first same-sex marriage in this country in recent history, as early as in 1971! A now retired minister, Roger Lynn, interviewed in the article, told the story of how two young men, Jack Baker and Michael McConnell, asked him to marry them in 1971. They had even, with just a little cheating, acquired a marriage license, using the name Pat Lyn on the line for the wife's name. (Their 1970 application for a marriage license made national news. They were turned down at that time.) "I knew they were stretching the law," Lynn said, "but as far as I was concerned, it was a legitimate marriage." Lynn performed the ceremony for the two men. But the Minnesota Supreme Court struck it down in a ruling that ended up actually banning gay marriage in Minnesota. Before, gay marriage had simply not been discussed. Thus, this case led to a step backward in the struggle for same-sex marriage. In the long run, however, it helped the cause, Dale Carpenter, professor at the University of Minnesota law school, said in the same article. "It is without question the first time a state supreme court addressed the issue of same-sex marriage. Legally it was a setback—culturally and politically it was a planting of a seed. It's the way change happens."[7]

Jack Baker and Michael McConnell are still together and live in south Minneapolis.

That Was Then. This Is Now.

President Obama, who, when running for president in 2008 endorsed a repeal of DOMA (meaning he did not want the federal government to overrule the laws of individual states regarding same-sex marriages), was soon accused by many of his fellow Democrats of dragging his feet on the topic of same-sex marriage, using the excuse that his views were "evolving." Nevertheless, on September 20, 2011, he did take a stand for LGBTQ rights when putting a stop to the 1993 Don't Ask, Don't Tell policy, which prohibited openly gay and lesbian persons from serving in the U.S. military.

Less than a year after the end of Don't Ask, Don't Tell (which kept LGBTQ persons closeted), Obama's vice president, Joe Biden, made a surprising comment

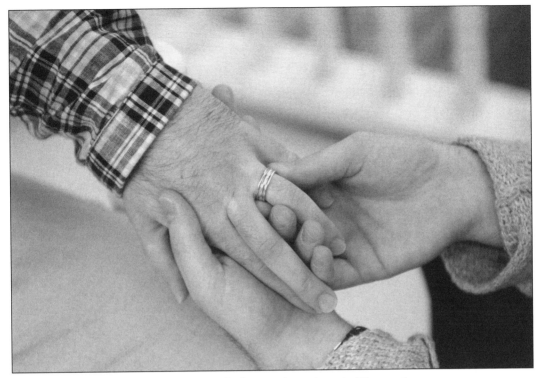

The very first same-sex marriage might have taken place in Minnesota.

Is Marriage Really Necessary?

Not everyone is excited about marriage. In a 2011 article in *Dick and Sharon's LA Progressive*, a daily online newspaper out of Los Angeles, Kivi Neimi wrote about her ambivalent thoughts on this topic: "Earlier this week, New York legalized gay marriage. I won't go into how I think marriage is a broken institution. It is an institution, with legal rights granted to it. As long as the United States government is going to grant privileges to people based upon entering into this institution of marriage then marriage should be open to all people, no matter how they unite. Black and white, man and woman, able-bodied and disabled, or man and man—everyone should be able to partake—IF THEY WANT. Here is the rub. Some of us don't want to."

Neimi went on to talk about how moved she was watching the vote in the New York senate, simply because of the symbolic value of taking away another obstacle to equality. Still, she is concerned that marriage equality not be seen as an end-all, that while allowing same-sex marriage does validate the relationships of LGBTQ persons, it is also, Neimi said, "an assimilation into a broken society."[8]

> ## ❗ Overcoming Invisibility
>
> In the introduction to his book *From the Closet to the Courtroom*, Carlos Ball compares African Americans' struggles for equality with the emerging rights of LGBTQ persons. "Overcoming invisibility," he writes, "is the first step in successfully demanding basic civil rights."
>
> Bell believes that it was not a coincidence that the Supreme Court finally "recognized the capabilities and hopes of the African Americans" in 1954 with its *Brown v. Board of Education* ruling only two years after Ralph Ellison's book *Invisible Man* was published (1952), a book that brought to light the invisibility of African Americans in this country. After *Brown v. Board of Education*, it was deemed no longer constitutional to segregate black and white students into separate schools.[9]

in an interview on NBC's *Meet the Press*. "I am absolutely comfortable with the fact that men marrying men, women marrying women and heterosexual men and women marrying one another are entitled to the same exact rights, all the civil rights, all the civil liberties," he said.[10] Then he added, as an afterthought, that of course, the president was the one in charge of policy making, not him.

After his statement, Biden was accused both of tying president Obama's hands in this matter, making it necessary for him to make a statement in favor of same-sex marriage, and of testing the water for the president, gauging the public's response to such a statement. Be that as it may, after years of procrastination, the president did, in fact, make a statement, only three days after Biden took his public stand in favor of same-sex marriage. "At a certain point, I've just concluded that for me personally it is important for me [*sic*] to go ahead and affirm that I think same-sex couples should be able to get married," President Obama said in a historic interview on *ABC News* on May 9, 2012.[11]

While the president's endorsement was an important step in the direction toward marriage equality, most states in the country (and most countries in the world) have far to go before LGBTQ families can enjoy the same legal rights and protection that most people take for granted.

Andrew, age eighteen, grew up with two dads in the state of Wisconsin. His dads travelled to California to get married in 2008, when it was legal there. Their marriage was not then, and is not now in 2012, legal in Wisconsin. Andrew feels that Obama's endorsements and support for gay marriage is very good news. But one of his dads "took the cynical approach" to the endorsement, Andrew says.

He felt that it was all about politics and timing and that this endorsement could have come a lot sooner.[12]

Don't Ask, Don't Tell—One Year Later

In an article in *Huffington Post*, Lila Shapiro revisits Don't Ask, Don't Tell one year after its repeal, reviewing a study by the Palm Center, a resource institute that specializes in studies of LGBTQ persons and the military. The study shows that the negative consequences of the repeal, feared by some, did not materialize. After interviews, research, and observations, Aaron Belkin, the founding director of the Palm Center and lead author of the study, said in the *Huffington Post* article, "For almost twenty years, experts predicted that allowing gays and lesbians to serve openly would harm the military. Now the evidence is in, and the conclusion is clear: repealing 'don't ask, don't tell' did not harm the military, and if anything made it easier for the Pentagon to pursue its mission."[13]

What about the Kids?

"They should be able to get married," Casey, seventeen, said about her two moms. "When I was a young kid my mom would not have been able to adopt me if something had happened to my biological mom."[14]

Jonathan, age fourteen, was also dismayed about the prejudice against his moms and the fact that they couldn't get married. Among other things, he finds it confusing to fill out forms. They are never designed for his family. No matter how you do it, it ends up making you feel dishonest, he said.[15]

Huda Jadallah and Deanna Karraa live in the Bay Area in California with their three children. As a part of the Marriage Equality Movement Family Story Quilt, Jadallah told their family story. Not being able to marry has brought considerable hardship to their family and perhaps particularly to their children, Jadallah said in her essay. "The inability to marry as lesbian mothers created economic, social, emotional, and legal challenges to our family. We were denied access to housing, healthcare, and our children have had the painful experience of having their family challenged [and] disrespected."[16]

Jadallah also talked about adoption costs related to cross-adopting their three children, but said that while the financial strain was difficult, the emotional burden was worse. "We were told that in order to complete the adoption we had to inform our four-year-old [twin] sons that they were being adopted. Our boys never questioned that we were a family until that moment. The internal disruption to their sense of self and family was irreversible. The process the [authorities] made us go through was not in the best interest of our children—rather it denied the legitimacy of the family they always had."[17]

Why the Ruckus?

So why does same-sex marriage seem like such a threat to the rest of society? Blogger Glennon Melton writes in an article titled "A Mountain I'm Willing to Die On," "I've been married for nine years and barely any gay people have tried to break up my marriage."[18]

Yet, the very idea of same-sex marriage seems to threaten the fabric of our culture. Jan LaRue, chief counsel for Concerned Women for America, a group that refers to itself as the nation's largest public policy organization for women, writes the following in one of her ten talking points for why same-sex marriage is bad:

> Homosexual marriage will devalue your marriage. A license to marry is a legal document by which government will treat same-sex marriage as if it were equal to the real thing. A license speaks for the government and will tell society that government says the marriages are equal. Any time a lesser thing is made equal to a greater, the greater is devalued. For example:
>
> If the Smithsonian Museum displays a hunk of polished blue glass next to the Hope Diamond with a sign that says, "These are of equal value," and treats them as if they were, the Hope Diamond is devalued in the public's eye. The government says it's just expensive blue glass. The history and mystery are lost too.[19]

LaRue then goes on to give a number of other lofty metaphors meant to show how heterosexual marriages will mean nothing if same-sex marriages are allowed. One not-so-logical example that LaRue uses is if someone were to use a robot as an employee, the real employees would be devalued as it would be obvious to them that anyone could do their job. Another example that she uses is one where the government (for inexplicable reasons) would give a babysitter the same rights over a child as a parent has, in which case, LaRue concludes, the parent would be devalued and become just like a babysitter.[20]

In this country, it is difficult to find examples of people opposing same-sex marriage without deep-seated religious reasons. This is also true for Concerned Women for America, which says on its website that it wants to "bring Biblical principles into all levels of public policy."

What Happens When Same-Sex Marriage Becomes Legal?

In an article on the *New York Times* website, "Motherlode," Lisa Belkin interviews M. V. Lee Badgett, director of the Williams Institute on Sexual Orientation, Law and Public Policy at the UCLA School of Law, about her book *When Gay People Get Married: What Happens When Societies Legalize Same-Sex Marriages.* She asks about what we can learn from the Netherlands, a country that legalized same-sex marriage in 2001. Badgett said in the interview that research findings showed that even though many of the Dutch couples had been together for a long time, the ability to get married changed their relationship. They felt more committed, more responsible for their spouse, and even more connected on a spiritual level. The couples who were able to get married also felt that other people saw them differently and took their relationship more seriously. It "reminded them that they're part of a larger social institution." Even more remarkable was the fact that people who chose to get married after new laws made it possible, were not the only people affected by the changes. Badgett found that "the right to marry even changed people who chose not to marry. Everyone I interviewed noted that they were glad the law had changed—they felt 'invited to the party' . . . and they said that they felt more a part of society as a result." She said that lesbian women and gay men's health were affected by being excluded from the institution of marriage and that when society takes these steps to rectify years of exclusion, it positively affects everybody. "I believe that the sense of increased social inclusion that I saw in the Netherlands has the potential to profoundly change all lesbian, gay, and bisexual people in a positive way in the U.S., too," she said in the interview.[21]

Badgett's conclusion in her study of same-sex marriages in the Netherlands was that instead of same-sex marriage changing or in any way threatening the idea of marriage—because, as it turns out, same-sex couples' marriages tended to be similar to heterosexual couples' marriages in all traditional ways—the Dutch culture had changed its view on same-sex couples. They have become a very integrated part of Dutch society.[22]

Notes

1. Andrew Sullivan, "Why Gay Marriage Is Good for Straight America," *Newsweek*, July 18, 2011, www.thedailybeast.com/newsweek/2011/07/17/andrew-sullivan-why-gay-marriage-is-good-for-america.html (accessed July 2012).
2. Zach Wahls, with Bruce Littlefield, *My Two Moms: Lessons of Love, Strength, and What Makes a Family* (New York: Gotham Books, 2012), 135, 144–45.

3. Kaley, Skype interview by author, October 30, 2012.
4. Philip S. Gutis, "Ideas and Trends; Small Steps Toward Acceptance Renew Debate on Gay Marriage," *New York Times*, November 5, 1989, www.nytimes.com/1989/11/05/weekin review/ideas-trends-small-steps-toward-acceptance-renew-debate-on-gay-marriage.html (accessed August 2012).
5. Gutis, "Ideas and Trends."
6. Carlos A. Ball, *From the Closet to the Courtroom: Five LGBT Rights Lawsuits That Have Changed Our Nation* (Boston, Mass.: Beacon Press, 2010), 3.
7. Doug Belden, "Gay Marriage Landmark? Minnesota Pastor Who Conducted 1971 Ceremony Thinks So," *Pioneer Press*, August 16, 2012.
8. Kivi Neimi, "Gay Pride," *Dick and Sharon's LA Progressive*, www.laprogressive.com/gay-pride-2/ (accessed October 5, 2012).
9. Ball, *From the Closet to the Courtroom*, 1–2.
10. Jackie Calmes and Peter Baker, "Obama Says Same-Sex Marriage Should Be Legal," *New York Times*, May 9, 2012.
11. Calmes and Baker, "Obama Says Same-Sex Marriage Should Be Legal."
12. Andrew, telephone interview by author, May 25, 2012.
13. Lila Shapiro, "Don't Ask Don't Tell Study Shows No Negative Effects on Military One Year after Repeal," *HuffPost Gay Voices*, September 10, 2012, www.huffingtonpost.com/2012/09/10/dont-ask-dont-tell-study_n_1868892.html (accessed February 19, 2013).
14. Casey, in-person interview by author, April 24, 2012.
15. Jonathan, in-person interview by author, May 30, 2012.
16. Huda Jadallah, "Hudah Jadallah and Deanna Karraa," *Marriage Equality USA*, www.marriageequality.org/Huda-Deanna (accessed August 22, 2012).
17. Jadallah, "Hudah Jadallah and Deanna Karraa."
18. Glennon Melton, "A Mountain I'm Willing to Die On," *Momastery* (blog), January 26, 2012, www.huffingtonpost.com/glennon-melton/a-mountain-im-willing-to-die-on_b_1223229.html (accessed January 26, 2012).
19. Jan LaRue, "Talking Points: Why Homosexual 'Marriage' Is Wrong," Concerned Women for America, www.cwfa.org/articledisplay.asp?id=4589 (accessed August 23, 2012).
20. LaRue, "Talking Points."
21. Lisa Belkin, "Dutch Views on Same-Sex Marriage," *New York Times*, November 9, 2009, http://parenting.blogs.nytimes.com/2009/11/09/how-the-dutch-work-same-sex-marriage (accessed March 18, 2013).
22. Belkin, "Dutch Views on Same-Sex Marriage."

OTHER LEGAL ISSUES

Conception

Egg Donation

Egg donation has become a common way for potential lesbian mothers to conceive children together. It is important that new laws to protect children also keep up with new rapidly evolving fertility techniques. *A Legal Guide for Lesbian and Gay Couples* describes how an egg donation, also called ovum donation, works. One partner donates an egg. The egg is then fertilized and placed in the other partner's womb. This way both women are more a part of the child than if the birth mother uses her own eggs. In many states, egg donation is used to legally ensure that the child belongs to both parents. There might still be paperwork to complete, but it can be done during pregnancy, so by the time the baby is born, both mothers are legally considered his or her parents. One negative side of ovum donation is that it is an expensive as well as a medically invasive procedure.[1]

A Disturbing Trend

In her 2009 book *Ties That Bind*, Sarah Schulman addresses what she calls "a budding trend of gay people using the courts to deny their partner's access to children that the two had raised together."[2] In an interview in the book with Kate Kendell, director of the National Coalition for Lesbian Rights, Schulman brought up this trend. Kendell said that though one might think that the religious right, homophobic parents, or disgruntled ex-husbands were the worst enemies trying to take away lesbians' parental rights, she had seen an increasing number of court cases where women who had raised children together were trying to deny each other access to the children. The biological mothers, Kendell said, sometimes even use the old argument that a family with lesbian mothers is not a real family and are, in this way, trying to deny basic parental rights to former lesbian part-

> ## An Egg Donor Court Case
>
> A child custody battle in Florida in 2012 brought to light a not often talked about aspect of lesbian parenthood. Eight years earlier, one mother provided an egg, which was fertilized and planted in her partner's uterus. The long and the short of this story is that a few years after the child was born the birth mother decided to end the relationship. She left with the child, claiming that her partner, the provider of the egg in this case, had no legal right to their daughter. She cited the Florida law that says that egg and sperm donors "relinquish all maternal or paternal rights." The judge grudgingly ruled in favor of the birth mother, but when the case went to appellate court the biological mother (as the woman who provided the egg referred to herself) won, as she was not considered an "egg donor" because the couple had, of course, intended to raise the child together.[4]

ners. Sometimes it works, and the nonbiological mother might be denied the right to see her children. Like Schulman, Kendell believes that some women, when they have the state on their side, might use the power of oppression, formerly used against them, to their own advantage.

As long as we have a system that allows some people to oppress others, Schulman believes, it is easy, even natural, for the oppressed to become the oppressor.[3]

The Sperm

Children with heterosexual parents, or even single parents, usually don't have to explain how they came to be. They can take the time to figure the birds and the bees out for themselves before they are challenged with the task of having to explain it to their peers. But children with two parents of the same gender are often asked how they were conceived.

There are, of course, many different ways in which a child may be conceived. Many women use the "turkey baster" method (it's not usually an actual turkey baster, but a syringe with a plunger as opposed to a bulb at the end). The sperm donor ejaculates into a plastic cup. The semen is collected from the cup with the syringe (the turkey baster) and then deposited inside the woman's vagina. (Often the sperm donor is a relative of the nonbiological mother, in order for the baby to be related by blood to both mothers.)

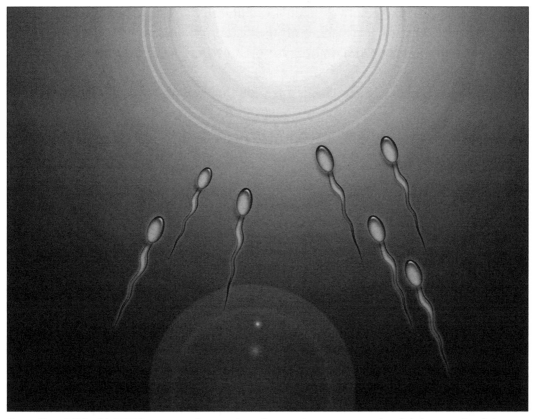

Even if a child of LGBTQ parents knows how he or she was conceived, it is somebody's personal choice whether to share this information when people ask.

Some women choose to have intercourse with the sperm donor in order to conceive, but this might, understandably, not always be an emotionally viable option. Since the creation of the Sperm Bank of California in 1982, a sperm bank dedicated to serving all women, regardless of marital status and sexual orientation, more fertility options are open to lesbian women. Still, donor insemination is probably the easiest and most common way for lesbian women to get pregnant today.[5]

According to the COLAGE *Donor Insemination Guide*, there are three kinds of sperm donors. First, there is the anonymous donor, who donates sperm but never intends to be known to the child. While this works well for some families, a majority of children born from donor insemination, even those who are very content with their families, seem to want to know who their donor is and find out about traits and characteristics they might have inherited from him. Some of the children interviewed in the *Donor Insemination Guide* did, however, change their mind about this as they got older. They concluded that much of their desire to know who their donors were stemmed from the wish to be able to answer people's questions, questions that other children don't have to worry about. Anonymous donors are usually extremely difficult for children to locate later. But the sperm bank might be able to share some of the "identifying numbers" with someone trying to locate a sperm donor because of a serious genetic condition or other health problems.

The second kind of donor is an open identity donor—a donor who agrees to have his identifying information released to the child when the child turns eighteen. While many children are excited to meet their donor, not all choose to do so. Some don't want the involvement of another adult in their life and some might simply not be curious. Some children feel it is disloyal to their parents to seek out the sperm donor, much as adopted children sometimes feel awkward about talking about their biological parents with their adopted parents.

The third kind of donor is the known donor. This refers to a donor that the child knows growing up, a man who may or may not play a big role in the child's life. Older donor insemination children interviewed in the *Donor Insemination Guide* warned other children against one particular aspect of their relationship with a known donor. They cautioned other children against allowing someone else to define their relationship with their donor. One person interviewed in the guide added to this sentiment: "Don't try to place a structure for dad/mom you learn in society—on tv etc.—onto your relationship with your donor. Take the relationship for what it is and nurture it as you become an adult." Another teenager interviewed for the guide talked about his ambiguity about meeting his donor and his concern about how to relate to him. "This person is your father, but not necessarily your dad," he said.[6]

Ry, age seventeen, interviewed in the documentary *Our House*, learned the hard way what can happen if you don't have the right donor arrangement and the right legal protection. While Ry's mothers knew that they did not want the sperm donors in their children's or their own lives and certainly did not view them as fathers to their children, they believed that it would be nice for their children to have known sperm donors. This way the children could learn about their other biological half. In what became a terrifying drama in their family's life, Ry's sperm donor—who was not the same as that of Ry's sister—ended up suing for paternity and visitation rights. "We were forced to articulate what it meant to be a family," Ry said. Ry was ordered to see a court appointed psychiatrist who asked, "Who is your family?" She remembers sobbing and sobbing. "I love my family," she said. "I love my sister. I don't want him to be my father. I could say the wrong thing and I would be on the plane to California." It took four years, a lot of money and a great deal of anguish for Ry's mothers to fight the suit. In the end they won, but much damage had been done. Ry's mothers said that both girls came away with the feeling that their mothers did not know how to protect them. But there is another side of this dark story. In the end, the children gained a whole new appreciation for their parents. "I love my parents so much," Ry said. "I have

Logan's Family

For Logan, age twenty-one, the lack of legal protection from her sperm donor is something that has thrown a dark cloud over her life. After what she went through, Logan would advise anyone to choose an anonymous donor for his or her child.

The first years of Logan's life were very difficult due to the sperm donor and the family's lack of legal protection. Logan's two moms, Jane and Beth, had been together for four or five years before they asked a gay friend to donate sperm for one of them to become pregnant. The donor, Steve, agreed to donate and was on board with Logan's moms' sentiment that he would have no part in the child's life. Today things tend to be more contractual, Logan said, but at the time, it was all by verbal agreement. When Logan was born, however, Steve changed his mind and very much wanted to be a part of Logan's life. In fact, he wanted full custody. Steve took Logan's moms to court and while he did not win full custody, he did get monthly visitation rights with Logan. "It was quite the hoopla in my town," Logan said. The newspapers wrote about it, ridiculing all involved.

Growing up, Logan had to visit with this man she hardly knew once a month. Each time he was scheduled to come and pick her up, she would agonize for days. Not because there was something wrong with Steve—when they were together, Logan said, he was "a nice guy, fun and athletic"—but because the entire setup was strange both for Logan and her moms. Logan began blaming her moms for the awkward visitations with her sperm donor. She felt that her childhood was tainted by these visitations. Eventually, Logan put her foot down, told her sperm donor how she really felt about him, and, finally, the visitations stopped. "I never felt I needed to have a third parent," Logan said. "Two was totally enough for me. I have no yearning to know that genetic part of me." Though, Logan added, she might have the luxury of feeling this way precisely because she indeed does know that genetic part of herself.

In addition to the contentious relationship with her donor, Logan's moms separated when she was quite young. In retrospect, she looks back with admiration on how her moms handled the separation. It would have been easy for her biological mom to dismiss her other mom and prevent her from having legal contact with Logan, but contrary to the women discussed in Sarah Schulman's book, Logan' moms took the high road. Logan grew up spending an equal amount of time with both her moms. She now credits her moms' civil behavior for her having a good relationship with both of them. "I still maintain a really amazing and strong and frequent relationship with both my moms," she said.

Though her childhood was complicated by the difficulties with her sperm donor and her moms' separation, Logan lived in an LGBTQ-friendly area, "a liberal pocket of the south," she called it, which in many ways made life easier. She also went to a private school. It was all "rainbow, peace, and love," she said. "I never felt different about having two moms. Just special. People would say, 'Wow, you have two moms. Man, you're so lucky.'" In many ways, Logan said, growing up with two moms is a huge part of her story now and very much affected the kind of person she turned out to be. "Most obviously by allowing me to be open-minded when it comes to not only alternative life styles but also to people's point of view and eccentricities. Nothing really shocks me." And she also learned much about women. "I didn't just grow up with two moms. I grew up with a tribe of women." This, Logan feels, has made her astutely aware of women's issues. And because she feels she was a struggling teen, she wants to go into social work when she grows up and help teens in need. "I am an advocate," she said. "I'm very loud."

Contrary to other LGBTQ teens who feel it is easier to come out as LGBTQ themselves because they know they have supportive families, Logan's own coming out as a lesbian woman was a great struggle. Even though she grew up in an LGBTQ-friendly community, she also knew how hateful the world could be toward LGBTQ persons. "I was really afraid of the whole right-wing thing," she said. "You know, the 'gay parents raise gay kids' thing." She worried about people judging her moms and believing that it was because Logan had lesbian mothers that she herself turned out to be a lesbian. "I had to really come to terms with that," she said. Today she is happy with who she is and is active in the LGBTQ community in her town. Logan feels it is important to view LGBTQ rights as a civil rights issue. "The community has come a long way," she said, "but there is still so much to be done. . . . It is very important to maintain visibility in the civil eye and push and perpetuate [LGBTQ rights]. This is very much a civil rights issue."[8]

so much respect for them for going all the way with the family they wanted in their hearts and in their minds. Having lesbian parents is not an issue in my life, but will it ever just be nothing?"[7]

According to the *Donor Insemination Guide*, one common question many children have about their donor is "Will he be LGBTQ friendly?" Usually the answer is yes. Donors tend to be aware of the fact that many of those seeking donor services are lesbians, and they will not be surprised that the child has LGBTQ parents.

Almost unanimously, donor insemination children interviewed in the guide urged others in their situation to keep an open dialogue with their parents and be understanding of their parents' possible discomfort when it comes to sperm donor contact. Sometimes the children interviewed were resentful and didn't understand why their parents would have chosen to go with an anonymous donor whom they could never learn about, but the parents often had good reasons for this. They might, for example, have been afraid of losing their child in a custody battle, or even of having their child taken away because they were LGBTQ.

Finding a donor might also add something else to a family, as discussed in Casey's interview in chapter 1: siblings, or "donor siblings" as they are sometimes called. Different sperm banks have different policies but www.donorsibling registry.com is a good place to try to track down donor siblings.

How to Answer Intrusive Questions

Donor insemination children should not be forced to explain how they were conceived—nobody should. Nonetheless, the question is often asked. In addition, even if children who are asked this question have learned a sex-positive approach at home where they have been encouraged to use correct words such as *penis*, *vagina*, and *sperm*, they might be ridiculed when they do, or even prevented from doing so, even though there is really no other way to describe how they came to be.

The COLAGE *Donor Insemination Guide* suggests three phrases for younger children with lesbian mothers to use when asked about their dad:

1. "Everyone has a biological dad, but not everyone has a dad in their family. My biological dad donated his sperm so my mom(s) could have me, but we've never met him.
2. Every baby grows from a sperm and an egg, but the sperm that made me came from a man outside my family.
3. My parents got sperm from a sperm bank to start me growing as a baby."[9]

We're Thankful for Turkey Basters

This section is taken from a blog post written by a child of lesbian and gay parents who was conceived at home, using a turkey baster. This post was written on his thirtieth birthday, which happened to fall on Thanksgiving.

Three decades ago, I was conceived through the ingenuity of three trailblazing queers and an amazingly versatile invention known as a turkey baster. As I reflect on the first three decades of my life, I feel overwhelmed with gratitude for my two moms and my dad, who conjured me out of the ether, immersed me in a community of forward thinkers, raised me with unconditional love, and supported my life's journey at every turn.

I'm grateful that these three individuals managed to think outside the boxes built around them, overcoming assumptions that their sexual orientation was incompatible with their desire to parent, and inventing a successful system of child rearing that spanned three loving households (where there was no established model for them to follow).

I'm grateful that they, through their activism and insistence on recognition, have constantly pushed boundaries, opened countless minds and hearts, and exposed scores of queer would-be parents to new possibilities.

I'm also grateful for the community of queerspawn that I discovered through COLAGE. You inspire me and help me imagine a world, thirty more years into the future, where governments, cultural institutions, and society at large not only recognize and protect, but also encourage and uphold families like ours. I believe that this world is within our reach and that we can help to manifest it through our collective activism and storytelling.

Finally, let me give thanks to the inventor of the turkey baster, whose name is lost to history but whose legacy is great: Your invention has brought Thanksgiving magic to millions of families—in more ways than one for this family.—Darnell Snyder Witt (son of Arvada Darnell, Steve Snyder, and Jeanette Witt)[10]

Many heterosexual couples use sperm donors as well, of course, but this is not obvious to the rest of the world so their children don't need to explain their existence in the same way as children of same-sex couples do.

What about the Sperm Donor?

According to sperm donor Sean Berkley in his blog, "Six Terrifying Things Nobody Tells You about Donating Sperm," the sperm donor gets paid fairly well, but the process of donating sperm is rigorous and not as effortless as it might seem. There are quite a few hoops to jump through before becoming accepted as a donor, such as documenting your own and your family's entire medical history. Among a great number of criteria, Berkley said, he had to be tall (over six feet), not have red hair, and be enrolled in college. He also said that he had lost dates because some girls would not go out with him after finding out that he had donated sperm. He understands their feelings and often considers the ethical issues involved in donating sperm. Still, in the end, he feels he is giving away a great gift, but he adds, "You should know going in that it's a hell of a lot more complicated than just jizzing into a cup." Feasibly, as Berkley is an open identity donor (they get paid more), twelve children might one day show up on his doorstep wanting to get to know their daddy. (Different services have different maximum numbers of children one donor can donate sperm for; the service Berkley worked for has twelve.[11])

Forms, Forms, Forms

In the *Donor Insemination Guide*, DeGroot talks about the emotionally bothersome issue of being handed a form where there is no way for you to honestly represent your family. On the college financial aid forms, for example (the FAFSA), only different-sex parents are recognized, so only one parent's income will be counted. A small break in the many financial disadvantages of same-sex couples, one might assume, but the truth is, many people feel dishonest putting just one parent down when there really should be two. DeGroot encourages applicants to contact the financial aid office to find out who they should list on their forms and how to truthfully represent their family.

Legal Issues Particular to Trans Persons

There is another complication with legal documents about which many are happily oblivious. For the trans population, one major legal barrier and a cause for much discrimination is some trans persons' lack of proper identification. When changing your sex on your passport, on your birth certificate, and in the social security office, for example, the current rule in most states is that you must first have gender reassignment surgery. Not all trans persons or gender nonconforming persons have had this surgery and not all wish to have it. (And there are those who wish to have it but are unable to for a number of reasons, financial reasons being one of them.)

Trans persons are often routinely rejected at the polling booths because the sex on their identification card does not seem in accordance with the gender of their person. The National Center for Transgender Equality calls for changes to these policies.[12]

Another obstacle in the everyday life of trans persons is that most states do not allow people to change their gender marker on day-to-day documents such as driver's licenses without having had "bottom surgery" (genital reconstructive surgery; for more information about this see chapter 3). And the surgery is usually a condition for changing the gender marker on a birth certificate, which in turn is the document we use in order to get *other* documents such as a passport.

Using public restrooms can be difficult for gender nonconforming persons.

JamieAnn, the TransWoman interviewed in chapter 3, mentioned the complications with public restrooms. While this seems a minor issue, JamieAnn said it was a difficult thing for her to negotiate. She often feared that she would get arrested for going into the "wrong" bathroom. She didn't like to tie up the family restrooms as they might be needed by young parents and their children. For a long time, JamieAnn carried a letter about gender identity written by her doctor, "anticipating that a security guard would show up anytime because there was a guy in the women's restroom." It took a long time for JamieAnn to realize that nothing was going to happen, and that people in fact saw her for who she was, a woman using the women's restroom.[13]

Another difficulty for trans persons in particular is convincing health insurance companies to agree to pay for certain medications they sometimes say should not be used by a person of that gender, for example, female hormones for someone transitioning from male to female.

Discrimination in the Workplace

In her book *Lesbian and Gay Parents and Their Children*, Abbie Goldberg discusses the role of the workplace in both helping and hurting LGBTQ families. She talks about several studies that found that a large number of sexual minorities experienced discrimination and prejudice in their workplace due to sexual orientation or gender identity. According to Goldberg, people seemed to hold particularly strong views and be especially hateful toward LGBTQ persons with children. Goldberg says that because of this, it is especially important for workplaces to not only adopt rules that protect LGBTQ persons from prejudice and harassment, but go even further and help ensure benefits for same-sex partners.[14]

Other Rights or Lack Thereof

While same-sex marriage has already been discussed extensively, many other rights denied LGBTQ persons and families are directly tied to this issue. Many of these rights would be taken care of by legalizing same-sex marriage, though this is certainly not a cure-all. For one thing, people should also have the right *not* to marry if they choose. Heterosexual parents don't have to be married for their children to be recognized as the children of both parents, for example.

The Movement Advancement Project is "an independent think tank that provides rigorous research, insight and analysis that help speed equality for lesbian, gay, bisexual and transgender (LGBT) people." In its pamphlet *All Children Matter*, it lists a number of ways in which LGBTQ families are disadvantaged and even kept in poverty. A few of the most important issues the pamphlet points out are that LGBTQ families have unequal access to healthcare (many employers don't recognize same-sex relationships and will not extend health insurance to partners and children); sometimes face unwelcoming healthcare environments; have a higher tax burden; don't have the same adoption rights as heterosexual persons; face hostility in school, the work environment, and the community; and don't have the right to sponsor a noncitizen (immigrant) for permanent residency.[15]

While it certainly seems as though LGBTQ families are fighting an uphill battle, the truth is a great number of organizations and citizen groups are working toward abolishing inequalities. Two very important ones for children with LGBTQ parents are Parents, Families and Friends of Lesbians and Gays (PFLAG) and Gay, Lesbian and Straight Education Network (GLSEN).

PFLAG was one of the first major support groups for LGBTQ persons. The organization was started by Jeanne Manford in 1972, in support of her son, who was beaten in public for being gay. PFLAG is deeply engaged in legal issues and in changing legislation in favor of LGBTQ persons. For example, in the 1990s it helped add gay and lesbian protection to Title IX, a portion of the Education Amendments of 1972 which states, "No person in the United States shall, on the basis of sex, be excluded from participation in, be denied the benefits of, or be subjected to discrimination under any education program or activity receiving federal financial assistance."

PFLAG urges people to be very active in working toward inclusive sensible laws, at the time when the laws are being written. It believes that it is much more difficult to change a law already in place than to try to get it right from the very beginning. On its website PFLAG provides a comprehensive list of political representatives down to the county level. It also has a special page with legislative alerts and updates where you can learn about issues currently up for a vote. And PFLAG provides tips on how to contact your congressman, gives talking points, and suggests the best way to state your case. In August of 2012, issues on the PFLAG website calling for attention included the Every Child Deserves a Family Act. The act would ensure that child welfare workers do not discriminate against adoption or foster parents on the basis of sexual orientation, marital status, or gender identity. Another issue that PFLAG draws attention to is LGBTQ persons in the military. While the repeal of Don't Ask, Don't Tell is a step in the right direction, PFLAG urges activists to work toward equal rights also for transgender service members and LGBTQ persons wishing to enlist. Then there is the Safe Schools Improvement Act, a bill that would potentially amend the Safe and Drug-Free Schools and Communities Act and help schools implement comprehensive anti-bullying policies.

GLSEN is another very active LGBTQ rights organization working first and foremost in the educational system. According to its website, GLSEN "strives to assure that each member of every school community is valued and respected regardless of sexual orientation or gender identity/expression." The organization does this by helping create a Gay-Straight Alliance (GSA) in schools, encouraging members to participate in the Day of Silence (to draw attention to bullying and hate crimes against LGBTQ persons and their families), providing research to help schools learn how to address issues like bullying, and much more.

There are many other organizations, too numerous to mention, that support LGBTQ rights. Some of them are, in no particular order, the Human Rights Campaign, which says it works for lesbian, gay, bisexual, and transgender equal rights; Queer Nation, which was started by AIDS activists in 1990 and is known for its boldness and confrontational tactics; and Lambda Legal, an organization committed to advancing the rights of lesbians, gay men, transgender people, and people with HIV, through litigation and education.

Notes

1. Denis Clifford, Frederick Hertz, and Emily Doskow, *A Legal Guide for Lesbian and Gay Couples* (Berkeley, Calif.: Nolo, 2012), 81.
2. Sarah Schulman, *Ties That Bind: Familial Homophobia and Its Consequences* (New York: The New Press, 2009), 81, 84.
3. Schulman, *Ties That Bind*, 81, 84.
4. James L. Rosica, "Same-Sex Custody Battle Could Change Florida Law," Associated Press, March 4, 2012, news.yahoo.com/same-sex-custody-battle-could-change-florida-law-141246936.html (accessed March 4, 2012).
5. Another, less suitable word for donor insemination is *artificial insemination*. Both terms refer to the process in which a woman gets pregnant by having a donor's sperm deposited inside her vagina, but the term *artificial* feels to some children as though the process by which they were conceived is yet another way to stigmatize them.
6. Jeff DeGroot, *Donor Insemination Guide* (San Francisco: COLAGE, 2010), 19–20, 33.
7. Quoted in Meema Spadola, dir., *Our House: A Very Real Documentary about Kids of Gay and Lesbian Parents* (Brooklyn, N.Y.: First Run/Ikarus Films, 2000).
8. Logan, telephone interview by author, November 1, 2012.
9. DeGroot, *Donor Insemination Guide*, 41.
10. Darnell Snyder Witt, "We're Thankful for Turkey Basters," COLAGE, November 23, 2011, www.colage.org/uncategorized/were-thankful-for-turkey-basters/ (accessed November 8, 2012); published with permission by the author.
11. Sean Berkley, "Six Terrifying Things Nobody Tells You about Donating Sperm," *Cracked.com*, November 12, 2011, www.cracked.com/article_19497_6-terrifying-things-nobody-tells-you-about-donating-sperm.html (accessed June 28, 2012).
12. National Center for Transgender Equality, "ID Documents and Records," 2011, transequality.org/Issues/federal_documents.html (accessed September 20, 2012).
13. JamieAnn, Skype interview by author, September 30, 2012.

14. Abbie E. Goldberg, *Lesbian and Gay Parents and Their Children: Research on the Family Life Cycle* (Washington, D.C.: American Psychological Association, 2010), 121–22.

15. Movement Advancement Project, "All Children Matter: How Legal and Social Inequalities Hurt LGBT Families, Executive Summary," October 2011, www.lgbtmap.org/policy-and -issue-analysis/lgbt-families (accessed July 2012), 2.

BULLYING

··

What Geography Has to Do with It

Wouldn't it be great if a book about LGBTQ issues did not have to include a chapter on bullying? Unfortunately bullying is a dark reality and a very important issue for LGBTQ families—for some, even the most pressing issue. Sadly, it is not unusual to see news stories of gay or gender nonconforming students being bullied so badly that they choose to end their own lives. "Bullied to Death: Victim's Stories," a 2012 episode on ABC's *20/20*, explored this painful topic and the frustration of parents of LGBTQ and other bullied students who were trying to get their children's schools to do something about this enormous problem. According to the show, there are no national guidelines or laws regarding bullying in schools. School districts around the country are pretty much on their own figuring out how to solve the problem or, for that matter, choosing to ignore it.[1]

While most of the students interviewed for this book denied being "seriously" bullied (that was often the very word they used) for having LGBTQ parents, most of their parents had the financial and emotional resources to settle in "safe" communities. Several of them, however, were homeschooled for longer or shorter periods of time, some were in private schools, and some had switched schools for unknown reasons. Casey, age seventeen, said that her moms taught her to stand up for herself, but bullying is not much of an issue for her because her family chooses where they go and who they socialize with. "We avoid places where that could be an issue," Casey said.[2] So while Casey didn't feel that bullying was a problem in her life, her family members did have to plan their life more carefully than people in general in order to avoid being bullied.

The same was true for Kaley, age twenty-one. Kaley went to magnet schools, was never in the public school system growing up, and never had to deal with bullying or heteronormative prejudice, she said. Yet, her moms would role-play with her, set up scenarios in which one of them would challenge her and teach her what to do in different situations. Kaley acknowledged that she was privileged and very much recognized that not all children with LGBTQ parents are lucky enough to live in an LGBTQ-friendly area.[3]

Research shows that children with LGBTQ parents are indeed more stigmatized and are more often the victims of bullying than children and teens in general (though this does not take into consideration children who identify as LGBTQ themselves or who are perceived to be LGBTQ). The Dutch-American study comparing children of lesbian mothers in the two countries showed that children with lesbian parents in the United States were more likely to be bullied than children with lesbian parents in the Netherlands. According to the study, this was due to the fact that the United States has a more macho culture and is less accepting of sexual orientation variation.[4] (Students identifying as LGBTQ or who have LGBTQ parents are, of course, not the only students getting bullied. People get bullied for all kinds of reasons: for being members of a racial or socioeconomic minority, for being handicapped, and for absolutely no reason at all. Yet, even when bullying has nothing to do with LGBTQ issues, slurs like *sissy* and *faggot* are often used.)

As we have learned from the preceding teen stories, where you live matters. There are definitely more or less LGBTQ-friendly areas in this country. California cities like San Francisco, Palm Beach Springs, and West Hollywood tend to be known as LGBTQ friendly. Orlando, Florida, and Cambridge, Massachusetts, are usually on the list, but so are, perhaps more surprisingly, cities like Austin, Texas; Salt Lake City, Utah; Kansas City, Missouri; and Minneapolis, Minnesota.

In her book *Lesbian and Gay Parents and Their Children*, Abbie Goldberg confirms that where you live matters. In fact, she says, gay and lesbian couples with higher education and socioeconomic status are often more flexible to move in order to avoid areas where their families will be oppressed.[5] The opposite side of that coin is, of course, that families without the educational, financial, and professional means have to stay where they are even if that means living in an LGBTQ-hostile area.

Andrew, age eighteen, is a perfect example of how living in an LGBTQ-friendly community can make growing up with gay dads a nonissue. While sad that his parents got a divorce when he was in preschool and that his mother moved away to Connecticut, living in Madison, Wisconsin, Andrew never reflected on the fact that his dad was gay. He was not bullied at school for having two dads, and even though he attended public school, his friends were accepting of his family.[6]

The attitude of your local community toward LGBTQ issues tends to matter in other countries as well. Australian psychotherapist Stephen Gunther says that his father was a fundamentalist Christian, and when he began coming out to his friends as a male-to-female transsexual, he lived in a conservative Tasmanian community. Gunther said his father's friends "dropped away one by one, until only a few remained." Then his father moved from the small conservative community to the more cosmopolitan Melbourne.[7]

What Is Bullying?

We tend to recognize bullying when we see it, but what is it really?

In the documentary *Our House*, fifteen-year-old Ryan was interviewed about her two moms. Not yet out in her school about her family (there had simply never been a reason to tell anybody that she had two moms, she said), she was very excited to tell her friends about it when her moms were getting married. "It was both their dreams," Ryan said. But after she told her friends at school that her moms were getting married, Ryan's life took an ugly turn. "She was put through hell," one of her moms said in the interview. "It's been going on forever." They described how Ryan got pushed and shoved in the school hallways. If Ryan would drop her books, for example, someone would kick them away. Before she told people about her moms' wedding Ryan had believed that she had four close friends. "I lost them, one by one," she said in the interview. At school, she was called *lesbo*, *whore*, *gayrod*. When the abuse had gone on for a long time, they all realized it would not blow over and one of Ryan's moms went to the principal. The principal asked her, "Have you ever thought of changing your lifestyle now that it is affecting your daughter's life at school?"

Ryan's moms took Ryan out of the public school and began homeschooling her.[8]

The world's first known scientific study of bully/victim problems among school children and youth was started by a Swedish man, Dan Olweus, in the 1970s. In his program, called the Olweus Bullying Prevention Program, Olweus explains bullying like this: "A person is bullied when he or she is exposed, repeatedly and over time, to negative actions on the part of one or more other persons, and he or she has difficulty defending himself or herself."[9]

Bullying differs from other kinds of aggression, the Olweus program specifies, in that it usually targets a certain individual, is repetitive, and has a power balance component between the person who bullies and his or her victim. And bullying can take many forms, among them "verbal bullying, social exclusion or isolation, physical bullying, bullying through lies and false rumors, having money or other things taken or damaged, threats or being forced to do things, racial bullying, sexual bullying, cyber-bullying (via cell phone or the Internet)."[10]

How Common Is Bullying?

One number often used in media to describe the enormity of the bullying problem in our schools is that every day, 160,000 students stay home from school because they are afraid to go. Regarding those identifying as LGBTQ, the numbers of students who reported being bullied is staggeringly high. A 2007 study found that approximately 86 percent of LGBTQ students had been verbally harassed. Forty-four percent had been physically harassed, and an alarming 22 percent had been physically assaulted *within the past school year* because of their sexual orientation. Similar numbers were reported for gender nonconforming students.[11] The 2011 *National School Climate Survey* showed that schools' anti-bullying efforts might actually be making a difference, even though the progress has been much too slow. In 2011, close to 82 percent of LGBT students reported being verbally harassed, approximately 38 percent had been physically harassed, and 18 percent had been physically assaulted within the past school year.[12]

Why Bullying Is Particularly Devastating to Teens

In his article about the brain in *National Geographic*, David Dobbs describes what goes on in the teen brain during the high school years. In addition to the physical harm that bullying can cause, Dobbs brings up another, very real and very destructive side of bullying. "Our brains react to peer exclusion much as they respond to threats to physical health or food supply," he writes.[13] This explains why such an appallingly large number of teens choose to end their lives when they no longer feel they are a part of the group. At any other time in their lives they might have been able to handle social rejection, but during the teen years, being excluded can be a matter of life and death.

Phobias of Hatred

Homophobia is when someone has strong feelings of aversion toward another person because of his or her sexual orientation, though often the word *homophobia* includes antipathy toward and prejudice against any person identifying as LGBTQ. It can, in other words, include people who do not identify as homosexual. Sometimes more specific words are used to describe dislike for different LGBTQ subgroups, such as *lesbophobia*, for those with a particular hatred toward lesbians; *transphobia*, for those who focus their aggression on trans persons; and *biphobia*, which is aimed at bisexual persons. Homophobia and other hatred toward LGBTQ persons have been likened to racism and hatred toward certain groups of people in history, such as Jews during World War II.

The antonym to all these terms is the word *allophilia*, which means embracing or feeling love for a group opposite or different from one's own.

Being bullied is difficult for everybody, but a teenager's acute need to be a part of the group is greater than at any other age and this makes bullying particularly devastating to teens.

Who Are the Bullies?

Many years ago, my friend Ivy told me that she was a bully in high school. She said that she relentlessly harassed gay and lesbian students so nobody would get the idea that *she* might be gay. Eventually, after a significant personal crisis Ivy transcended her fear of her own sexuality, found a wonderful same-sex partner, and got back to the business of living a full life. She said she will always regret her misguided anger toward the other gay and lesbian students in her high school.

Many of us know stories like that; people who bully because they fear their own sexuality (though this is, as we will see, far from the only reason that people bully—bullying is a complex issue with complex reasons). There is increasingly more research to back this theory.

An article in *LiveScience*, for example, discusses research that indicates that among many other reasons for homophobia, one important cause for bullying aimed at LGBTQ persons might indeed be the bully's own repressed same-sex attraction. Richard Ryan, a professor of psychology at the University of Rochester and co-author of the 2012 study discussed in the article, established a number of interesting things in his research. First, he looked at his subjects' view of their own sexual orientation. The students (who were German or American) with supportive parents were the most likely to be accepting of their own sexuality. Those with authoritarian parents often showed a discrepancy between their reported sexual orientation and the behavior the researchers observed that might indicate same-sex attraction. And here is the gist of the study: the students from authoritarian homes who showed a discrepancy between what they *said* their desires were and *the conclusions that the researchers drew about them* in the study, were the students who were the most likely to be hostile toward gays and lesbians. They were also the most likely to support antigay policies.

While Ryan sees homophobia and hate crimes as a very serious societal problem, he also came away from the study with a measure of compassion for the bullies. "We laugh at and make fun of such blatant hypocrisy," he wrote. "But in a very real way, these people may often themselves be victims of repression and experience exaggerated feelings of threat."[14]

Popular parenting blogger Glennon Melton holds the same belief that both Ryan and Taylor do, that the bully is first and foremost a repressed individual. She writes in her much-read *Momastery* blog, "The kids who bully are those who are afraid that a secret part of themselves is not okay." But Melton also believes that children are really only mirrors of the adults in their lives. "What kids are doing in the schools," she writes, "is what adults do in the media. The only difference is that children bully in the hallways and the cafeterias while we bully from behind the pulpits and legislative benches and in one-liners on sitcoms."[15]

Other Reasons for Bullying

In a 2012 episode of the television show *20/20* some students who identified as bullies said they bullied because they were afraid to be bullied themselves. If they bullied, they figured, they would not become victims. And here is another shocking reason they said they bullied—because they could! Nobody stopped them.[16]

Dreams and Repression

Jeremy Taylor, a Unitarian Universalist minister and founder of the Association for the Study of Dreams, has traveled around the country for many years and taught people about dream interpretation and the roles dreams can have in helping foster a healthy psychological being. Getting rid of our own repression (repression is when we hide parts of who we really are, even to ourselves) is key to battling outside oppression, according to Taylor. That means, in short, that in order to stop oppressing others or treat others badly, we need to face our own psychological problems. When we repress our true feelings, Taylor believes, we inadvertently project those same, to us undesirable, feelings onto others, meaning that we see our own flaws in other people, but not in ourselves.

"The sad but constantly repeated truth of the matter is that whenever anyone denies some aspect of his/her own fundamental, flawed, unfinished humanness, it is inevitable (because it is a natural unconscious process), that the person will then deny the essential humanity of others—particularly when they have the 'bad taste' to look like the thing they are rejecting and denying in themselves," Taylor writes.[17]

Taylor then goes on to use the example of a racist who projects characteristics on other people that he or she sees in him- or herself, such as "too lazy," "too irresponsible," "too sexually active," "too stupid," "too violent," "too sneaky," "too secretive," "too closed off," or just plain "too different" to be seen as individual fellow human beings. Taylor sees these outspoken dislikes as a "confession" of the things people consider unflattering in themselves, characteristics that, he says, "the person has driven 'underground' in the process of repression."[18]

If we willingly face our own repressed issues—and one way of doing this, according to Jeremy Taylor is via dream interpretation—we are a lot less likely to oppress or hate other people.

In his book *My Two Moms*, Zach Wahls talks about the importance of recognizing the sometimes fine line of when a victim becomes a bully. When Wahls was fairly young and had just started a new school where he was bullied for having two moms, he also had the sad burden of having to worry about the failing health of his biological mom. Nobody would talk to him about it, he said, and he worried alone. Back then, the kids at school sometimes gave each other a "Vulcan neck pinch," something they had learned from *Star Trek*. Wahls pinched the neck of a peer a few times, justifying it in his mind as "roughhousing." Later, the boy he had pinched showed up at Wahls's house with his mom and accused him of being a bully. Wahls's moms confronted him and he experienced a moment of absolute horror when he realized that he had, in fact, been a bully. "Now, this is my realization: Most people don't consider themselves bullies," Wahls writes about the incident. "They don't really think about what they're doing. They just do what they do—bully, tease and mock others—because it feels good and can sometimes make their own pain go away."[19]

The lesson from Wahls—that people don't always know that they are being bullies—might also be true for verbal bullying. In our telephone interview, Cindy (interviewed in chapter 8) said that despite the fact that her dad was gay, despite the fact that her parents had taught her about tolerance and acceptance, she and her friends still used the word *gayrod*. "We used it all the time," she said. "We didn't know what it meant."[20] (According to the urban dictionary *gayrod* means someone who acts in a way that is perceived as gay.)

One Sadly, Not-So-Atypical School District

By the 1970s, the Olweus Bullying Prevention Program established that "environmental factors such as attitudes, routines, and behaviors of important adults (in particular teachers and administrators) play a major role in determining whether there will be bullying in a certain classroom or a certain school."[21] Despite this knowledge, harassment and bullying of LGBTQ students and students with LGBTQ parents is rampant across the country.

The Anoka-Hennepin School District in Minnesota, a district served (at the time of this writing in 2012) by congresswoman Michele Bachmann, notorious for her outspoken antigay stance, has been called a "suicide contagion area." The district has been noted for its many incidents of bullying and lack of staff intervention. Between 2009 and 2011, nine students in the district committed suicide, several of whom had been bullied for openly identifying as LGBTQ or being perceived as such. In 2011, six of the Anoka-Hennepin School District bullying victims brought a harassment lawsuit against the district. They felt that the district policy requiring teachers to stay neutral regarding all issues related

> ## Choosing Sides
>
> "We must take sides. Neutrality helps the oppressor, never the victim. Silence encourages the tormentor, never the tormented."—Elie Wiesel, *The Night Trilogy: Night/Dawn/Day*[22]

to sexual orientation in the classroom harmed the students. Some of the bullied students felt that these policies "hamper teachers from effectively preventing bullying of students who are gay or perceived as gay." The school district defended its position by claiming that the policy "respects the views of families and students who believe homosexual conduct is immoral." One document presented to the school board in defense of the "Respectful Learning Environment" policy felt that it was not the job of the district to "pick sides" when it comes to "contentious political, religious, social or economic issues." Teachers should not be placed in the role of persuading students to adopt a particular viewpoint on any topic, it says.[23]

Faced with a lawsuit, the Anoka-Hennepin School District was finally forced to take the problem seriously. The school board made a financial settlement with the students in question, but as a part of the suit it also began a comprehensive revision of its policy on harassment and bullying. District Superintendent Dennis Carlson confirmed in an e-mail interview that changes were indeed being made, but emphasized that the new guidelines had been in the works long before the lawsuit necessitated it.[24] Among the initiatives that the school district took was to hire an equity consultant to help the district track incidents of harassment, teach the district how to best respond when incidents did happen, and show the district how to best involve parents in anti-bullying efforts. The district also hired an equity coordinator to aid it in implementing the new policies and to help make sure that staff follows them. And it hired professionals who could immediately respond to complaints and be available at the schools for bullying victims at all times. In addition, the lawsuit dictated that the school district establish a five-year partnership with the Department of Justice and the Office for Civil Rights, which was to oversee the school district's progress in regards to curbing the number of bullying incidents.[25]

While most of them ended up transferring out of the school district, the students involved in the lawsuit nonetheless felt relieved that the district implemented all these changes. Damian McGee-Backes, who does not identify as gay but was bullied because his fathers are gay, said he was very happy about the changes: "I am very proud the school district agreed to do this. I am glad other kids won't have to go through what I went through," he said.[26]

Superintendent Carlson feels he learned a lot from speaking with hundreds of gay students over the past few years, things that other school districts could learn as well. "GSA [Gay-Straight Alliance] clubs and gay student support groups are essential," he said in an e-mail interview. "So is customized staff training, mental health support, security cameras, frequent monitoring and tracking of bullying information, and firm discipline of student and staff discrimination toward others." While Carlson feels that focusing on a special group of students, such as those identifying as LGBTQ, can be perceived as discrimination, there are a great number of things that school districts can do to ensure the safety of all students, he said. School districts should "develop a comprehensive plan of action to address [bullying]. This will require clear policies (at the federal, state and local school district level). . . . The emphasis needs to be on all students—none are to be excluded from the public school family. Our gay students need to speak up and to be heard in the area of bullying and ill treatment by others. Staff and administration need to listen and take immediate positive steps to eliminate any sign or act of discrimination."[27]

In other words, the Anoka-Hennepin School District in Minnesota—unfortunately far from the only school district in this country battling bullying and homophobia among students and staff—found that passively waiting for bullying to go away or not choosing sides when it came to "contentious, political, religious, social or economic issues" did not work. The school district had to adopt a very proactive and aggressive role in combatting bullying in order for anything to change.

Nabozny v. Podlesny

Another school district that ended up in the news because of bullying of LGBTQ students was the Ashland School District in northern Wisconsin. When he first started being harassed at his school, James Nabozny was a gay seventh-grade student with a difficult home life. Through the seventh and the eighth grade and later in high school, Nabozny was harassed so badly that he actually ran away from home to avoid having to go to school. He had no support from his family (his parents were alcoholics, though later they both stopped drinking in order to be better support for their son). According to Carlos A. Ball, author of *From the Closet to the Court Room*, Nabozny was beat up, berated, and urinated on. When he ran to the principal's office for help, he was told, that "if he insisted on being openly gay in school, then he had to expect that these kinds of incidents would take place." During these years, Nabozny tried to kill himself a number of times, yet received very little, if any, support from the Ashland School District. He was repeatedly told that he was provoking the other boys into harassing him. Yet, during these years, when no action was taken to stop Nabozny's tormentors, several students in the school district were suspended for other reasons. One student was suspended for calling another student a bitch. Another was suspended for scratching someone and pulling the person's hair, smoking on school property, and calling people bad names. None of these incidents came even close to the abuse that Nabozny suffered at the hands of his tormentors—who were never suspended for what they did to him.

Miraculously, Nabozny survived high school (though left Ashland before he could graduate from there). He tried to sue the school, but the case was thrown out. It was determined that schools could not be liable for the actions of its students, and that LGBTQ (or other) students had no right to protection from their peers while in school.

Three years later, Nabozny brought his case to Lambda, an organization that works with legal measures and education to promote LGBTQ rights. He wanted to ensure that students going to school in the Ashland School District and in school districts like it all across the country would never have to suffer the kind of torture that he did and not get any support from the school. The attorneys at Lambda knew that no lawsuit had ever been successful in protecting LGBTQ students from bullies at schools. But . . . there was something called the Ku Klux Klan Act of 1871. This act had to do with the southern states' failure to protect its black citizens against hate organizations like the Ku Klux Klan. Lambda took Nabozny's case to the Seventh Circuit Court of Appeals where it was established that yes, the schools do in fact have a responsibility to protect its LGBTQ students from harassment and violence. With that, the case was sent back to a lower small-town court where the jury found that the school officials indeed failed to protect Nabozny against bullies. The case was settled in 1996 before it reached a verdict, and Nabozny was awarded close to a million dollars in the settlement.

The *Nabozny v. Podlesny* case became an important landmark in gay rights because it established that LGBTQ students have equal right to protection. Students don't get to bully someone because he or she identifies as LGBTQ or have a nontraditional family, and it is the school's responsibility to protect students from being bullied.[28]

Today, Jamie Nabozny is a public speaker who travels around the country talking about bullying. A documentary movie *Bullied* was made about him in 2010 (for more information about this movie, see the resources section).

What to Do about Bullying

What Institutions Can Do about Bullying

As we have learned from anti-LGBTQ incidents at the Anoka-Hennepin School District and many other sad stories around the country, bullying does not go away by itself. Changing things for the better takes energy and consistent effort by all involved. But is it necessary, or even helpful, to put all this attention on the bullies, rather than nurturing the victims and teaching them strategies for dealing with bullies? Teacher and educational consultant Christer Mattsson believes that it is indeed important to pay attention to the bullies. He even goes so far to say that people should be "respecting also the intolerant students." In his small community of Kungälv in southwestern Sweden, administrators of the school in a very troubled community decided to focus their attention on the social structures of students believed to cause social unrest in the schools. According to Mattsson, understanding the perpetrating students' motivation is core to succeeding in creating a more tolerant atmosphere. In his *Kungälv Model*—where he spells out methodology for other school districts—he likens the interdependence of the different group of bullies in a school to a cluster of grapes held together by various social motivations.

After carefully studying the dynamics of the bullies at the school, the researchers divided the students into core group and followers; then the followers were subdivided into groups as well. With the help of adult supervision and by involving parents and some of the more tolerant students in the school, through education and increased communication, the different student groups in the power structure were split (which was accomplished by isolating some students from others). At the same time the strengths of the individuals in the bully groups were inventoried and used to rebuild a more tolerant student structure. In the end, the bullying students were offered special educational opportunities to make them stronger and less destructive members of the community.[29]

According to the Olweus Bullying Prevention Program, some schools attempt to address bullying by using peer mediation and conflict resolution. (Even though the *Kungälv Model* does in fact involve positive student interaction, the staff of the school is very much in charge at all times.) The reason this is not a good idea, according to the Olweus program, is that these methods "assume there is a bit of both right and wrong on both sides. Such programs may place some blame on the student who is being bullied, and free the student or students who are bullying from some responsibility."[30]

Pink Triangles and Rainbow Stickers

The symbol that can sometimes be seen on teachers' and administrators' windows at school—a combination of the LGBT pride flag, a pink triangle referring to gay, and a black triangle referring to lesbian—is meant as a safe space symbol. When a teacher or an administrator places a symbol like that in his office or classroom, it means that he considers himself an ally to LGBTQ persons and that this is a safe place and that LGBTQ-hostile language and bullying will not be tolerated. Perhaps more importantly, this small sticker sends a message to LGBTQ students and students with LGBTQ parents that they are not alone. The symbol itself is taken from World War II and Nazi Germany, where prisoners in concentration camps were made to wear different symbols that explained why they were there: pink triangles for gay men and black triangles for lesbians. Like the word *queer*, this is an example of taking back symbols used by the enemy in order to make them harmless or even benign.

Members of the school staff who display rainbow stickers have often been educated in LGBTQ issues. Some of the things adults in the school should learn to do if they haven't already, according to the Gay, Lesbian and Straight Education Network (GLSEN), is to quickly intervene when they see bullying or hear name calling by immediately addressing the issue, naming what they see, making sure they support the student who was the target of name calling or bullying, and holding the bully accountable.[31]

And it may be good to remember that students often don't know what they are actually saying. Even kids who don't want to hurt others might sometimes use hurtful language. When students use the phrase "That's so gay," for example, they often defend themselves by saying they didn't refer to "homosexual." Jonathan, age fourteen, who has two moms, defends people using the expression. "It's just a euphemism," he said. "Not used in a context. It has nothing to do with LGBTQ."[32]

What Students Can Do

Even the most empowered students are rarely going to start an entire anti-bullying program by themselves. There are, however, things individuals can do and should do. Zach Wahls talks about how his moms taught him about fogging, using words to confuse your assailant, moving attention away from yourself.[33]

Abbie Goldberg talks in her book about the various ways in which children at different ages have learned to deal with the bullying they encounter due to having LGBTQ parents. She writes that the very youngest children in her study, even up to middle school, would talk to their siblings and their parents when something happened at school or on the playground. Sometimes they would talk to other children or to a teacher. When they got older they might sometimes fight people who said mean things. The older they got, however, the more they would start hiding their LGBTQ families from their peers, not invite friends over, and become increasingly more selective with whom they chose to share information about their family. Then when they became juniors and seniors in high school, students once again tended to be more open and directly confront people who used offensive language with or around them.[34]

There are times when the adults closest to us fail to help. Students who are bullied and can't get help from parents or other family members or guardians need to contact someone else who can help, such as teachers and school administrators. It Gets Better is a Web-based organization that, for the sad reason that it is needed, has grown exponentially over the past years. While some high school students get angry at the thought that they should have to wait for things to get better, others find solace in knowing that bullying is not going to follow them to college where there are many other out students who either identify as LGBTQ or who have LGBTQ parents. Visit www.itgetsbetter.org.

In case of an emergency, call, for example, the Trevor Project Lifeline at (866) 488–7386. The operators answering that phone line are trained to prevent suicide in LGBTQ youth and are available twenty-four hour a day.

Notes

1. "Bullied to Death: Victims' Stories," *20/20*, season 31, episode 6, October 14, 2010, abc.go.com/watch/2020/SH559026/VD5592259/bullied-to-death-victims-stories (accessed February 20, 2013).
2. Casey, in-person interview by author, April 27, 2012.
3. Kaley, Skype interview by author, October 30, 2012.
4. Henny M. W. Bos, PhD, Frank van Balen, PhD, Nanette K. Gartrell, MD, Heidi Peyser, MA, and Theo G. M. Sandfort, PhD, "Children in Planned Lesbian Families: A Cross-Cultural Comparison between the United States and the Netherlands," *American Journal of Orthopsychiatry* 78, no. 2 (2008): 211–19.
5. Abbie E. Goldberg, *Lesbian and Gay Parents and Their Children: Research on the Family Life Cycle* (Washington, D.C.: American Psychological Association, 2010), 137.
6. Andrew, telephone interview by author, May 31, 2012.
7. Stephen Gunther, "My Transsexual Father," *Australian Humanities Review* (August 1997), 1.
8. Quoted in Meema Spadola, dir., *Our House: A Very Real Documentary about Kids of Gay and Lesbian Parents* (Brooklyn, N.Y.: First Run/Ikarus Films, 2000).
9. *Olweus Bullying Prevention Program* (Center City, Minn.: Hazelden, 2008), 1.
10. *Olweus Bullying Prevention Program*, 1.
11. Gay, Lesbian and Straight Education Network, *National School Climate Survey*, 2007.
12. Gay, Lesbian and Straight Education Network, *Key Findings of the 2011 National School Climate Survey*, www.glsen.org/cgi-bin/iowa/all/library/record/2897.html?state=research&type=research (accessed February 20, 2013).
13. David Dobbs, "Beautiful Brains," *National Geographic* 220, no. 4 (October 2011): 55.
14. Jeanna Bryner, "Study: Homophobes May Be Hidden Homosexuals," *LiveScience*, April 9, 2012, news.yahoo.com/study-homophobes-may-hidden-homosexuals-194806808.html (accessed April 9, 2012).
15. Glennon Melton, "A Mountain I'm Willing to Die On," *Momastery* (blog), January 26, 2012, www.huffingtonpost.com/glennon-melton/a-mountain-im-willing-to-die-on_b_1223229.html (accessed January 26, 2012).
16. "Bullied to Death."

17. Jeremy Taylor, "Educating to Counter Oppression: Some Important Unconscious Psychological Considerations," 2004, www.jeremytaylor.com/pages/socialjustice.html (accessed July 26, 2012).
18. Taylor, "Educating to Counter Oppression."
19. Zach Wahls, with Bruce Littlefield, *My Two Moms: Lessons of Love, Strength, and What Makes a Family* (New York: Gotham Books, 2012), 49.
20. Cindy, telephone interview by author, May 24, 2012.
21. *Olweus Bullying Prevention Program*, 2.
22. Elie Wiesel, *The Night Trilogy: Night/Dawn/Day* (New York: Hill and Wang, 2008).
23. "Anoka-Hennepin Teachers Endorse New Policy on Discussing Sexual Orientation," *Pioneer Press*, February 6, 2012, www.twincities.com/localnews/ci_19906578 (accessed February 7, 2012).
24. Anoka-Hennepin School District Superintendent Dennis Carlson, e-mail interview by author, July 23, 2012.
25. Sue Austreng, "Anoka-Hennepin Settles Lawsuit, Board Member Resigns," *ABC Newspapers.com*, March 5, 2012, abcnewspapers.com/2012/03/05/anoka-hennepin-settles-lawsuit-board-member-resigns/ (accessed March 5, 2012).
26. "Anoka-Hennepin Teachers Endorse New Policy on Discussing Sexual Orientation."
27. Superintendent Carlson, e-mail interview by author.
28. Carlos A. Ball, *From the Closet to the Courtroom: Five LGBT Rights Lawsuits That Have Changed Our Nation* (Boston, Mass.: Beacon Press, 2010), 71, 67–98.
29. Christer Mattsson, *Kungälvsmodellen: Att bemöta social oro och inolerans i skolan* (To Address Social Unrest and Intolerance in School, my translation), 2006 (available from me).
30. Karin Lindgren, "Respektera även intoleranta elever" (Respect Also Intolerant Students, my translation), *Lärarnas tidning*, March 19, 2010.
31. GLSEN, "Safe Space Kit, Guide to Being an Ally to LGBT Students," www.glsen.org/cgi-bin/iowa/all/library/record/1641.html (accessed August 28, 2012), 2, 16.
32. Jonathan, in-person interview by author, May 30, 2012.
33. Wahls, *My Two Moms*, 43.
34. Goldberg, *Lesbian and Gay Parents*, 137.

MEDIA, POPULAR CULTURE, AND LGBTQ FAMILIES

Now and Then and Now

Today, LGBTQ persons and families appear more and more often on television and in other media and are less often portrayed in a derogatory way. LGBTQ parents with children appear on mainstream shows like *Modern Family* and *Glee*, and prominent media personalities like CNN journalist Anderson Cooper, actor Jesse Tyler Ferguson, and singer Ricky Martin are coming out en masse and finding that being out doesn't necessarily make their ratings or popularity drop.

But it wasn't always so. And you don't even have to go far back in time to find famous people struggling with their careers after coming out. According to *Rolling Stone* magazine, when Elton John came out in 1976, many people stopped buying his albums and his career definitely took a turn for the worse.[1] (Though we all know it recovered quite well in the 1980s.) In short, with some exceptions, before the 1970s famous people simply did not come out.

When Rock Hudson died from AIDS in 1985, people were shocked to learn that such a handsome man could be gay. Twelve years later, in 1997, when standup comedian and talk show host Ellen DeGeneres came out, media ridiculed her to the point that she fell into a depression. Her personal relationship suffered so badly that she and her partner broke up.[2] In 2002, prominent media personality Rosie O'Donnell came out, confirming what was already fairly well-known, that she was in a same-sex relationship; in 2006, Neil Patrick Harris came out in *People* magazine.

Then, in 2009, Chaz Bono came out as a female-to-male transsexual. While Bono wasn't the first well-known trans person to come out, he certainly got media attention and in many ways helped educate the public on what it means to be transsexual. Growing up as Chastity, the daughter of the famous singing duo Sonny and Cher, she early on became an LGBTQ activist and lived in a same-sex relationship for many years. In 2009, Chastity became Chaz. Since then, Chaz has put a very public face on trans. He has been on the *Oprah Winfrey Show*; made a documentary, *Becoming Chaz* (2011), about his transition; written a book—a New York Times best-seller—*Transition: Becoming Who I Was Always Meant to Be* (2011); appeared on *Dancing with the Stars*; and become even more of an activist social networker.[3]

It is more difficult to find famous children with LGBTQ *parents*, perhaps because, at least as an adult, it is easier to be in the closet about your parents than about yourself. (And how many people really discuss their parents' sexual orientation anyway? Unless there's a reason, it might just not come up.) But there certainly are some famous children of LGBTQ parents who are open and proud of their families, and others whose families have been outed in the media for negative reasons. Actress and movie director Jodie Foster grew up with two moms. Infamous football running back O. J. Simpson had a father who was a drag queen (and died of AIDS in 1986), actress Jena Malone was raised by two mothers, British actress Vanessa Redgrave had a famous bisexual father. It is likely that the unusually high number of media personalities and movie stars who come out about their LGBTQ parents is due to the fact that it has always been more acceptable to be out in the television and movie industry than in the rest of society.

Stereotypes

In her young adult novel *Personal Effects*, E. M. Kokie's homophobic seventeen-year-old main character, Matt, meets a gay man for the first time in his life. He is still unaware of his own stereotypes and looking at the man, he thinks, "He doesn't even look like a faggot, maybe his clothes, maybe, but he's strong, and he's big. He doesn't sound like a faggot. His hands look strong, not girly at all." Later, when confronted with the fact that someone very close to him might be gay, he is once again rattled by this prospect and can't quite reconcile in his mind what he thinks of as two vastly opposite concepts—gay and military: "He was in the freaking Army. He wore T-shirts and jeans. His hair was pretty short. He didn't even own any mousse or gel or anything. He never wore jewelry. He hit harder than anyone I've ever met, except Dad. And he was so fierce. He dated girls. Didn't he? In high school?"[4]

The stereotypes and the homophobia that Matt perpetuates in *Personal Effects* were an important part of showing where Matt was coming from; not hatred, but ignorance. Kokie also confirms this in an e-mail interview. "Matt's homophobia was based on ignorance," Kokie wrote. "But I felt it was important to be true to his character at the beginning of the book. I hoped readers would recognize and even experience his transformation from fear and prejudice, through confusion and anger, to understanding. Seeing Matt's confusion—stereotypes and prejudices crashing into reality—is an important part of that transformation."[5]

Casey, age seventeen, said that while LGBTQ persons on television, like Emily in *Pretty Little Liars* and Kurt in *Glee*, have been portrayed in a stereotypical manner, it is still better to have stereotypical gay people on TV than none at all. Casey also said that she hoped that the stereotyping of LGBTQ persons would change. "Eventually, it won't always be like, 'Oh, it's the gay guy and he likes musical theater,'" she said.[6]

"When I see *Modern Family*," said Cindy, who is now an adult but grew up with a gay dad, "I see this really rich family. It surprises me. I don't usually see gay families that are well-to-do. And everybody is having so much fun at how flamboyant [Cam] is. I wonder if it's necessarily that funny to the gay populations. There are a lot of stereotypes there."[7]

But like Casey, Cindy felt that stereotypical LGBTQ individuals on television are better than none. That is how it began with African Americans, she said. You might have to have the stereotypes before there is room to advance and create more dimensional characters of all kinds.[8]

Thomas, age fourteen, who lives with his two moms and his brother, has a more philosophical approach to stereotypes. He believes that one reason that we have these stereotypes of gay men in particular, like Kurt on *Glee*, is that this bold, vivacious personality might be exactly what one needs to be brave enough to come out. It might be more difficult, Thomas believes, to come out for young gay people who are not the ones we see "painted with the same brush" on television shows. Still, Thomas believes that if the characters are likeable, it's probably good to have them on the shows in order to help people get used to the idea [of LGBTQ persons].[9]

Kaley, age twenty-one, feels very much like Thomas and Casey. "*Modern Family* is my guilty pleasure," she said. "I love that show, but it's not completely truthful. I've had this conversation many times before." Kaley feels that having LGBTQ persons on TV is definitely a step in the right direction but that we really only show one kind of LGBTQ person. "Most queers and trans folks are not on television," she said. "Their stories haven't been told."[10]

JamieAnn, a sixty-five-year-old TransWoman, feels that media very much influenced her family's expectations of what she would look like and how she would act when she first presented as a woman. And not in a good way.

The first time JamieAnn's daughter and daughter-in-law met her as JamieAnn, not Jim, they were nervous. JamieAnn's daughter-in-law said later that she hadn't known what to expect, but judging from the crazy-looking men in dresses and high heels she had seen on TV, she was pretty sure it would be horrific. But JamieAnn chose a very conservative look the first time she met her family as JamieAnn, a simple black top and jeans, nothing like trans persons in the media. Her family, especially her daughter-in-law, was greatly relieved. Together, the family had managed to transcend media stereotypes.[11]

For less stereotypical portrayals of LGBTQ persons, watch a few late-season episodes of *Glee*; for example, season 3. Here are a few gems: the genuine relationship between two friends, Santana and Brittany, who discover that they feel more for each other than friends usually do; the coming out of former jock and bully Karofsky; and the "Saturday Night Glee-ver" episode, featuring a very nuanced portrayal of Unique, a male-to-female trans teen.

Sarah Schulman, author of *Ties That Bind*, also feels that gays and lesbians in the media, perhaps television and movies in particular, are not well represented. She feels that showing gays and lesbians in a more universal in-depth manner means to also portray homophobia and acts of hostility that LGBTQ persons are constantly victims of in order to "force an acknowledgement of heterosexual cruelty as a constant and daily part of American life."[12]

The word *stereotype* is two hundred years old and originally had to do with printing presses. According to *Merriam-Webster's Collegiate Dictionary*, a stereotype was "a plate cast from a printing surface."[13] This gives a pretty good picture of how the word is used today as well. It is usually used as a generalization of a group of people and does not allow for individuality or variation. As a verb, *stereotype* could mean, for example, making a certain group of people more alike in your mind than they really are.

Writer Brittney Weber writes on the Gay/Gender Issues page of the Canadian social network and blogsite *Suite101* that stereotyping can also be a good thing. It can help us categorize and organize things in our brains. She writes, "The television series *Will & Grace* has been examined and sometimes criticized for pigeonholing gay men. While most people know that the promiscuous, 'flaming' character, Jack, is not the epitome of what it means to be a gay man, they can't help but laugh because the character reminds them of their flamboyant Uncle Bob. If stereotypes can be separated from unbending fact, they can serve to be helpful rather than harmful." Weber writes that while stereotyping paired with ignorance can be polarizing, an open mind should be able to distinguish the good from the bad and stay critical when confronted with stereotyping. According to Weber, it isn't the stereotyping in itself that is a problem; it is the judgment that sometimes comes with it.[14]

How Does Famous LGBTQ People Coming Out Help LGBTQ Families?

When high-profile television journalist Anderson Cooper came out in 2012, media had long speculated that he was gay. Some LGBTQ activists even accused him of hiding at a time when they felt it was getting increasingly more important for LGBTQ persons to come out of the closet. Cooper seems to have been swayed by that argument. In a frank letter to the online newssite the *Daily Beast* on July 2, 2012, he wrote, "Recently, however, I've begun to consider whether the unintended outcomes of maintaining my privacy outweigh personal and professional principle. It's become clear to me that by remaining silent on certain aspects of my personal life for so long, I have given some the mistaken impression that I am trying to hide something—something that makes me uncomfortable, ashamed or even afraid. This is distressing because it is simply not true."[15]

Cooper goes on to explain that he has been reminded of the fact that the advancement of minority groups, increased rights, and more inclusiveness only happen when people become more visible. He also said that he is concerned about closeted young people in schools across the country and the bullying that these youths are victims of. He concludes that while his privacy is important to him and he is cautious about mixing his private life with that of his very public persona, it is time for him to speak out. "The fact is, I'm gay, always have been, always will be, and I couldn't be any more happy, comfortable with myself, and proud," he ended his letter.[16]

Famous People Coming Out: A Cynical Look

In a 2012 article in the *Atlantic*, Alyssa Rosenberg takes a cynical look at celebrities coming out, juxtaposing this phenomenon with the very harsh reality for many teens unable to do the same thing. "Coming out remains a fraught process for many Americans—particularly for young people who still rely on their parents for emotional and financial support—but for some famous, secure people, official confirmation of their sexual orientation isn't just a matter of honesty: It's a highly valuable commodity," she writes in the article "How Coming Out Became Cool for Celebrities." Rosenberg goes on to explain what she means by this. As a pop culture blogger she keeps a close eye on contemporary media. Of the many famous people ending up on the cover of *People* magazine announcing that they're out, she believes that very few of them would be famous enough to end up on the cover for any other reason. Rosenberg went back in time to the coming out of Ellen DeGeneres, which, while causing some bumps in the comedian's career, eventually led to more fame and fortune. She also assumed that Neil Patrick Harris landed some good new roles after coming out. However, she said, and here is the gist of her story, many LGBTQ youth who come out without having a good safety network risk things like homelessness, poverty, and suicide. This, she emphasizes, is indeed more real and more dire than lower viewer ratings. The risk of coming out for people like Anderson Cooper, Rosenberg says, is an entirely different thing than it is for LGBTQ youth. She ends her article with: "For young gay people, not much has changed in America. But just because the coming-out process has become beneficial for some celebrities doesn't mean we're required to buy what they're selling."[17] One might, of course, argue that no matter what their reason for coming out, celebrities being open about being LGBTQ will, in the long run, be helpful also to these youth at risk by making all things LGBTQ less marginalized.

We All Need to See Our Own Families out There

In author, editor, and journalist Andrew Sullivan's *Newsweek* article "Why Gay Marriage Is Good for Straight America," he writes about the moment when he realized that his life did not fit in with the culture he saw around him, a revelation that also told him that the Hollywood movies that he watched, the ones with glitz and happy endings, had nothing to do with him. "For some reason, I knew somewhere deep down that I couldn't have a marriage like my parents. . . . At the very moment you become aware of sex and emotion, you simultaneously know that for you, there is no future coupling, no future family, no future home. In the future, I would be suddenly exiled from what I knew: my family, my friends, every household on television, every end to every romantic movie I'd ever seen."[18] Sullivan felt this, of course, because he did not see himself or any LGBTQ families reflected in media around him growing up.

Rainbow Rumpus

Laura Matanah is the founder and publisher of *Rainbow Rumpus*, "the world's only online literary magazine for children and youth with lesbian, gay, bisexual, and transgender (LGBT) parents," as its website states. Matanah is passionate about providing children and older youth with reading material in which they

Everybody wants to see their families reflected in the world around them.

recognize themselves. In fact, that is why the site was first launched. The website says: "Rainbow Rumpus was conceived in 2005 when publisher Laura Matanah's daughter found a small photo in the Human Rights Campaign magazine *Equality* and exclaimed, 'Look Mommy! Two moms and twins! Just like us!' A light bulb went off for Ms. Matanah, and *Rainbow Rumpus*, the world's only Web-based literary magazine for youth with LGBT parents, was born."[19]

Rainbow Rumpus provides stories, art, and social networking opportunities for children and youth with LGBTQ parents. In an e-mail interview, Matanah explained why it is so important for children to have something like *Rainbow Rumpus* in their lives:

I think that the lack of books and videos about our families, and the homophobia and transphobia that we have to deal with, can lead kids from

Andrew's Family

Andrew, age eighteen, lived with his mom in an LGBTQ-friendly community in the Midwest at the time of our 2012 interview. His parents got divorced when he was in preschool and his mom moved to the East Coast. As a younger child, Andrew mostly lived with his dad and his dad's partner. His parents didn't really explain to Andrew why they separated, but when Andrew was in elementary school, his dad's partner moved in with them. Andrew was young enough at the time of the divorce that, while missing his parents being together, he never wondered about the fact that his father lived with a man. His mom was very liberal and never said anything derogatory about his father's moving in with another man, so for Andrew, while he didn't know many other kids in the same situation, his father being gay was never an issue. Andrew said he never felt defined by having two dads, but by the time he wrote his college essay he had begun to realize that, in some very important ways, it had indeed shaped him. He mentioned his family in his essay as well as his belief that having grown up with two dads made him more accepting of diverse people and families. As a senior in high school, Andrew didn't consider himself particularly active regarding LGBTQ issues, though he was a part of his high school's Gay-Straight Alliance (GSA). His dads were trying to get him to be more involved, he said, and "when it comes time, I will be more politically active." When he graduates from college, Andrew wants to be a high school history teacher.[20]

our families to feel alone and sometimes scared. I think seeing our experiences reflected in media is vital because it is affirming in a world that often puts our families down, it helps us to tell our own stories, and it helps us to be fully who we are. I also believe that when other people hear our stories they come to understand the things that affect us. Once they understand us, they are more likely to be welcoming and try to make the world more fair. The best stories show all of our complexity and liveliness. We started *Rainbow Rumpus* and *Rainbow Riot* [the special teen edition of *Rainbow Rumpus*] so kids and teens from LGBT-headed homes could read great stories and share great stories about their lives. I hope you'll visit the sites, share the stories you find there with others, and, if you're growing up in an LGBT-headed home, consider sharing your story with us.[21]

Dear Abby

One prominent media personality is quietly using her fame to help further LGBTQ causes. In a 2012 column, Jeanne Phillips, or "Dear Abby" as most of us know her, published the following letter from a reader:

Waiter's Use of Makeup Shocks Surprised Diner

DEAR ABBY: Last night at a restaurant, my husband and I were surprised to see a male server wearing a blond wig and full makeup. I was, to say the least, shocked and very glad we hadn't brought the children, ages 11 and 14, with us. How do you explain something like that to an 11-year-old? The 14-year-old would be able to "get it."

What kind of policies are in place for restaurants in cases like this? What if customers are offended? Could I request a different server or just leave? Your comments would be appreciated.—TAKEN ABACK IN CALIFORNIA

Dear Abby's response:

DEAR TAKEN ABACK: In California, people have the legal right to dress in a style not typical of their gender without fear of discrimination or retaliation. That right is protected by state law. If customers find it offensive, they can either request a different server or take their business elsewhere. Presumably, the customer would pay for food that had already been prepared.

Because children today grow up quickly and are less sheltered than in past decades, I recommend you explain to your 11-year-old that not all people are alike, and the importance of treating others with respect. It's called *reality*.[22]

Dear Abby's scathing reply was probably not surprising for those who have followed her column for the past ten years or so, in fact, ever since she took over for her mother, Pauline Phillips, who started it in 1956. Dear Abby has quickly become known as a loyal proponent of LGBTQ rights. And, according to an article in *USA Today*, Phillips's mother should be remembered as an LGBTQ ally as well, as she started this trend and even "helped put PFLAG [Parents, Families and Friends of Lesbians and Gays] on the map in 1984 when she first referred a distraught parent to the organization."[23]

Back in 2007, it was not yet common for media personalities to speak out as allies of LGBTQ causes, but Dear Abby, who had always treated LGBTQ persons with respect, finally burst out in an interview with *USA Today* regarding same-sex marriage: "I believe if two people want to commit to each other, God bless 'em. That is the highest form of commitment, for heaven's sake."[24]

PFLAG responded by giving Phillips their very first Straight for Equality Award, an award designed to engage more allies. PFLAG director Jody Huckaby said of the choice to give the award to Jeanne Phillips, "She is such a mainstream voice. If 'Dear Abby' is talking about it, it gives other people permission to talk about it."[25]

Popular Culture and Words

Hardly any topic in media goes unnoticed and untouched by *South Park*. This animated television series, written by Trey Parker and Matt Stone, has aired since 1997. With its irreverent and, to some, highly offensive humor and profane language it has, for better and for worse, addressed the entire spectrum of cultural conflict. With its propensity for controversy, *South Park* has also, of course, dealt with many LGBTQ issues. In a 2009 episode called "The F-Word," *South Park* writers explored the word *faggot*. The (animated) children on the show decide to take the word *faggot* and change its meaning from a derogatory word used against gay men to make it refer to inconsiderate burly riders of Harley-Davidson motorcycles. While the other characters on the show find this offensive at first, the word eventually gains approval in this new usage.

The Gay and Lesbian Association against Defamation (GLAAD), however, found this episode harmful to LGBTQ causes, according to an article in the *New York Times*. "The creators of 'South Park' are right on one important point: more and more people are using the F-word as an all-purpose insult," GLAAD wrote in a statement in the *New York Times*. "However, it is irresponsible and wrong to suggest that it is a benign insult or that promoting its use has no consequences for those who are the targets of anti-gay bullying and violence. This is a slur whose meaning remains rooted in homophobia. And while many 'South Park' viewers will understand the sophisticated satire and critique in last night's episode, others won't—and if even a small number of those take from this a message that using the 'F-word' is OK, it worsens the hostile climate that many in our community continue to face."[26]

Whether or not one agrees with GLAAD's assessment that the *South Park* episode worsens the situation for LGBTQ persons, it does bring up, again, the important issue of words and how we use and abuse them, and leaves us with the thought that intentionality is key.

Thomas's Family

Thomas, age fourteen, lived with his seventeen-year-old brother and his two moms in a rural area outside a college town in the Midwest. Thomas loves to sing and play the violin. His moms have been together since he was born and it is the only family he has ever known. Before entering high school, Thomas was home-schooled for five years. He calls his moms either by their first name or just mom, in which case both heads often turn. He feels that most people in his world are accepting of his family, but adds that this might be because they choose not to be around people who are not accepting. "I am comfortable telling people about my family," he said. "Then again, I don't go around telling people I don't know."

Thomas feels like most of the social taboos and problems with intolerance stem from the older generation. "The majority of people my age," he said, "either support [LGBTQ issues] or don't care enough to be against them." He believes that it was much harder some years back, before Stonewall, and that imminent change is at hand. "I have a feeling that the country will come around in the next ten years." Thomas feels that while it is sad for those who suffer injustice right now and who for different reasons will not be around to see the day when LGBTQ persons have equal rights, "the people who don't have the benefits now can take pride in being pioneers."

Thomas said he didn't get bullied "very often" (living close to a liberal college town helps), but there were times when he was younger when other kids made fun of him and talked about his parents in a mocking way. He never got beat up but felt that people didn't understand. Now his school has a "no bullying" policy and a principal who is acutely sensitive to bullying issues. Thomas, who is gay himself, said that the most important step toward a safe school is to have a GSA there. Most teachers at his school also have safe room stickers on their doors or windows, he said. And the school participates in a Day of Silence every year (organized by the Gay, Lesbian and Straight Education Network to draw attention to bullying in schools, particularly as it pertains to LGBTQ students). The teachers don't participate in this, Thomas said, because it would be difficult for them not to talk all day, but they are supportive of students who want to do it.

Regarding media portrayal of LGBTQ persons, Thomas believes that Kurt in *Glee* is indeed a bit of a stereotype and that painting everybody with the same brush is not a great idea because it can be polarizing. The rest of the world simply learns that there is only one way to be a gay man. Thomas believes that quiet, introverted gay men might have a more difficult time coming out to begin with and even when they *are* out, people might not think of them as gay because they don't fit our stereotypes. This allows us to keep our stereotype of a gay vivacious flamboyant man—we simply don't see the gay men who are not like that, not in the media and not in real life.[27]

Famous Out Olympians

In a 2012 blog in the online *Huffington Post* magazine, college student and *Huffington Post* blogger Kevin Burra complains about the ridiculously low number of openly gay Olympians, twenty-three out of eleven thousand athletes! However, Burra does mention that this number more than doubled since the previous Olympics two years earlier.[28] Another article on *Gaynet,* an online magazine and newsletter for gay men, speculates about the reason for the low number of out male Olympians in particular. It suggests that there are financial reasons for gay male athletes to avoid coming out. Being openly gay, the author reasons, might lessen the athletes' opportunities for getting endorsements. Other reasons cited in the article for keeping out of the public eye were privacy, the "jock-factor" in sports, shame, shyness, and sadly, fear—coming out brings for some a very real risk of harassment and violence.[29]

Nevertheless, some Olympians (mostly women) have chosen to come out, and, perhaps not surprisingly, a large percentage of them come from the relatively small countries of Sweden (three, plus the former women's U.S. soccer coach who is Swedish) and the Netherlands (five)—countries that have legalized same-sex marriage. Statistically, this means that nine out of twenty-three, thus 39 percent, of all out Olympians come from just two countries.

Movies[30]

While the pendulum swings back and forth when it comes to the advancement of rights, LGBTQ families and persons are definitely popping up more and more in popular media and with fewer negative characteristics attached. It is not unusual to see a movie with a gay or lesbian character who is not even central to the story, but just appears in the background—in other words, the movie is not *about* LGBTQ issues; it just uses LGBTQ persons to reflect real life. The movies listed here are a few examples of mostly mainstream movies that deal with LGBTQ families and issues, using LGBTQ characters either as main protagonists or sidekicks.

Beginners (2011)—Oliver (played by Ewan McGregor) is an adult professional dealing with the imminent death of his father (wonderfully played by award-winning actor Christopher Plummer) and the fact that his father has just come out as gay. The father is now pursuing and finding love. Oliver, while a bit confused and perplexed, comes to understand and respect his father for—even at this late time in life—breaking away from convention in order to live fully. This movie, though quiet, is charged with emotion and is full of love.

Brokeback Mountain (2006)—This movie, starring Jake Gyllenhaal and Heath Ledger, is a sad and beautiful love story between two cowboys who can't accept being gay and are, for very real reasons, afraid of repercussions in a society that would not accept them. They try to move on and live their lives as spouses and fathers, but their love story continues and they meet again, years after they first fell in love. In a better world, this movie could have been simply a deeply resonant love story, but sadly, being gay in a homophobic world catches up with the two cowboys and very much determines the ending of this movie.

The Kids Are All Right (2010)—Like *Beginners*, *The Kids Are All Right* is also about the children of LGBTQ persons. The two children of a lesbian couple, played by Annette Bening and Julianne Moore, set out to find the sperm donor of the younger sibling (who is under eighteen and thus not supposed to be able to find her sperm donor yet). Like many of the children interviewed in the *Sperm Donor Guide*, these children learn that finding your donor does not necessarily turn out the way you thought it would or should. Basically, this film shows a family with LGBTQ parents that is just as messed up as most other families are, and yet, the kids end up just fine, like most kids do in the end.

Milk (2008)—The story about Harvey Milk, California's first openly gay elected public official, starring Sean Penn, is both uplifting and sad. Penn's acting and the compelling story of perseverance make it worth every moment.

Our Idiot Brother (2012)—In this movie Paul Rudd plays a loving but naïve and not very ambitious young man who ends up in jail for selling pot to a police officer. One of his sisters in the movie is a bisexual woman. Rudd's character lovingly says about his sister that she is able to love anybody, no matter who they are. The movie isn't about the sister, but the presence of her and her no-nonsense, fun same-sex partner and their troubled relationship add much to this feel-good movie.

The Perfect Family (2012)—While the movie *The Perfect Family* with Kathleen Turner is slow moving, it well portrays the genuine struggle of a mother whose daughter is getting married—to a woman—and the mother's stubbornness when it comes to accepting this new reality in her life.

The Importance of Learning about Media

In its *Speak Out* guide, COLAGE encourages its members to learn all they can about media, including the news, because news, it says, "influences public opinion and policy about youth with LGBT parents." One very important point it also shines a light on is that while not everything you see on television, in the movies, or on the Internet is true, and while you might very well know this, people in general believe that anything they see online is true. This means that a stereotypically portrayed LGBTQ mom or dad on television or YouTube might be seen by the general population as the epitome of an LGBTQ parent. Media also often serves corporate interests, the guide reminds us, not people, which means that we have to be vigilant in making sure people don't get trampled in the process. LGBTQ persons, while gaining some ground, are still underrepresented in media (which makes it all the more important that the ones who do appear are not stereotyped). COLAGE hopes that children and young adults with LGBTQ parents will educate themselves and will someday have the power to change how they are represented in media.[31]

Notes

1. "The 25 Boldest Career Moves in Rock History: 15—Elton John Comes Out of the Closet," *Rolling Stone*, www.rollingstone.com/music/lists/the-25-boldest-career-moves-in-rock-history-20110318/elton-john-comes-out-of-the-closet-20110323 (accessed September 4, 2012).
2. Bridget Foley, "Ellen DeGeneres," *W Magazine* 36, no. 3 (March 2007), www.wmagazine.com/celebrities/2007/03/ellen_degeneres (accessed June 9, 2012), 496–501.
3. Section based on Chaz Bono's website, www.chazbono.net (accessed September 5, 2012).
4. E. M. Kokie, *Personal Effects* (Somerville, Mass.: Candlewick Press, 2012), 251, 257.
5. E. M. Kokie, e-mail interview by author, October 27, 2012.
6. Casey, in-person interview by author, April 27, 2012.
7. Cindy, telephone interview by author, May 24, 2012.
8. Cindy, telephone interview by author.
9. Thomas, in-person interview by author, June 6, 2012.
10. Kaley, Skype interview by author, October 30, 2012.
11. JamieAnn, Skype interview by author, August 15, 2012.
12. Sarah Schulman, *Ties That Bind: Familial Homophobia and Its Consequences* (New York: The New Press, 2009), 6.
13. *Merriam-Webster's Collegiate Dictionary*, 11th ed., s.v. "stereotype."
14. Brittney Weber, "Is Stereotyping Bad? Examples of Good Stereotypes," *Suite101.com* (blog), February 26, 2010, suite101.com/article/is-stereotyping-bad-a206755 (accessed September 17, 2012).
15. "Anderson Cooper: 'The Fact Is, I'm Gay,'" *Daily Beast*, July 2, 2012, www.thedailybeast.com/cheats/2012/07/02/anderson-cooper-i-m-gay.html (accessed September 4, 2012).
16. "Anderson Cooper."
17. Alyssa Rosenberg, "How Coming Out Became Cool for Celebrities," *Atlantic*, January 10, 2012, www.theatlantic.com/entertainment/archive/2012/01/how-coming-out-became-cool-for-celebrities/250895/ (accessed November 12, 2012).
18. Andrew Sullivan, "Why Gay Marriage Is Good for Straight America," *Newsweek*, July 18, 2011, www.thedailybeast.com/newsweek/2011/07/17/andrew-sullivan-why-gay-marriage-is-good-for-america.html (accessed July 2012).
19. From the *Rainbow Rumpus* website, www.rainbowrumpus.org (accessed September 17, 2012).
20. Andrew, telephone interview by author, May 31, 2012.
21. Laura Matanah, e-mail interview by author, September 17, 2012.
22. Jeanne Phillips, "Dear Abby," *Detroit News*, September 7, 2012, http://www.uexpress.com/dearabby/?uc_full_date=20120907 (accessed September 7, 2012).
23. Lisa Leff, "'Dear Abby' Says She's for Gay Marriage," *USA Today*, October 10, 2007, usatoday30.usatoday.com/news/nation/2007-10-09-abby-gay-marriage_N.htm (accessed September 7, 2012).
24. Leff, "'Dear Abby' Says She's for Gay Marriage."

25. Leff, "'Dear Abby' Says She's for Gay Marriage."

26. Dave Itzkoff, "Gay Advocacy Group Objects to 'South Park' Episode," *New York Times*, November 6, 2009, artsbeat.blogs.nytimes.com/2009/11/06/gay-advocacy-group-objects-to -south-park-episode/ (accessed February 21, 2013).

27. Thomas, in-person interview by author.

28. Kevin Burra, "Gay Olympians Competing at 2012 London Olympics," *Huffington Post*, July 27, 2012, www.huffingtonpost.com/2012/07/27/gay-olympians-london-2012-olympics _n_1710329.html (accessed July 27, 2012).

29. Daniel Villarreal, "POLL: Why Do Most Gay Male Olympians Stay Closeted?" Gay.net, September 1, 2012, www.gay.net/sports/2012/08/01/poll-why-do-most-gay-male-olympians -stay-closeted (accessed September 17, 2012).

30. See also the resource section at the end of this book for more information about movies.

31. COLAGE, *Speak Up, Speak Out!* December 1, 2010, www.colage.org/resources/speak-up -speak-out/, 9 (accessed August 10, 2012).

RELIGION, POLITICS, AND CORPORATIONS

Religion—Helping or Hurting?

When Zack Wahls was growing up and the rest of the world was not always accepting of his family, he found solace in his church, where he felt entirely accepted and affirmed. In his Unitarian Universalist congregation, people did not ask questions about his two moms, and it felt like a safe haven for Wahls and his sister.[1]

Not all children with LGBTQ parents are as lucky as Wahls in finding a religious home that accepts them and their families. Danna, age fourteen, and Ember, sixteen, interviewed in the film *Our House: A Very Real Documentary about Kids of Gay and Lesbian Parents,* were in their early teens when their dad came out as gay and their parents divorced. This might not have been quite as traumatic had it not been for the fact that the Mormon Church, to which they belonged, vehemently objects to homosexuality. "When he first came out, I didn't tell anyone," Ember said. "Me being little miss Mormon girl. This was evil. It was bad, especially in the Mormon Church." Her mother, Jan, who now supports her ex-husband, said that the Mormon Church views homosexuality as "an abhorrence, an abomination against the normal order of man."[2]

Ember left the Mormon Church because she could not accept the fact that it considered her father evil. "How can you go to a church that hates your father?" she said. And it upset her greatly that people kept telling her to forgive him. "I didn't want to forgive him," she said. "What had he done wrong?"

But Ember's sister, Danna, and her mom were willing to overlook these flaws of the church and its parishioners. Danna felt that even though the antigay talk bothered her, all her friends were in the church and the church gave her something to fall back on in life. This didn't mean that she accepted what the church taught regarding homosexuality. She really disliked it when they read

Using the Bible to Justify Your Position

While Christianity is far from the only religion where large groups of its followers vilify LGBTQ persons and their families, it is, in this country, the most vocal one. Some Christians use the Bible to justify hatred and bigotry and find Bible verses to support their views. Some Bible verses often used for this purpose include the following:

> Leviticus 18:22–23[3]—"Thou shalt not lie with mankind, as with womankind: it *is* abomination."
>
> Leviticus 20:13—"If a man also lie with mankind, as he lieth with a woman, both of them have committed an abomination; they shall surely be put to death; their blood shall be upon them."
>
> 1 Corinthians 6:9—"Know ye not that the unrighteous shall not inherit the kingdom of God? Be not deceived; neither fornicators, nor idolaters, nor adulterers, nor effeminate, nor abusers of themselves with mankind." ("Abusers of themselves with mankind" refers to homosexuals.)

The argument that you can find almost anything to support your view in the Bible is often true. Yet, there are Bible verses that nobody would even consider taking seriously today, such as these:

> Psalm 136:9—"Happy shall he be, that taketh and dasheth their little ones against the stones."
>
> Deuteronomy 23:1 (which suggests that someone whose genitals are not intact shall not be able to enter the kingdom of heaven)—"He that is wounded in the stones, or hath his privy member cut off, shall not enter into the congregation of the LORD."

Later on, after Jesus enters the picture in the Bible, there seems to have been a policy change, and not only will you be welcome in heaven if your penis has been cut off, but this verse even encourages you to mutilate yourself—Matthew 19:12: "For there are some eunuchs, which were so born from *their* mother's womb; and there are some eunuchs, which were made eunuchs of men: and there be eunuchs, which have made themselves eunuchs for the kingdom of heaven's sake. He that is able to receive *it*, let him receive *it*."

While the Bible holds many spiritual truths and much comfort, it can indeed be used to promote hatred and prejudice.

the scripture in church and would come upon a passage where it talked about homosexuality being bad. Her friends and others in the church tried to be accommodating though, and usually avoided talking about antigay matters around her, she said.

But there are preachers and houses of worship that are even more vehement in their opposition to LGBTQ persons. Scott Lively, a pastor with a large following in this country (and in Uganda), is a media personality who has made it his mission to preach against LGBTQ families. Lively calls his movement a "pro-family" movement and uses very strong rhetoric in condemning LGBTQ persons and their families. In fighting bills that would give LGBTQ persons and families equal rights, he says that his followers need to stop "acting nice and trying to persuade the public officials through reason." Instead, Lively says, the politicians listening to what he calls "the leftists" and the "gay fascists" "need to see angry crowds with tar and feathers coming to run them out of office!"[4]

Casey, age seventeen, who constantly tries to understand why her family is ostracized in society and media, believes that this prejudice against LGBTQ persons has its roots in religion. "There is a societal prejudice that has been pushed by religion," she said. "I'm not sure why religion makes it such a big deal. We're not hurting anybody. I feel like we're a very non-threatening group. People take out different quotes from the Bible. If we went by everything in there, there would be no football and people would have a bazillion wives. I feel like my big thing about organized religion is that people use it as a veil for intolerance. They want to cover up that they are scared of the unfamiliar," Casey said.[5]

Yet, Casey and her family managed to find a religious home that is not intolerant. "The First UU Church has been awesome," she said. "Nobody has ever batted an eyelash. I've grown up in that church. It's a very big part of who I am. It's a safety net to know it's there."[6]

Searching for a Church Home

JamieAnn, a TransWoman, comes from a deeply spiritual background. Her father was a Lutheran minister. She respected him very much and feels grateful today for her strong spiritual Christian tradition. When JamieAnn was still a man, Jim, who had just begun to realize that he must make some major changes in life, he turned to his spiritual home, the Lutheran church. "I needed pastoral care," JamieAnn said. But when Jim met with his minister, the meeting was a great disappointment. Jim was unable to share his pressing personal crisis, and the minister was not sensitive enough to recognize that Jim very desperately needed help—or worse, he might have chosen to not see it. It would take another ten years for Jim, now JamieAnn, to approach that church again, longing to return to what she felt was her spiritual home. JamieAnn reintroduced herself to her old pastor and said that she was interested in reestablishing her old faith home. "And these words stick with me forever," JamieAnn said of the pastor's response. "It is a sign of how exclusive and not Christian the church can be. He said, 'I can think of one or two churches in town where you'd be welcome. Certainly, the Congregational Church is one.' Hypocrite, I thought to myself. What in the world are you doing ministering to God's people? The bread that you talk about sharing, that's Christ's body, Christ's blood. But I couldn't say any of those things. I wound up leaving."[7]

JamieAnn struggled with the rejection by what she had always considered her religion. And she struggled with her faith and with people calling themselves Christians, yet rejecting her. "I was embarrassed to be called a Christian," she said. "People were exclusive, as opposed to being inclusive. I completely lost my interest in religion."

JamieAnn blogs for the *Huffington Post*, and this is another place where she sees the dark side of people who call themselves Christians. "I get a lot of crap," she said. Responding to her blog, people will say things like, "We don't hate you, we love you and because we love you, we need to save you. Surely, you don't think God created you the way you now are. You went against God's plan for you." By their very actions, JamieAnn said, these people show her that as much as they talk about hating the sin and loving the sinner, they do indeed hate what they consider "the sinner." "It is a culture that is nourished in the church," she said.

If you are a progressive Christian and you try to argue using the Bible, you will always lose, JamieAnn believes. People use anti-LGBTQ passages from the Bible, she says, but nobody ever brings out the fact that the Bible also tells you that you're going to hell for eating shellfish or for wearing fabric made from more than one material.

In JamieAnn's struggles to find a church home she learned that sometimes congregations could be friendly and open and welcoming, but the church mission statement might leave a lot to be desired. Other times, the opposite was true—the mission statement professed a welcoming attitude but the congregation and some-times the minister did not live up to those expectations. In order for JamieAnn to feel at home in a church, both things had to be true—the congregation and the congregational leaders have to show that LGBTQ families and persons are wel-come, and the church has to be very intentional about welcoming diverse people and families in its mission statement.

It is easy to be flippant and say that if a house of worship does not accept your family the way it is, you can always find another religious home that will be more accepting. This, however, may be difficult for a number of reasons. A person may,

Some houses of worship support LGBTQ families, some do not.
Learn the difference.

for example, have grown up in the very same church where he or she still worships, and the church may indeed have become like a second family, in which case it is not quite so easy to dismiss it. This was certainly true for Danna, whose father was rejected by the Mormon Church because he was gay. Danna was a part of a youth group to which most of her friends belonged. Leaving the church would have meant leaving most of her friends behind.

Someone may also strongly believe in the teachings or his or her house of worship, something that might make it more difficult to leave but that could also wreak havoc with one's spirituality. If you believe most of the things that your church or mosque or synagogue teaches, then it may be especially difficult to sort out its prejudice against LGBTQ persons. If the religious institution is correct in everything else, then how come it has this one piece wrong? And perhaps more frighteningly, if you reject this particular idea, then what else might be wrong?

Many LGBTQ persons do indeed leave their churches when they meet with a lack of support or even rejection after coming out. Others, like Carol Curoe, who grew up Catholic and felt Catholic to her very core, did everything she could for a long time to find an accepting Catholic congregation. "Being Catholic was the reference point for our lives," she wrote in her book *Are There Closets in Heaven?* After a long search, her family found a Catholic parish that was accepting and affirming, but Curoe still has difficulties relating to the Catholic Church and is careful to represent the church to her sons in as truthful a light as possible, with all its flaws.[8]

It is true for many churches that they officially reject LGBTQ persons and families, but the individual congregations within the denomination might still be welcoming; so also for the Catholic Church. Many Catholic priests and many individual churches and groups, such as New Ways Ministry and Catholic Rainbow Parents and Dignity, are supportive of LGBTQ issues, while still upholding strong Catholic values.

To Curoe, her Catholic faith was so important that even when its condemnation of who she was felt overwhelming, she did not want to abandon it. For many years she worked hard at finding Catholic congregations that would be nurturing and accepting.[9]

Curing Homosexuality

There are those who believe that gender and sexuality are something you choose. This sentiment is particularly common when religion is used to argue against LGBTQ persons and issues. The argument is that LGBTQ persons are bad because they *choose* to live a life considered "unnatural" by some, and if they are parents, it might be believed that they are putting their children in harm's way.

Cindy's Family

Sometimes it feels like not much has changed for LGBTQ families in the last half century, but Cindy was only eleven years old some forty years ago when her father came out to his family, and her story is markedly different from that of the other people interviewed for this book.

Cindy was the middle child of three girls and lived in a number of different small towns in southern Wisconsin. Her father was a Methodist minister and life was picture-book perfect. Well, maybe not. It turned out that Cindy's father, who had been in the air force, was going to therapy on and off. He later confessed to Cindy that "he had feelings he did not consider normal." After the air force, he thought that if he got married, those disturbing feelings would go away. They didn't.

"When Dad came out," Cindy said, "we lived in Wauwatosa. I was eleven."

Cindy's dad told her mom first. The girls—Cindy and her seven-year-old younger sister and her fourteen-year-old older sister—knew something was up. "They clearly weren't happy," she said of her parents at the time. Cindy does not remember much about the particular moment when they told her, only that it was confusing. And the part about her dad being gay went way over her head. "Sexuality was not a big part of my life at that point. It was a lot for me to wrap my little brain around. They took us to therapy to try to help us get through it."

The fact that her father came out as gay was, in the end, a nonissue for eleven-year-old Cindy, perhaps even for the adult Cindy. "It was a much bigger deal that they were getting a divorce," she said. "That affected me for the rest of my life."

When Cindy's friend Sheila came for a visit, Cindy's parents sat Sheila down and told her the entire story. "She felt awkward and sad," Cindy said. "It ruined the whole visit." Yet, in a way, Cindy felt that it was good to have a friend who knew of her parents' divorce, someone she could later write letters to in order to vent.

The next step for Cindy's dad was to break the news to his Methodist congregation. Cindy believes that the church administration had not dealt with issues like this before and that they might have been a bit bewildered. In what could possibly be considered a generous attitude at the time, the church offered Cindy's dad a position in a small town in northern Wisconsin—a job yes, but not the greatest place for a gay man to relocate to. Not then, and not now.

Still, Cindy never felt that people cared or even knew that her dad was gay. "I suppose people at the church knew," she said. "But they didn't go around telling people." Nor did other people in their life seem to know. "When my parents got a divorce, people asked me why," she said.

During an interim period, Cindy's dad worked at another Methodist church and had a live-in boyfriend, Bob. There were problems with Bob, but they had nothing to do with him or Cindy's dad being gay, Cindy emphasized. It was all about Bob's personality, which was not great.

"We got to know Bob pretty well," Cindy said. "He didn't seem real happy that we girls were around. He put up with us but he wasn't really nice to us." Cindy tells a story of coloring Easter eggs and holding one up that she was particularly proud of. "Bob smashed it with his fist," she said. "Then I threw it in his face and ran off. Things weren't easy. Other times he would play with us, but it was really intense when he was around."

This stepparent story does not seem that unusual, but it hammers home the fact that children with LGBTQ parents have the same divorce issues that children in heterosexual parent households do—the drama has to do with parents' separation, lack of communication, the consolidation of two families, and having a new stepparent.

"Eventually, my dad decided to leave the church," Cindy said. "He became a counselor for troubled teens and later worked with Interfaith."

After her dad moved out, the family didn't see him much. The girls had regular visitations, every other weekend or so in the beginning, but Cindy saw her father less and less. "I was only twelve and I kept wondering, why is he doing this?" Cindy said. "Then he moved to Chicago. And we didn't see him at all."

A few years later Cindy's dad moved back to Wisconsin, and she was able to see him on a regular basis again. He now had a new partner. "Don was extremely nice," Cindy said.

Cindy's dad died from Hepatitis B at the age of sixty-one. She misses him. In many ways she always felt especially close to him. "His birthday was the day before mine," she said. Their particular bond was perhaps why his distancing himself from his family was so difficult for Cindy. But in a way his illness provided Cindy and her dad with an opportunity to get close again.

"Our relationship toward the end was fantastic," she said. "A lot of that had to do with him being in the hospital. I knew where to find him. We had long talks. By the time he passed away we were really, really close again."

Her dad's partner, Don, was good to the family. "He had been loving toward my dad and he was loving toward us," Cindy said. "After Dad died he took care of his affairs, making sure we all got what we should, us girls and Mom."

Growing up, Cindy did not have friends with LGBTQ parents—in fact she didn't even know any LGBTQ persons other than her dad and his partner until she was an adult. Now she has close friends who are gay parents themselves. She doesn't believe that growing up with a gay dad has defined her in any way. Her family was always extremely accepting, which might explain why her father being gay was never an issue for her. Today, though, Cindy does not go around telling people about her father. "I would if it came up in a conversation," she said. "In this political climate though, I would be careful. I don't want people judging my dad. I don't want to see that in their eyes."

Cindy believes that things might slowly be getting better for LGBTQ persons. "The fact that there are more people openly admitting it and wearing it on their shirts and flags is a good thing," she said. "And kids in school are more accepting of other kids. But I know there is still bullying going on."

The biggest obstacle standing in the way of change, Cindy believes, has to do with the prejudices that adults pass on to their children. "Kids are coming home from school hearing their parents say hateful things. So things are not wonderfully better, but a little."

It occurred to Cindy that she had never actually told her husband's (of eight years) parents and sister that her dad was gay. She marvels at her realization. "I know they wouldn't judge me," she said. "It just hasn't come up."[10]

People who identify as LGBTQ usually resent the thought that being homosexual is a choice (some also reject the term *sexual preference* because it indicates that there is a choice involved).

In their 2012 movie *Chasing the Devil: Inside the Ex-Gay Movement*, filmmakers Bill Hussung and Mishara Canino-Hussung explore and expose the ex-gay movement and its claims of "curing" homosexuals from "same-sex leanings." In the movie, Joanne Highley of Abundant Life Bible Institute says that she heard a voice from God telling her that she needed to minister to homosexuals and Jews. It isn't entirely clear what she had to say to Jews, but in regards to homosexuals she feels that the "lifestyle" is 100 percent choice and that we must learn to resist it. On the Abundant Life Bible Institute website Highley wrote that she had "suffered" from lesbianism in her younger years, but is now free of "all homosexual evil desires and activity" and has been "for over fifty years, all glory and praise to our loving Father." She now believes it is her calling in life to help other people out of homosexuality.[11]

Richard Cohen is a conversion therapist (conversion refers to converting people from homosexual to heterosexual). He was expelled from the American Counseling Association because of ethics violations, but in 2012 was one of the leaders of the ex-gay movement. He was interviewed extensively for *Chasing the Devil*, and it is obvious how he so quickly rose to power in the movement. Cohen has a great sense of humor and likes to be the center of attention. He is funny and quirky and affable. But his behavior, as well as that of many of the others filmed by the Hussung/Canino-Hussung team, goes from odd to bizarre when confronted with his own issues. Like Highley, Cohen claims that God spoke to him. God told him to move to Seattle; get help for his marriage, which was rocky; get an education; and help people. (The fact that his marriage was rocky might not be surprising considering that, as a gay man, he not only married a woman, but a woman he didn't know, one whom Sun Myung Moon of the Unification church chose for him.) This is how Cohen became an integral part of the ex-gay movement and perhaps the most famous (or infamous) ex-gay leader.

It is obvious from the interviews that all men in this documentary (other than Highley, not many women have a prominent position in it) spend most of their time fighting their same-sex sexual urges, such as looking at gay pornography. Peterson Toscano, one man interviewed in the movie, joined the ex-gay movement because he hated himself. The group promised him a new beginning and a clean slate, he said in the interview, a new life with Jesus. But unfortunately, it never addressed the fact that he had suffered terrible abuse in his childhood. Highley "counseled" Toscano in a way that felt extremely intimate and inappropriate, he said, and when he recognized this as another form of abuse, he left the movement.

John Sterback is considered by Richard Cohen as one of the greatest success stories of the ex-gay movement. At the end of the documentary, Sterback was successfully suppressing his urges (to look at porn or to hook up with other men) 100 percent of the time, and he had also become a coach helping people out of their homosexuality. When asked about his future, Sterback said, looking very sad, that all he wanted was a woman, or maybe even a man, to be chaste with for the rest of his life.

According to the filmmakers, the men involved in the ex-gay movement are troubled individuals, often with a highly abusive past. They are in great need of therapy, but instead they have stumbled upon the ex-gay movement.[12] (Ex-gay therapy was outlawed for minors in the state of California in September 2012, the motivation being that the therapy was deemed dangerous, as it could cause mental anguish to the point of suicide.)

In addition to the importance of understanding the pain that some LGBTQ persons feel and the extent to which they are willing to go in order to be "cured" of their homosexuality to fit into society, it is particularly relevant to consider the effects that the ex-gay movement might have on their children, teenage children in particular, who are dealing with their own budding sexuality and gender identity. While it has been shown that teens with LGBTQ parents tend to have an easier time coming out as LGBTQ themselves (though not always, as we have seen), there are no readily available studies on teens with ex-gay parents, but it is probably safe to assume that children of ex-gays who are LGBTQ would have a more difficult time with sexual orientation and/or gender expression.

Separation of Church and State

In the previously mentioned Michele Bachmann interview in *Meet the Press* in August 2011, in addition to emphasizing that marriage should only be between a man and a woman, Bachmann also clarified her views on sexual minorities. "It's a very sad life," she said. "It's part of Satan, I think. . . . It leads to the personal enslavement of individuals. Because if you're involved in the gay and lesbian lifestyle, it's bondage. It is personal bondage, personal despair, and personal enslavement. And that's why this is so dangerous. . . . . We need to have profound compassion for people who are dealing with the very real issue of sexual dysfunction in their life and sexual identity disorders."[13]

Bachmann is a U.S. congresswoman who was a candidate for the Republican nomination for president in 2012. What Bachmann and other politicians who are eager to use the Bible to defend their politics fail to remember is that in this country, there is a constitutional separation of church and state, and using religion in political circumstances like this is not constitutional.

Cindy, who grew up with a gay dad, is appalled at how some politicians get away with using the Bible as a tool to foster hatred. "It is scary," she said, "that we can be considering some of those people for the highest office in the country."[14]

"It's disgusting to hear people hate so openly," Andrew, who has two dads, said of politicians using the Bible to justify prejudice against his family. "And it's scary to know that people listen to them. A part of me wants to fight back."[15]

Thomas, age fourteen, who has two moms, has a slightly different view of politicians and religious leaders working against LGBTQ rights. While he is not a fan of them, he believes that strong LGBTQ supporters who are not gay—in other words, allies—"get a lot more worked up than people who are gay." Gay people, Thomas believes, tend to look at people like Bachmann and Santorum, and say, "OMG, that is so ridiculous." On the other hand, he adds, if these people actually get into a higher political position, "we're so screwed."[16]

Politics Matter, But How?

The November 2012 elections brought what many people on both sides of the fence feel was a tidal change in gay-rights issues. The sentiment after the election was that a majority of LGBTQ and non-LGBTQ voters felt that it was time to grant all families the same rights. While it is still true that most states in the union do not allow same-sex marriage, the election brought major changes around the country. Minnesota voters voted down the marriage ban amendment on their ballot, an amendment trying to ensure that only marriages between a man and a woman were legally recognized. (Same-sex marriage became legal in Minnesota in 2013. The rejection of the 2012 amendment meant that there would be no permanent legal ban against same-sex marriage.) In addition, three new states (Maine, Maryland, and the state of Washington) passed same-sex marriage laws, making it legal for same-sex couples to marry, and Wisconsin voted in the first ever openly gay senator, Tammy Baldwin, to the U.S. Senate.

So, what happened? Some say a shift in demographics happened—more young voters and more voters from formerly small minority groups that have now grown to a substantial contingency—critical mass—are to thank for these changes. But what about politics? In a 2012 Minnesota poll, 49 percent of the voters said they would vote against the marriage ban amendment. Forty-three percent of the voters said they supported the amendment (meaning that they did not want LGBTQ persons to be able to marry, ever). The surprising issue here, and the reason why this Minnesota example is used, is that less than six months earlier, 48 percent of Minnesotans supported the very same amendment. Something happened between January 2012 and June 2012 to increase the general public's support of same-sex marriage.

Indeed, something did happen! In May of 2012, first Vice President Biden and later President Obama voiced their support for same-sex marriage. It is believed that at least among African American voters, this might have helped change some minds.[17]

And if politics can change the public opinion in favor of LGBTQ issues (as in the preceding example), it can surely also do the opposite. Zach Wahls was in the eighth grade when he watched a Republican National Convention for a class assignment. While he certainly knew by then that some people did not respect his family, he remembers being shocked at the viciousness of the political discourse. Well-groomed men would go up to the podium and speak about the threats of terrorism and gay marriage, all in one breath—as though his family posed the same threat to society as a terrorist did. Wahls also realized at that time that the speakers who vilified his family were playing politics. They wanted to portray his family as very different, with different values and ideas, because it is easier to vilify someone who is not like you. At that time, and again later when Wahls testified in support of same-sex marriage in the Iowa legislature in 2011, he was struck by the polite tone with which hatred toward his family was presented. Even when someone in the legislature called for the *death* of homosexuals, it was with a very polite tone of voice. Wahls had been introduced to the game of politics.

Wahls makes an important point in his book when he discusses the fact that it is easier to make laws against people you don't know, don't see, and are unfamiliar with. He believes, for example, that his moms could be active in the Boy Scouts because it would be impossible for people to discriminate against them when they knew them. (It would be good if this were *always* true, but we all know it isn't.) This brings us back to the invisibility issue discussed in chapter 2, and the importance of being seen.[18]

LGBTQ Rights and the Republican Party

The question begs to be asked: Can you be a Republican and pro-LGBTQ?

The Republican Party, which has been against same-sex marriage and for the preservation of the Defense of Marriage Act (DOMA, signed into law by a Democratic president, Bill Clinton), took its anti-same-sex marriage sentiment up a notch during the 2012 Republican National Convention. Gay conservative leaders such as R. Clarke Cooper, the head of the gay and lesbian grassroots organization Log Cabin Republicans, were disappointed with the antigay marriage plank written into the Republican Party's program in 2012 by Tony Perkins, president of the Family Research Council, a Christian lobbying group. Under the Defense of Marriage heading, in addition to chastising the current administration's refusal to, for example, uphold DOMA, and for allowing same-sex marriage on military

Some Republicans feel that old Republican tradition is very much in line with allowing same-sex couples to marry.

bases, it states: "We reaffirm our support for a constitutional amendment defining marriage as the union of one man and one woman. We applaud the citizens of the majority of States which have enshrined in their constitutions the traditional concept of marriage, and we support the campaigns under way in several other states to do so."[19]

In an interview in the *Advocate*, a news magazine for LGBTQ persons, Cooper said, "The obsessive exclusion of gay couples, including military families, from the rights and responsibilities of marriage, combined with bizarre rhetoric about 'hate campaigns' and 'the homosexual rights agenda' are clear signs of desperation among social conservatives who know that public opinion is rapidly turning in favor of equality." Yet, Cooper, a proud Republican, is willing to stick with his party. He even feels that there have been some improvements in the Republican platform since earlier years, mostly because Log Cabin members were, for the first time, a part of the drafting of the marriage plank. Some improvements Cooper sees are the exclusion of anything that calls for a return to Don't Ask, Don't Tell. He is also pleased that the language regarding refugees does not interfere with LGBT people's possibility of asylum in this country in case of persecution and danger. And he approves of the formulations that recognize that "all Americans have the right to be treated with dignity and respect."[20]

The small group of Republican pro-LGBTQ people invited as a group to the Republican National Convention for the first time was vocal about its place in the Republican Party. In fact, the Log Cabin and Young Conservatives for the Freedom to Marry took out a full-page ad in the *Tampa Tribune* during the Republican National Convention, an ad emphasizing that same-sex marriage is very much in line with Republican values. It read: "The freedom to marry is directly in line with the core ideals and principles of the Republican Party—less government, more individual freedom, personal responsibility and the importance of freedom."[21]

Jesse Levey is another pro-LGBTQ Republican. In a CNN interview in 2009, he talked about growing up with two moms. He said he believes in "family values, small government and his lesbian mothers' right to marry."[22]

Industrialist billionaire David Koch, one of the Republican Party's most avid financial supporters, and, according to the *New York Times*, "one of the most influential men in American politics," surprisingly came out in support of same-sex marriage in 2012. When confronted with the fact that the Republican Party in general and then presidential candidate Mitt Romney in particular oppose same-sex marriage, Koch said simply, "Well, I disagree with that."[23]

Clint Eastwood, actor, director, film producer, and former mayor of Carmel, California, is another well-known Republican who has chosen to speak out on marriage equity. In an interview on the TV show *Ellen* he indicated that he had no problem with same-sex marriage whatsoever; in fact, he even said that it is a part of the old Republican values to "leave everybody alone."[24]

Kaley, age twenty-one, said "Some of my closest friends are a gay Republican couple. . . . They're great guys. I think it might be a tough situation. They are pro-LGBTQ of course, but come from old money. They are of the old Republicanism. Still, I think it's a tricky identity to have."[25]

Corporations

LGBTQ persons are not only attacked by politicians and churches but also, in some cases, by corporations. In 2012, the head of Chick-fil-A, Dan Cathy, said, according to an article in the *Los Angeles Times*, that he supported "the biblical definition of the family unit." While the wording of that statement was vague and could mean anything, we have been polarized enough in the past few years to become savvy to this kind of language. Most will conclude that Cathy's comment meant he opposes same-sex marriage.

After Cathy's pronouncement, mayors of big cities like Chicago, Boston, and San Francisco quickly announced that Chick-fil-A was not welcome in their towns, while some religious leaders like Mike Huckabee and Billy Graham, and political leaders like Rick Santorum, came out in Chick-fil-A's defense. While the controversy and the following boycotts were not believed to have made a major dent in the $4.1 billion a year corporation, the statement lost Chick-fil-A its partnership with the Jim Henson Company, creator of the Muppets. And in September of 2012, after boycotts, kiss-ins, and unfortunately, extensive vandalism to its restaurants, the company issued a statement saying it would reconsider its donations to anti-LGBTQ organizations and causes.[26]

Minnesota-based Target is another corporation with a troubled attitude toward LGBTQ rights. In 2012, Target came under fire for donating $150,000 in cash and services to the political action committee MN Forward, known for its anti-LGBTQ stand, though it actually had been donating to organizations and politicians working against LGBTQ rights for some time.[27] Lady Gaga, while negotiating a commercial contract with the retail giant, tried to get Target to commit to donating to LGBTQ rights causes as well. After intense negotiations, however, Target and Lady Gaga failed to come to an agreement and parted ways.[28]

But not all, probably not even a majority of corporations, are anti-LGBTQ. In 2012, Starbucks coffee, for example, officially declared that it was pro-same-sex marriage. It followed a number of other organizations that have taken the same position, such as Nike, Google, and Microsoft.

Today, no organization would consider declaring that it is pro–African American or pro-Hispanic because it is understood. It is no longer acceptable to treat racial minorities differently than the rest of the population. There might soon come a day when it is no longer necessary for organizations to declare themselves "pro" any minority group, including LGBTQ, because we will no longer be allowed to treat people differently.

Nonprofits—Girl Scouts and Boy Scouts

In 2011, the Girl Scouts of the USA (GSUSA) struggled with a controversy over a seven-year-old transgender child who wanted to join the Girl Scouts. The Girl Scouts in Colorado, while originally rejecting the male-to-female (MTF) trans child's request to join the troop, eventually came around and allowed the child to join. "If a child is living as a girl, that's good enough for us. We don't require any proof of gender," said Rachelle Trujillo, the vice president for communications for the Colorado branch. The Girl Scouts also released a statement through the Gay and Lesbian Alliance against Defamation (GLAAD) saying, "If a child identifies as a girl and the child's family presents her as a girl, Girl Scouts of Colorado welcomes her as a Girl Scout."[29]

But a fourteen-year-old Girl Scout, not in Colorado but in California, would not let the conflict die. In a YouTube video she urged her fellow Girl Scouts and others to boycott Girl Scout cookies in protest of the Colorado branch allowing seven-year-old Bobby Montoya to join the troop. On her YouTube video, which sparked as much anger as it did support, the fourteen-year-old said she believes that the GSUSA "cares more about promoting the desires of a small handful of people than it does for my safety and the safety of my friends and sister Girl Scouts and they are doing it with money we earned for them from Girl Scout Cookies."[30] She did not specify what threats the seven-year-old MTF trans child posed to her.

The fourteen-year-old YouTube girl is far from the only one condemning the Girl Scouts for its tolerance. Family Watch International, a conservative Christian organization that, according to its website, aims to "preserve and promote the family, based on marriage between a man and a woman as the societal unit that provides the best outcome for men, women and children," wrote about the Girl Scouts' position regarding the trans child in its "Position Statement":

> We recognize the basic human rights of all people, including lesbian, gay, bisexual and transgender individuals. All citizens, regardless of sexual orientation or gender identity, have the right to housing, employment, and to be free from violence and harassment.
>
> While we condemn violence or harassment of anyone, we do not accept that individuals should be given *special* rights based on sexual orientation or gender identity.
>
> We have provided the information in this section to make parents aware that Girl Scouts of the USA is increasingly promoting LGBT issues to girls by featuring prominent LGBT rights activists as role models at Girl Scout events, in Girl Scout materials, and by referring girls to websites that aggressively promote special LGBT rights.
>
> We believe it is inappropriate to promote LGBT issues to children.[31]

While it is not correct to say that the GSUSA "promote LGBT issues to children," the organization is generally known for being tolerant and inclusive.

How about the Boy Scouts? The Boy Scouts of America (BSA) has long had a troubled relationship with LGBTQ issues. Zach Wahls, author of *My Two Moms*, while well aware of the LGBTQ controversies of the Boy Scouts, is an Eagle Scout and speaks warmly of his Boy Scout troop and his Boy Scout experience growing up.

In the summer of 2012, however, when most organizations tended to be adopting nondiscriminatory policies and working toward greater inclusion, the BSA voted to uphold its ban on gay members and leaders. Opponents of this renewed confirmation of intolerance in the Boy Scouts said this vote stemmed from the misinformed belief that homosexual scout leaders are placing children in danger. The American Psychological Association confirms that "homosexual men are not more likely to sexually abuse children than heterosexual men are. . . . There is no scientific support for fears about children of gay or lesbian parents being abused by their parents or their parents' gay, lesbian or bisexual friends or acquaintances."[32]

A Boy Scout troop in Kentucky launched a controversy in September of 2012 when it dismissed a Scout leader for being gay. Greg Bourke raised two children (a Boy Scout and a Girl Scout) with his partner of thirty years. When the Boy Scouts learned that he was gay he was dismissed as its leader. Bourke is still a leader in his daughter's Girl Scout troop. Co-leader of that troop, Kim Haydon, said in a July letter to Boy Scout officials that to "discount all that he has done for our youth only because he is gay is absurd. Shame on you and your small mindedness."[33]

The Boy Scouts' refusal to change its policy caused its largest corporate sponsor, Intel, to withdraw its sponsorship in 2012, stating that the Boy Scouts are not in agreement with Intel's nondiscriminatory policy.[34]

Zach Wahls's experience in his Boy Scout troop does show us that, just as with different congregations in the same church, Boy Scout chapters can vary in inclusivity, and even LGBTQ-hostile organizations may have chapters or parts of the organization that are safe and welcoming for LGBTQ persons and their families.

The good news here is that the Boy Scout position is controversial today because most organizations and corporations are moving toward pro-LGBTQ policies, which is why the Boy Scouts stand out.[35]

Notes

1. Zach Wahls, with Bruce Littlefield, *My Two Moms: Lessons of Love, Strength, and What Makes a Family* (New York: Gotham Books, 2012), 63.
2. Quotes by Ember, Danna, and their mom are from Meema Spadola, dir., *Our House: A Very Real Documentary about Kids of Gay and Lesbian Parents* (Brooklyn, N.Y.: First Run/Ikarus Films, 2000).
3. All Bible quotes are from the King James Version.
4. Scott Lively, "Has the Worm Finally Turned?" *Scott Lively Ministries* (blog), September 7, 2012, www.scottlively.net/2012/09/07/has-the-worm-finally-turned/ (accessed September 25, 2012).

5. Casey, in-person interview by author, April 27, 2012.

6. Casey, in-person interview by author.

7. JamieAnn, Skype interview by author, August 15, 2012. Information about JamieAnn in the following paragraphs comes from this same interview.

8. Carol Curoe and Robert Curoe, *Are There Closets in Heaven? A Catholic Father and Lesbian Daughter Share Their Story* (Minneapolis, Minn.: Syren Book Company, 2007), 153.

9. Curoe and Curoe, *Are There Closets in Heaven?* 153.

10. Cindy, telephone interview by author, May 24, 2012.

11. Joanne Highley, Abundant Life Bible Institute website, www.albiw.com/faculty/Joanne_ Highley.htm (accessed April 11, 2012).

12. Bill Hussung and Mishara Canino-Hussung, dirs., *Chasing the Devil: Inside the Ex-Gay Movement* (New York: Coqui Zen Entertainment, 2008).

13. David Gregory, "Bachmann, Branstad, Murphy, Robinson, Martin, Todd," *Meet the Press*, NBC, August 14, 2011, www.msnbc.msn.com/id/44136028/ns/meet_the_press-transcripts/t/meet-press-transcript-august/ (accessed August 20, 2012).

14. Cindy, telephone interview by author, May 23, 2012.

15. Andrew, telephone interview by author, May 25, 2012.

16. Thomas, in-person interview by author, June 6, 2012.

17. Tom Kludt, "Poll: Minnesota Gay Marriage Ban Losing Support," *Talking Points Memo*, June 5, 2012, http://2012.talkingpointsmemo.com/2012/06/minnesota-gay-marriage-amendment-poll-losing-support.php (accessed November 5, 2012).

18. Wahls, *My Two Moms*, 45, 106, 108.

19. "We the People: A Restoration of Constitutional Government. Republican Platform, We Believe in America," GOP.com, www.gop.com/2012-republican-platform_we/ (accessed November 12, 2012).

20. Julie Bolcer, "Gay Conservatives Disappointed in Republican Party Platform," *Advocate.com*, August 12, 2012, www.advocate.com/politics/election/2012/08/22/gay-conservatives-disappointed-republican-party-platform (accessed September 18, 2012).

21. Jen Christensen, "Gay Groups and 'Homocon' Welcomed to GOP Convention Despite Platform," *InAmerica* (CNN blog), September 1, 2012, inamerica.blogs.cnn.com/2012/08/31/gay-groups-and-homocon-welcomed-to-gop-convention-despite-platform/ (accessed September 18, 2012).

22. John Blake, "'Gayby Boom': Children of Gay Couples Speak Out," *CNN Living*, June 29, 2009, www.cnn.com/2009/LIVING/wayoflife/06/28/gayby/index.html (accessed September 18, 2012).

23. Kenneth P. Vogel and Priyanka Goghani, "David Koch Breaks from GOP on Gay Marriage, Taxes, Defense Cuts," Politico, August 30, 2012, www.politico.com/news/stories/0812/80483 .html (accessed November 12, 2012).

24. "Clint Eastwood Talks Gay Marriage, RNC Speech Controversy," *Ellen*, NBC, September 18, 2012.

25. Kaley, Skype interview by author, October 30, 2012.

26. The section about Chick-fil-A is based on three different sources: Tiffany Hsu, "Chick-fil-A Loses Muppets, Gains Mike Huckabee in Gay Controversy," *Los Angeles Times*, July 23, 2012, articles.latimes.com/2012/jul/23/business/la-fi-mo-chick-fil-a-muppets-huckabee-20120723 (accessed July 26, 2012); Bill Barrrow, "Chick-fil-A Sandwiches Become Political Symbol," Associated Press, July 26, 2012, www.huffingtonpost.com/2012/07/26/chick-fil-a-sandwiches -_n_1707511.html (accessed August 29, 2012): Lester Brathwaite, "Chick-fil-A Stops Anti-Gay

Donations, Adopts Anti-Discrimination Policy," *Queerty*, September 19, 2012, www.queerty
.com/chick-fil-a-stops-anti-gay-donations-adopts-anti-discrimination-policy-20120919/ (accessed November 12, 2012).

27. John Rogers, "Target's Anti-Gay Political Donations Are Not Actually New: A History Lesson," *Queerty*, August 5, 2010, www.queerty.com/targets-anti-gay-political-donations-are
-not-actually-new-a-history-lesson-20100805/ (accessed September 13, 2012).

28. Chris Geidner, "Lady Gaga and Target End Deal, Say Sources," *Metro Weekly*, March 8, 2011,
www.metroweekly.com/poliglot/2011/03/lady-gaga-and-target-end-deal.html (accessed November 12, 2012).

29. "Girl Scouts' Inclusion of Bobby Montoya, 7-Year-Old Transgender Child, Prompts Troops
to Disband," *Huffington Post, Gay Voices*, December21, 2012, http://www.huffingtonpost
.com/2011/12/21/girl-scout-troops-transgender-child-disband_n_1163971.html (accessed
November 12, 2012).

30. Leslie Dobbins, "Girl Scout Disgruntled over Trans Inclusion Urges Cookie Boycott," January 11, 2012, www.shewired.com/news/2012/01/11/cookie-boycott-urged-disgruntled-girl
-scout (accessed November 12, 2012).

31. "100 Questions for the Girl Scouts. Girl Scouts and the Lesbian, Gay, Bisexual, Transgender
(LGBT) Agenda: Position Statement," Family Watch International, www.familywatchinter
national.org/100/lgbt_agenda.cfm (accessed November 12, 2012).

32. "Editorial: Boy Scouts' Anti-Gay Policy Teaches Wrong Lesson," *USA Today*, July 29, 2012,
usatoday30.usatoday.com/news/opinion/editorials/story/2012-07-29/Boy-Scouts-anti-gay
-policy/56579714/1 (accessed September 14, 2012).

33. Dani Heffernan, "Local Girl Scouts Troop Supports Kentucky Dad as Boy Scouts of America Kick Him out for Being Gay," GLAAD, www.glaad.org/blog/local-girl-scouts-troop
-supports-kentucky-dad-boy-scouts-america-kick-him-out-being-gay (accessed November
12, 2012).

34. "Intel Halts Boy Scout Donations over Anti-Gay Policy," *Huffington Post*, September 22,
2012, www.huffingtonpost.com/2012/09/22/intel-stops-boy-scout-don_n_1905856.html (accessed September 25, 2012).

35. At the time of this writing in 2013, after pressure from, among others, Bill Gates, BSA is
seriously reconsidering its position.

ACTIVISM

According to Wikipedia, "Activism consists of efforts to promote, impede, or direct social, political, economic, or environmental change. Activism can take a wide range of forms from writing letters to newspapers or politicians, political campaigning, economic activism such as boycotts or preferentially patronizing businesses, rallies, street marches, strikes, sit-ins, and hunger strikes."[1]

In her book, *Let's Get This Straight*, Tina Fahkrid-Deen also writes about activism. "In a nutshell," she writes, "activism is what you do to make the world a better place." According to Fahkrid-Deen you become an activist when you are passionate and angry enough about an issue to want to make a difference.[2]

Activism among LGBTQ Families

There are many powerful arguments for activism, the strongest one might be that if you *can* speak out, you *should*. There are, however, times in our lives when it may be more difficult to speak out for justice. In the book he wrote with his daughter Carol Curoe about her coming out as a lesbian, Robert Curoe talks about the early days after his daughter had just come out, when he was too ashamed to speak out. He would listen in silence as people told jokes in bad taste. He said nothing because he was afraid that if he did, people would suspect that he had a *reason* for it. Which, of course, he did.

Carol Curoe herself felt forced into activism, not when she came out, but when she and her partner started a family and suddenly faced discrimination wherever they turned.[3]

"When you have a cause that close to home, you're gonna be motivated," said Cindy, age fifty-three, the daughter of a gay father. "[LGBTQ families] are already feeling like they're out there. They have a lot to fight for." This is why, according to Cindy, LGBTQ persons and their families are more politically active than people in general. Though while she doesn't feel that growing up with a gay dad per se made her an activist, she does believe that she pays closer attention to LGBTQ issues because she has gay friends and that perhaps she has gay friends because she had a gay father. Cindy hates to see her friends suffer injustices. She believes that things are very difficult for LGBTQ persons and that "the pendulum has swung far in the wrong direction." In many places it is now acceptable to be rude and condescending to LGBTQ persons, she said in our 2012 interview. "It makes things really difficult." These issues, she believes, are likely to make LGBTQ persons and families motivated to be politically active.[4]

Thomas, age fourteen, who has two moms, said he is as politically involved "as I can be at age fourteen." Thomas said he watches the news on television. He was excited to be involved in Youth in Government at his high school (in most states called Youth *and* Government), a program that aims to teach civic engagement to youth. Once a year Thomas's group goes to the capitol for a long weekend and stages a mock government. "It's really cool," he said. "And I keep up with the news. I advocate. I tell people to vote. But I can't do a whole lot more yet. Only prepare myself, and I definitely do that."[5]

Like Cindy, Thomas believes that LGBTQ persons are active because they have to be. His moms are active, he said, because they can't legally marry. That motivates them. And if you're raised by politically active people, Thomas believes, you are very likely to become politically active yourself.[6]

Casey, age seventeen, definitely follows politics and issues. But her activism extends far beyond LGBTQ issues. Even though one of her pet issues is definitely gay rights, she is also concerned about immigration issues, she works for pro-choice, and she is educating herself about human trafficking because injustice and oppression concern her very much.[7]

Speak Out with COLAGE

When it comes to organizations working for the political interests of children with LGBTQ parents, none equals COLAGE. In a 2005 video, Meredith Fenton talks about the early days of COLAGE and the urgent need for a place to connect regarding LGBTQ activism. "There was all of a sudden this unprecedented amount of teenagers who were looking for community, and who had grown up in the community, and they wanted to do more than just meet others like them. They wanted to really make change in the world," she said. COLAGE picked up the ball and ran with it. They developed ways in which children with LGBTQ parents could be a part of creating a better world for themselves and their families. In a program called Speak OUT, COLAGE teaches children and youth how to be activists. Here are a few of the organization's tips and suggestions on how to educate yourself.[8]

Speaking in Public

1. Make eye contact with your audience (and if this is too difficult then *pretend* that you are looking at someone in the audience). Let your eyes scan from one end of the room to the other.
2. Speak loudly. And, since we tend to speak too fast when we are nervous, practice speaking extremely slowly, then, when you speak in front of an audience, you will speak at regular speed.
3. Make sure that your body language is not betraying you—this means that you should try to look confident even if you're not. Practice using confident hand gestures and make sure you are not pacing or rocking back and forth.
4. Keep your speech short and to the point, and when you get a question, don't worry if you can't answer it immediately. Take your time and think about what you want to say.

Answering Questions

1. The Speak OUT Program brings up questions that children of LGBTQ parents often get when they speak in public and suggestions of how to

Practice looking confident before speaking in public.

answer them. The first and perhaps most annoying question that children with LGBTQ parents tend to get is, "Are you gay?" Speak OUT says you may or may not want to answer this extremely personal question—it is indeed an acceptable option not to. If you want to, however, you can answer in generalities, such as referring to the percentage of the general population that is gay. The probability of you being gay is the same as the probability of anyone being gay, so you may tell the audience to draw its own conclusion. The most "activist" answer suggested by Speak OUT is "I am not going to answer that question and let me explain why—if I tell you that I identify as an LGBT person, the assumption will be made that my parents somehow made or influenced me to be gay. However, if I tell you that I am straight—it somehow reinforces the notion that straight equals more normal than other types of sexual orientations or gender identities because people will be 'relieved' to know that my parents haven't influenced my . . . sexuality."

2. COLAGE strongly advises speakers to avoid getting into religious arguments about whether or not it is wrong to be LGBTQ. Instead, Speak OUT suggests that if confronted with the issue of religion and you did grow up in an accepting church, you might reply that your church taught you that it is right to love all people. Again, just because somebody asks you a question doesn't mean that you have to answer.

3. Another question that potential COLAGE activists should expect is the one about whether they sometimes wish that their families were more "normal." The suggested way to reply to this question is to emphasize that the thought that some families are more normal or desirable than other families is nothing but an assumption, and we should learn to see all different families around us as acceptable.

Preparing Sound Bites[9]

Potential public speakers are also encouraged to prepare their own "sound bites" to be used in media and public speaking contexts. A sound bite is a short message that you practice before your speech but that can also be delivered on its own, without a context. The purpose of a sound bite is to give people something to remember after your talk or interview or performance is over. Your sound bite should be short and personal, simple, convincing, and upbeat. Two good examples of sound bites from the Speak OUT Program guide are: "The problem isn't that I have a lesbian mom. The problem is that I live in a homophobic society so that I am vulnerable to harassment in my community and discrimination from my government," and, "My parents love and support me the way that all capable

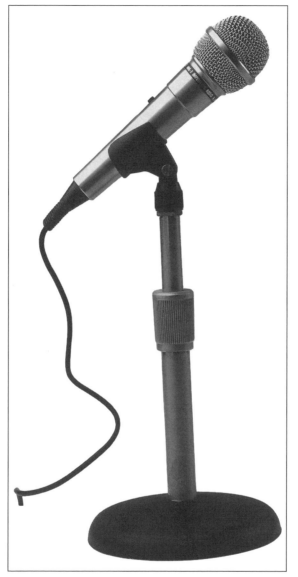

Preparing "sound bites" ahead of time can make your talk more memorable.

parents should love and support their children. My parents and my family deserve the same rights and responsibilities given to all capable parents."

Giving Interviews[10]

1. Giving interviews can be another powerful way to get LGBTQ families' stories out, though it should not be assumed that your story will be told only from the point of view that you are telling it or even intending it.

Still, this does not mean that you should not give interviews. Do, and be yourself, be relaxed, and if you don't know the answer to something, tell the person who interviews you that you will find out and provide them with resources later.

2. If the interview will be televised, wear bright but solid colors, avoid white or black clothing, or clothing with slogans on it. Wear simple jewelry, if any, and avoid buttons or pins.

3. Presenting your best self on TV is very similar to presenting your best self in a public speech, though you will usually be sitting down on television. Remember to sit up straight and avoid slouching and overly active or nervous hand gestures. If you want to learn more before your appearance, television anchors and preachers are good professionals to observe. The best advice regarding the television interview, as well as public speaking, is to be yourself, allow your personality to shine through, and express yourself in a natural way.

Other Ways to Be an Activist[11]

Other ways for children with LGBTQ parents to be activists is to write letters to the editor (make them timely, personal, and short) or to create your own media venue such as writing a book, a blog, a radio show, a movie, or a website. And if you are still eager to do more, you might do research on political issues and lobby politicians, join forces with other local LGBTQ groups and work with them on locally pressing issues, and meet with politicians who can change policy.

Zach Wahls and Another Side of Activism

It is one thing for children of LGBTQ parents to choose to become activists, and quite another to be pushed into it. Zach Wahls was tumultuously thrown into activism in 2011 when he, as a college student, testified in the Iowa House Judiciary Committee about what it was like to grow up with two moms. He cautions against pushing children of LGBTQ parents into activism.

I hear from many LGBTQ parents who tell me that they want their children to turn out just like me and to do the advocacy work I do. Every time I hear this, I wince and my heart goes out to those children. One of the reasons I'm an effective advocate today is because my moms did not ever want me to do advocacy work. . . . They never pressured me, never pushed me to do that, and hearing from parents who *are* doing that makes me very uncomfortable.

Activism versus Fanaticism

Most people recognize fanaticism when they see it (though often not in themselves) and most people would agree that fanaticism is not a good thing. A fanatic is someone we think of as so blinded by self-interest that he doesn't see the needs of others.

A child of the ongoing Israeli-Palestinian conflict, Israeli lecturer and journalist Amos Oz, author of *How to Cure a Fanatic*, would probably add to the idea of the self-interested fanatic. In many ways Oz sees the fanatic as the ultimate altruist, though perhaps someone who is altruistic in a selfish way, if that makes sense. "The essence of fanaticism," he writes in his book, "lies in the desire to force other people to change."[12]

We all know people who want what's best for everybody. In our sphere of acquaintances they may be the kindest, most loving people. They are full of compassion and understanding (at least that is the perception), and *they want to change us*. Oz writes that the fanatic "is more interested in you than in himself. He wants to save your soul, he wants to redeem you, he wants to liberate you from sin, from error, from smoking, from your faith or from your faithlessness."[13] Or, one might add, though it is not included in Oz's book, from homosexuality or life as a transgender person.

Oz believes that fanaticism begins at home, with the urge to change those you love, and that as an activist it is easy to "catch" fanaticism. Fanaticism, writes Oz, is "more contagious than any virus. You might easily contract fanaticism even as you are trying to defeat or combat it."[14]

According to *Merriam-Webster's Collegiate Dictionary*, a fanatic is "marked by excessive enthusiasm and often intense uncritical devotion."[15] The keyword here is "uncritical." In order to prevent ourselves from slipping into fanaticism, even as we combat it, we must look at our own behavior and the beliefs that we hold to be true, and put them under close scrutiny.

While it is easy to see that those who oppose us are fanatical, it is very difficult to see how we might ourselves be fanatical when demanding, for example, equal rights. But we can always benefit from examining our own beliefs and the *methods* we use when we demand change. Oz believes that looking at the world with a sense of humor helps and can be very effective in working toward change. When we laugh at ourselves, we don't take our own beliefs too seriously.

Oz also believes that a fundamental part of fanaticism comes from lack of imagination. If you are able to imagine what life is like for others, you would simply not insist on your own way as the only solution. If we could only inject him with a little bit of imagination, Oz writes, it would "cause the fanatic to feel uneasy."[16]

We've come a long, long ways. But we still have a long ways to go. Gay and lesbian parents who think that, magically, things have gotten better overnight are fooling themselves and are potentially putting their children in danger. They *have* to be conscious of what the reality is, and they *have* to be willing to take responsibility for the safety of their kids. Now, when kids are being harassed, it's not the fault of the parents—after all, we don't blame the victim. Parents do, however, have a responsibility to prepare their children and to, for God's sake, let them be kids. I'm [advocating for LGBTQ causes] so other kids of gay parents *don't have to*. I've met quite a few gay and lesbian parents who have chips on their shoulders—for whatever reason—but when you're raising kids, that chip has to be removed.[17]

Wahls is not, of course, discouraging activism—his own activist successes speak for themselves—but he emphasizes that activism must come from within, not from outside pressure.

What Activism Can Accomplish

Sometimes it is helpful to look at an organization with a long history of activism to get a sense of what is possible. Parents, Families and Friends of Lesbians and Gays (PFLAG) is such an organization. With a long history of activism, members can now step back and see what their particular activism has actually accomplished. In the 1990s PFLAG helped pass Safe Schools legislation, which prohibited bullying of students based on sexual orientation. It helped ensure that Title IX, legislation that prohibits discrimination on basis of sex, would also cover LGBTQ students, which means that students may not be discriminated against

Ashley's Family

Ashley, age eighteen at the time of our Skype interview, grew up with her mom and dad and brother in the suburb of a large metropolitan area in the Midwest. When she was sixteen, her father sat Ashley and her brother down and said he had something to tell them. Had they noticed that their grandpa had been putting clear nail polish on his nails? he wondered. "My first thought was, Papa is gay," Ashley said. "I was going off the stereotypes I had learned. I had not been exposed to the gay or trans community so I was going off what little I knew." But Ashley's grandpa was not gay. He was in the process of becoming a woman. At first, Ashley was shocked and curious all at the same time. She remembers wondering what it even meant. How does a man become a woman? What does that mean? And she was wondering why she hadn't noticed, but mostly, what would happen to her grandma and to her grandparents' relationship? "It was the first time I saw my grandma cry," she said. "It was hard in the beginning. It's better now, after counseling."

Ashley's grandpa was trying to be gentle with the family and started presenting as a female very slowly, adding more and more female clothing and features, but once Ashley had accepted her grandpa's new identity she felt that he should just go for it. "We might as well pull that Band-Aid off," she said.

The family started learning more about transgender and transsexual. Ashley found a documentary that was helpful, where trans persons were interviewed about their lives. The rest of what she found in media, however, wasn't so helpful, she said.

While referring to her grandpa as Jamie, Ashley, idiosyncratically perhaps, said she still calls her Papa to her face. It was a name that Ashley made up for her grandfather as a baby, and while she is not sure how Jamie now feels about being called Papa, she believes it might be a little bit like a badge of honor because she came up with the name.

Ashley's grandfather coming out as a trans woman changed a lot of things for Ashley, though it took time, she said. She is much less likely to go by stereotypes these days, and she feels that "gender does not have to be so sacred. There is a lot of variety around us." Jamie's transition also made Ashley look more closely at her own gender expression. "Could I be wrong about my own identity?" she wondered. She feels that being forced to examine that question about herself has added depth to her life. "It gives me more freedom to choose, not only gender but also how to express gender. It's not as fixed as it used to be," she said. And while she concluded that yes, she is and wants to be a woman, it is not as set in stone as it used to be. "Cis gender people never have to think about those things," she said.

Even though she is in college where the atmosphere is more accepting in general, Ashley doesn't tell just anybody about Jamie. "I look at the climate," she said. "If I see the right indications, I can tell." She also tries to prepare people before she introduces Jamie to them. She believes it helps her as well as Jamie and those who are introduced to her. Sometimes, Ashley said, things are awkward when she first introduces the topic, because people just don't know how to talk about gender, but then they talk some more and things get less awkward. Ashley introduced Jamie to her roommates fairly soon after she went off to college and she felt that it went well. Her roommate's boyfriend was there as well and the two of them are in theater, something Ashley believes helped, as she believes that theater people might be more open. She does know, however, that not everyone is going to be cool with the fact that she has a trans grandparent. "I have to not let it bother me," she said.

Though Ashley feels fortunate that the people around her are accepting, it isn't necessarily strangers or friends who have caused the most grief in Jamie's coming out. "The only really interesting situation was with my maternal grandmother," Ashley said. "She was close-minded at first. She would talk about our family as broken. My mother took a lot of slack." But after some time, Ashley could tell things were changing. "I don't know what in the world happened," she said. "[My maternal grandmother] started having these long conversations about life and then she came to the realization that she should interact with [Jamie] for the sake of the grandkids. And as more and more of these things were happening, [Jamie and my other grandmother] were talking more and more, not just about gender but about childhood experiences, things they had in common."

While Ashley was frustrated at times with the inability of her maternal grand-mother to accept Jamie's transition, she spoke with Jamie about it and told her to be patient with her other grandmother. And patience, Ashley very much feels now, is what made her grandmother finally come around and accept Jamie as a woman.

When talking about those early days after Jamie came out, Ashley feels that she has to learn to forgive herself for all the thoughts she had back then; they came from not being exposed and educated, she says. Sometimes she was feel-ing intolerant but she recognized later that it is all a growth process. "You just have to be really patient with each other," she said. She also told Jamie that she needed to be more patient with all of them and that they needed more time to adjust and learn. Sometimes they would use the wrong pronoun about Jamie, out of habit. "She was making a huge deal out of it," Ashley said, but then they would talk about it and Jamie recognized and acknowledged that this was not an easy process. In public, the family tried harder to not refer to Jamie as Jim or Dad. But sometimes, Ashley said, not even Jamie remembered her name and someone might call 'Jim,' to get her attention. "It just takes time," Ashley said. "Everybody goes through a process, the spouse, the children, the grandchildren, the siblings and the parents as well."

Jamie's dad had Alzheimer's when Jamie came out to the rest of the family and everybody decided that they were not up for the experience of having to tell him about Jamie every single time they came to the house, as though this was something that had just happened. Jamie's mother, however, was told after her husband died. Ashley knew it was a difficult adjustment for her great-grandma. "Sometimes in the middle of the dialogue Grandma Mary would switch the topic completely to something else." For the rest of them, by now, Ashley said "this is just the new normal."

While Ashley feels that she has moved on and is comfortable with this new way to be a family, she still has difficulties in one particular place: her grand-parents' home. Somehow, being in a certain environment, she feels, sets you up for certain expectations, and seeing Jamie's wigs in their house still shakes her up a bit.

Ashley studies gender roles at the university. She is politically aware and active and she has started participating in some LGBTQ events with Jamie. Once, she and Jamie and her aunt Karen went to a panel discussion about trans issues. While she is happy to talk about those issues and what it was like to have a trans grandparent, she also feels that you learn an incredible amount just from listening to other people's concerns and issues.[18]

for identifying as LGBTQ. PFLAG has prevented hate speeches, instituted scholarship programs, and started programs like the Welcoming Faith Communities, Bringing the Message Home, and PFLAG Diversity Network, all to improve safety and equality for LGBTQ students and families.[19]

Straight Allies

Jack Antonoff writes in *Gay Voices*, a blog on the *Huffington Post*, about the importance of being a straight ally. He begins his blog with the well-known poem by German theologian and anti-Nazi Martin Niemöller:

> First they came for the Socialists, and I did not speak out—
> Because I was not a Socialist.
> Then they came for the Trade Unionists, and I did not speak out—
> Because I was not a Trade Unionist.
> Then they came for the Jews, and I did not speak out—
> Because I was not a Jew.
> Then they came for me—and there was no one left to speak for me.

If that poem doesn't spell it out clearly enough, Antonoff also emphasizes the importance of interfering *every time* you see injustice. In reference to our more and more polarized political climate he writes: "We have reached a moment in which wavering apathy is simply a non-option, as it is an endorsement in itself of the treatment of LGBTQ Americans as second-class citizens. As straight allies, we have to realize that the time is now to take a critical look at ourselves and to question how and where we are allowing hate to exist and, therefore, to breed."[20]

But it isn't easy. Antonoff discusses how, as a straight ally who points it out every time you hear coworkers or family members or friends make crude or insensitive jokes or comments, you might well become known as a "buzzkill" or a wet blanket, and people might not want to invite you to their parties. They might even ask you to refrain from speaking out.[21]

It can be awkward indeed to point out "the elephant in the room." The story of *The Emperor's New Clothes*—where a little boy says out loud what everybody sees but is too afraid to say, that the emperor's new clothes are not at all made from the finest silks in the country, but actually don't even exist, and the emperor is naked—would hardly have been such a classic if there weren't an enormous amount of truth behind our awkwardness in speaking out.

"We would rather let hate speak linger among us than endure the awkward moment when someone points out that something is simply not acceptable," Antonoff writes. Antonoff believes that in order to learn to speak up, we have to get over our social paralysis. He brings up racism to prove his point. While still prevalent, racism is no longer socially acceptable (in most places). Yet, the social acceptability of hate speech toward LGBTQ persons is still debatable, he feels. But LGBTQ rights are not, Antonoff believes, a "gay issue." It is a human rights issue, and "straight apathy" is a great stumbling block in the pursuit of equality.[22]

Even though he emphasizes the importance of doing the right thing, Antonoff does not believe that things are or should necessarily be easy for straight allies. He feels that straight people should be willing to make sacrifices to stand up for human rights for all citizens. "No matter how we rationalize the oppression of fellow citizens, we will inevitably be faced with one question in the near future: How did we as Americans allow our LGBTQ citizens to be treated as second-class ones? It is a question that all Americans will ask in the future but should ask today," he writes.[23]

A few times while interviewing teens with LGBTQ parents, I was reminded of my status as an ally. One teen said to me, regarding comments made by Michele Bachmann that indicated that she thought of his family as wrong, "You people get much more upset about these things than we do. We mostly laugh and find it ridiculous." That is the difference between someone who is confronted with prejudice at every turn, and someone like me, who has the luxury of walking away from it. While not all LGBTQ persons are able to take the humor approach—for a variety of reasons, oppression is different for different people and also, as we have seen, varies greatly from one geographical area to the next, and for some, there is a very real threat of violence—LGBTQ persons and families clearly have to develop coping mechanisms that allies don't even have to consider.

Logan, age twenty-one, feels there is a great need for straight allies. "You can be told over and over again that a movie is good by a movie critic, but if a close friend or someone you trust says you should go see it, you are more likely to see the movie. That's what allies do for the community. They have greater access to a broader community that may not understand the gay community." By allies telling people about gay people they know, it normalizes it, Logan feels. Logan

> ### ? Are Children of LGBTQ Parents Allies?
>
> According to the Gay-Straight Alliance (GSA) Network, children with LGBTQ parents don't usually think of themselves as "allies." For many of them, from the time they could walk and talk they have a long and unique history of being a part of the LGBTQ rights movement, willingly or not so willingly fighting for their families' rights. They are immersed in all things LGBTQ. Recognizing the unique knowledge and insights of this group will help strengthen all GSAs.[24]

doesn't feel that a straight ally has to be particularly educated or a member of PFLAG to speak out. She feels that all that matters is that they "perpetuate positivity to the world about the LGBTQ community."[25]

In the memoir they wrote together about Carol Curoe coming out as a lesbian and their subsequent struggle with the Catholic Church and their own faith, Curoe and her father, Robert Curoe, discuss their newfound activism. Robert Curoe felt that he was suddenly confronted with intolerance in places where he least expected it and realized that it was more difficult for him to accept intolerance toward gays and lesbians in people who were otherwise open-minded. When Robert Curoe was a child, his parents fought for equal rights for African Americans. But, perhaps because they were devout Catholics and the church condemned it, they considered homosexuality a sin and could not recognize that LGBTQ persons too were oppressed and worthy of their social justice activism.[26]

On a positive note, it might also be true that even though Robert Curoe's parents were homophobic and set in their ways, Curoe's seeing them fighting for justice might be exactly what made him overcome his own Catholic beliefs that homosexuality was a sin, and in the end, take a stand for justice and the daughter that he loved.

How Do You Become an Ally?

Straight Allies in Everyday Life

In PFLAG's *Guide to Being a Straight Ally*, Katie, age twenty-nine, says she feels confused about how to be an ally. "I remember learning about the civil rights movement and other social movements for equality in school and thinking to myself, 'Well, if I had been an adult then, I would have stood up and done the right thing.'" But she continues, "Now I'm an adult, I see inequality and I know

I should do something, but it is just not that easy. I have so many questions and fears and I am just not sure where—if anywhere—I belong in the gay rights movement."[27]

The easy-to-read PFLAG guide, addressing allies and potential allies, is a great tool to help in figuring it all out. First of all, when you feel ready to take that step and start making a difference, the guide advises: educate yourself.[28] In other words, read all you can, talk to friends who have LGBTQ parents or who identify as LGBTQ. Don't be afraid to ask questions. The PFLAG booklet also advises allies to be prepared for things to take time. Change doesn't happen overnight, not in us and not in others. But it also says, don't be afraid to push yourself. And while you're at it, learn some new LGBTQ-friendly vocabulary. Muster your courage to speak up when someone makes an offensive joke. There are tricks to help us speak up when it feels difficult, such as using humor or even plain facts (which is why it is important to educate yourself). Try to catch yourself (or others) using stereotypes, such as "He dresses so well; he must be gay." And try to be as accurate as you can with words. If you don't know how to refer to someone's partner, for example, ask. One important place to focus your activism is where *you* have a voice but a person with LGBTQ parents or someone who identifies as LGBTQ might not, such as in a church setting. The guide says:

1. "First, many of these places still have policies or culture that remain unfriendly or restrictive to GLBT people. But the one-on-one, honest and informed conversations that you have can help change this fact.
2. "Second, as an ally, you bring a different perspective to the conversation. Your insistence on equality has a different ring. It isn't about you—it is about others, and about doing the right thing."[29]

The next step that the PFLAG guide suggests is . . . coming out! The guide means, of course, coming out as an ally. Even while you might have already been doing this in small ways, coming out as an ally means that you are taking it up a notch, that you tell people in plain language that you support LGBTQ rights. Some straight allies hesitate to come out as they are afraid to be seen as gay. Yes, it might happen, and if it matters to you, you can always emphasize the *straight* in *straight ally*.

Straight Allies at School

The Gay, Lesbian and Straight Education Network (GLSEN) also has an excellent resource for people wishing to be straight allies called the Safe Space Kit, which includes a book titled *Guide to Being an Ally*. The kit is aimed at school staff,

Can a School Be an Ally?
What about Other Institutions?

We have already mentioned how individual students and school staff can be allies, but the GLSEN guide takes this one step further and teaches schools *as institutions* how to become allies to LGBTQ students. The most obvious way for a school to become an ally is by being intentionally inclusive, the guide says. Schools should make sure that their health and sexuality education is inclusive when it comes to sexual orientation and gender nonconforming. They should order library books and material that reflect LGBTQ issues, and make sure that the school curriculum covers LGBTQ history, persons, and events. For athletes who identify as LGBTQ, it is especially important to ensure safety during athletic events, which can be a particularly rough environment for these students. Homecoming and athletic events should have gender-neutral alternatives to the "king" and "queen." When celebrating Mother's Day and Father's Day make sure that the celebration affirms all families. When it comes to filling out forms at school, make sure that all forms have alternatives to "father" and "mother" such as "parent" or "guardian." If there is a school dress code, there should be gender-neutral alternatives; girls should not, for example, be forced to wear skirts if they are not comfortable wearing them.

There are also things that allies can do in other institutions to help and affirm people from the LGBTQ community. Abbie E. Goldberg suggests that those who work in hospitals display small inconspicuous rainbow stickers or other LGBTQ-friendly indicators somewhere in the hospital to allow for LGBTQ-identifying persons to speak out if they choose to, or to let the staff know that they identify as LGBTQ if it is relevant to their treatment. The same should be true, according to Goldberg, in adoption agencies, places where parenting classes are held, and many other public locations.[30]

especially teachers and administrators, but it can be used by anyone wishing to be an ally.

An ally, the GLSEN guide says, is "an individual who speaks out and stands up for a person or group that is targeted and discriminated against. An ally works to end oppression by supporting and advocating for people who are stigmatized, discriminated against or treated unfairly." As with the triangles or rainbow stickers on the door or window of a school office, the GLSEN ally guide also encourages the use of a supportive button or wristband to make it known to students in the school that you are an ally to them and their families.[31]

And don't underestimate the importance of rainbow stickers in the window. In an interview in *PrideSource*, LGBT activist Laura Sorensen said that queer youth, even those living in more accepting areas, very much appreciate knowing that there are allies.

"It's been my experience with queer youth that when we're on field trips or in the car, if they were to see a rainbow sticker on another car, they'd get really excited," she said. "Or they'd go out of their way to tell me that the second year French teacher in their high school has a rainbow on their door, even if they've never met that teacher. It can be really isolating in high school and so, especially for youth who don't know a lot of LGBT people, it can be really exciting to see."[32]

The Unitarian Universalist Association (UUA) has made being an ally to LGBTQ persons and families one of its foremost concerns. On its website it has an extensive list of things to do to support what it calls "people with marginalized identities." Many of the things suggested have to do with—yes, here it is again—educating yourself regarding acceptable vocabulary and history. It is also important to learn to recognize oppression when you see it and take a stand against it. Keep your ears and eyes open to people's stories, and never assume that you know what is best for a group of which you are not a part.

The UUA page also encourages allies to learn how to challenge power structures, but also to not try to make big changes alone. Perhaps the most important thing for an ally, according to the UUA, is to learn to look at your own cultural assumptions and prejudices.[33]

Notes

1. *Wikipedia*, s.v. "Activism," en.wikipedia.org/wiki/Activism (accessed February 22, 2013).
2. Tina Fakhrid-Deen, with COLAGE, *Let's Get This Straight: The Ultimate Handbook for Youth with LGBTQ Parents* (Berkeley, Calif.: Seal Press, 2010), 157.
3. Carol Curoe and Robert Curoe, *Are There Closets in Heaven? A Catholic Father and Lesbian Daughter Share Their Story* (Minneapolis, Minn.: Syren Book Company, 2007), 92, 131–132.
4. Cindy, telephone interview by author, May 24, 2012.
5. Thomas, in-person interview by author, June 6, 2012.

6. Thomas, in-person interview by author.

7. Casey, in-person interview by author, April 27, 2012.

8. The following tips on public speaking and answering questions are based on COLAGE's guide *Speak Up, Speak Out!* December 1, 2010, www.colage.org/resources/speak-up-speak-out/, pages 1–8 (accessed September 8, 2012).

9. COLAGE, *Speak Up, Speak Out!* 10.

10. COLAGE, *Speak Up, Speak Out!* 12–13.

11. COLAGE, *Speak Up, Speak Out!* 17–20.

12. Amos Oz, *How to Cure a Fanatic* (Princeton, N.J.: Princeton University Press, 2010), 57.

13 Oz, *How to Cure a Fanatic*, 57.

14. Oz, *How to Cure a Fanatic*, 66.

15. *Merriam-Webster's Collegiate Dictionary*, 11th ed., s.v. "fanatic."

16. Oz, *How to Cure a Fanatic*, 89.

17. Zach Wahls, e-mail interview by author, September 12, 2012.

18. Ashley, Skype interview by author, October 15, 2012.

19. PFLAG website, community.pflag.org/page.aspx?pid=267 (accessed October 1, 2012).

20. Jack Antonoff, "Straight Allies: The Importance and the Realities," *HuffPost Gay Voices* (blog), February 16, 2012, www.huffingtonpost.com/jack-antonoff/straight-allies_b_1280498.html, (accessed August 29, 2012).

21. Antonoff, "Straight Allies."

22. Antonoff, "Straight Allies."

23. Antonoff, "Straight Allies."

24. GSA Network, www.gsanetwork.org (accessed September 21, 2012).

25. Logan, telephone interview by author, November 1, 2012.

26. Curoe and Curoe, *Are There Closets in Heaven?* 51.

27. PFLAG, *Guide to Being a Straight Ally* (Washington, D.C.: PFLAG, 2007), community.pflag.org/document.doc?id=139 (accessed November 12, 2012), 2.

28. There is an extensive list of resources toward the end of this book. It is a good place to start.

29. PFLAG, *Guide to Being a Straight Ally*, 19.

30. Abbie E. Goldberg, *Lesbian and Gay Parents and Their Children: Research on the Family Life Cycle* (Washington, D.C.: American Psychological Association, 2010), 86.

31. GLSEN, "Safe Space Kit: *Guide to Being an Ally to LGBT Students*," GLSEN, www.glsen.org/cgi-bin/iowa/all/library/record/1641.html (accessed August 28, 2012).

32. Jessica Carreras, "A 'Rainbow' of Possibilities, LGBT Symbols—What Are They? What Do They Mean? Does the Community Still Need Them?" *PrideSource*, June 4, 2009, www.pridesource.com/article.html?article=35356 (accessed October 1, 2012).

33. "How to Be a Strong Ally to People with Marginalized Identities," Unitarian Universalist Association of Congregations, www.uua.org/lgbtq/witness/26942.shtml (accessed April 1, 2012).

IT'S A SMALL WORLD AFTER ALL

....

The World

In 2012, the small west-central African country of Cameroon celebrated something it called Gay Hate Day. The same year, the southeast African country of Zimbabwe arrested forty-four members of the Zimbabwean organization Gays and Lesbians of Zimbabwe for being . . . gays and lesbians. And also in 2012, Russia tried to eliminate gay pride marches by making it illegal to direct "homosexual propaganda" toward minors. These are just a few countries that, as late as 2012, still blatantly disregarded the rights of large segments of their population.

But many things that are happening in the world regarding LGBTQ are positive and can be studied and copied in this country. Studies about the welfare of LGBTQ families in the Netherlands, for example, where same-sex marriage became legal in 2001, can be used in the United States in trying to accomplish the same thing. Swedish laws dictating that everybody has the right to change sex/gender can be emulated in this country (though there have been problems with that law that are currently being rectified).

Nonetheless, we should pay attention to the negative events in the world as well. Accomplishing change is easier when many people push for it, which is why we should support human rights organizations working for the welfare of LGBTQ families around the world.

If things seem to be happening at a breathtaking speed in areas of LGBTQ rights in this country, this is true for many other countries. The International Lesbian, Gay, Bisexual, Trans and Intersex Association (ILGA) writes on its website,

In recent years, many States [around the world] have made a determined effort to strengthen human rights protection in each of these [LGBTQ rights] areas. An array of new laws has been adopted—including laws banning discrimination, penalizing homophobic hate crimes, granting recognition of same-sex relationships, and making it easier for transgender individuals to obtain official documents that reflect their preferred gender. Training programmes have been developed for police, prison staff, teachers, social workers and other personnel, and anti-bullying initiatives have been implemented in many schools.

In the coming years, much more needs to be done to confront prejudice and protect LGBT people in all countries from violence and discrimination.[1]

In an effort to help guide countries around the world, the United Nations Human Rights Office in 2012 published an extensive booklet spelling out suggested guidelines for issues concerning LGBTQ. The five areas of concern in the booklet are (1) protecting individuals from homophobic and transphobic violence; (2) preventing torture and cruel, inhumane, and degrading treatment of LGBT persons; (3) decriminalizing homosexuality; (4) prohibiting discrimination based on sexual orientation and gender identity; and (5) respecting freedom of expression, association, and peaceful assembly.[2]

Trouble Spots

Obviously, not all countries around the world follow United Nations guidelines. In fact, even the countries that have made great strides toward LGBTQ equality have their dark spots. There are, however, some particularly difficult places around the globe for LGBTQ persons and families to live.

Madonna in Russia

While it is probably safe to say that most countries are moving toward greater equality for LGBTQ persons and families, others have taken huge steps in the other direction. In 2012 in Saint Petersburg, Russia's legislature passed a law making it illegal to direct homosexual propaganda toward minors. This, supposedly, was in reaction to gay-rights activists' demands for more rights. Suddenly, things like gay-rights demonstrations and gay pride parades were outlawed.[3]

Some years ago, Madonna was accused of giving a concert in Russia and not acknowledging the Russian government's blatant disregard for LGBTQ rights. In August of 2012, however, she once again gave a concert in Russia, in Saint Petersburg. This time Madonna loudly protested the new anti-LGBTQ law, drawing great ire from the Russian government and causing gay-rights opponents to sue

The United Nations makes guidelines regarding LGBTQ rights for all the countries of the world to follow, but it is not always easy to ensure that the guidelines are followed.

her. "Maybe someone does not see the link but after Madonna's concert maybe some boy becomes gay, some girl becomes lesbian, fewer children are born as a result and this big country cannot defend its borders—for me it causes moral suffering," said Alexei Kolotkov, one of the activists filing a suit against Madonna, in an interview in the British newspaper the *Guardian*.[4]

Igor Kochetkov, a Russian gay-rights activist, discussed the new Saint Petersburg law in a 2012 article in the *New York Times*. He called it absurd. "You can also adopt a law against turning off the light of the sun," he said, "but no one has the ability to do this. Even if someone wanted to, no amount of propaganda is going to turn a heterosexual gay." Russia had a law making same-sex relations punishable by prison until 1993.[5]

An American Pastor in Uganda

Uganda is another trouble spot for LGBTQ families. Its grim LGBTQ rights record seems to have been influenced by Christian American evangelists. Within the last couple of years, a truly frightening legal bill was proposed in Uganda, making homosexuality and certain sexual acts by homosexual men and women punishable by death. It turns out that this proposed bill was not only the work of Ugandans. Scott Lively, a pastor, the director for the conservative Christian California organization Abiding Truth Ministries, and an antigay activist, helped start what he calls a "pro-family" movement in Uganda. By *pro-family* Lively means: "We believe that the natural family was created by God to be the starting place and model for all human relationships. The natural family is one man and one woman and their children by birth or adoption, or the surviving remnant thereof. Marriage is God's institution to protect the natural family from forces such as promiscuity which would otherwise destroy it. To be pro-family is to actively promote and protect the natural family as the foundation of human society and culture."[6])

In an interview on *Current TV*, Lively said he *probably* does not approve of homosexuals in Uganda being executed, but he did take credit for being consulted in the drafting of the bill. In fact, he said he felt privileged to be a part of it. In an essay called "The Death Penalty in Uganda," on the Defend the Family website, he said he "urged [the Ugandans] to pattern their bill on some American laws regarding alcoholism and drug abuse." Lively himself claims that in an earlier, pre-Christian existence, he was happy to have been forced into treatment to stop drinking and driving. Lively views homosexuality the way he views alcohol and drug abuse—with the right kind of treatment it can be cured.[7]

In the same interview on *Current TV* Lively said that he believes that American and European gay activists have flooded Uganda. "If we [the anti-gay movement] don't do something, we will end up with a powerful gay movement basically overruling everybody else's values, forcing them . . . down everybody's throat." One of the things that Lively refers to when he says "doing something" is to write legislation that severely punishes homosexuals. But when, in the interview, he is confronted with the question of actually executing gays and lesbians, Lively squirms. After starting his sentence over a few times, he finally says that he would *rather* see the country take a nonpunitive approach and forcefully teach its young that marriage is the most important thing.[8]

Contrary to the logical conclusion of his statement about marriage, Lively was not suggesting that gays and lesbians be allowed to marry.

LGBTQ Ugandans have not sat idly, however, allowing a homophobic American evangelist to persuade their government to vilify them and put their lives and families in danger. A group of East African gay-rights advocates filed a lawsuit against Lively for "helping spread propaganda and violence against Uganda's gay people." The group wanted Lively's speeches in Uganda, condemning homosexuals as genocidal and pedophilic, to be deemed illegal for "violating international law and human rights."[9]

In November of 2012, the "Kill the Gays" bill was scheduled to pass as a "Christmas gift to the [Ugandan] population." In February 2013, it had been altered, and the death penalty removed, but homosexuality still carried a sentence of anything from five years to life in prison. It had yet to be voted on. A Pew Research Center survey from 2010 indicates that 89 percent of Ugandans oppose same-sex relationships.[10]

In addition, in the summer of 2012, a British theater producer, David Cecil, was imprisoned in Uganda (he was later released though put on trial, but let go, and in January of 2013 he was extradited to Great Britain) for putting on a play with a sympathetic gay protagonist. Yet, in the midst of threats against their community and under the very real possibility of getting arrested, Ugandan LGTBQ persons held their first gay pride parade in the summer of 2012 in the city of Entebbe. It was a festive and joyous event until Ugandan ethics and integrity minister Simon Lokodo, known for his anti-LGBTQ policies, sent in the police to crash the parade. Several people were arrested. But Ugandan LGBTQ activists vow not to give up. "This is who we are. We are here to stay. We are not going anywhere," one activist on site said.[11]

In a comment post to the *New York Times* online article "Gay and Proud in Uganda," melnathan wrote,

> The importance of this Pride event cannot be understated. The fact that these brave activists could pull this off in this milieu of persecution is a great victory for the community. Visibility like this notes the ongoing legacy of late activist David Kato, it defies the export of American Evangelical hate, and it helps ensure defeat of the Bahati Bill [the Ugandan bill discussed above that suggested executing people for being homosexual]. It shows leadership for all of Africa, and above all it shows that the LGBT people of Uganda simply refuse to give up their right to exist and to live their natural born sexual orientation.[12]

Cameroon—Just One Short Text Message

In 2011, a Cameroonian man, Roger Jean Claude Mbede, was arrested for sending a text message to another man saying, "I'm very much in love w/u." After he served a year and half in prison, where he was abused by fellow prisoners for his "perceived and unproven sexual orientation," an appellate court upheld his conviction and insisted that he serve the rest of his three-year sentence. In a 2012 article in the British newspaper the *Guardian*, a Human Rights Watch researcher, Neela Ghoshal, said this is not unusual in Cameroon. That same year "two men were convicted of homosexuality because of their 'effeminate' appearance and because they were drinking Bailey's Irish Cream, which was viewed as a drink favoured by gay men."[13] In 2011, more than twenty persons were arrested in

Cameroon for being gay. Section 347a of the Cameroonian Penal Code states: "Whoever has sexual relations with a person of the same sex shall be punished with imprisonment from six months to five years and with a fine ranging from 20,000 Francs CFA to 200,000 Francs CFA" (or 40 to 400 U.S. dollars).[14] A youth rally organized by an antigay group in Cameroon in 2012 said they were rallying to protect African values and that homosexuality is a "crime against humanity." The Catholic archbishop of Yaoundé stated that he believes homosexuality is opposed to the ideal of human reproduction and is a danger to the family unit, "an affront to the family, enemy of women and creation."[15]

Pan African ILGA members are deeply concerned about the lack of gay rights in Africa. "The lack of gay rights in Africa is becoming an increasing cause for concern among human rights groups. Cameroon's sodomy legislation contradicts international agreements that guarantee all citizens freedom from discrimination, the right to privacy, the right to freedom of association and assembly that the country is signatory to. These laws have been used to punish private sexual activity between consenting adults. Under these laws, law officials have also been known to harass and extort money from the LGBTI community."[16]

Asylum in the United States for LGBTQ Persons in Danger of Persecution

There is no doubt that there is a need for the United States and other countries to allow more LGBTQ refugees within its borders. In 2012 it became a little easier for LGBTQ persons persecuted in their own country to seek asylum in the United States, or rather, it became a little easier for immigration officials to recognize someone qualifying for asylum. U.S. Citizenship and Immigration Services issued *Guidance for Adjudicating Lesbian, Gay, Bisexual, Transgender and Intersex (LGBTI) Refugee and Asylum Claims.* The guidance is intended to make it easier for immigration officials to recognize LGBTQ persons at risk in order to, for example, learn to avoid stereotypes like "looking gay" (which sometimes is accompanied with the thought that if someone *doesn't* look gay, they can't be gay) or assumptions that someone who is or has been in a heterosexual marriage can't be LGBTQ.[17]

The new guide aims to teach immigration officers to ask asylum seekers the right questions in order to determine if they were indeed persecuted for being LGBTQ. It also discusses things like persecution and what it means. According to the guide, persecution can include violence, such as rape and other physical harm, but it can also be things like being forced into ex-gay therapy or an opposite-sex marriage. Immigration officers are also learning new ways to question asylum seekers to determine if they are at risk of being persecuted in the future (even if

> ## Not Only Christianity
>
> As mentioned before, Christianity is not the only religion whose teachings have been used to condemn LGBTQ persons and their families. Islam's Sharia Law dictates how to live as a Muslim. It forbids homosexuality, and in some Muslim countries such as Iran, Saudi Arabia, and Yemen, homosexuality is punishable by death.

they were never persecuted in the past). This might concern, for example, someone coming out who has not been out before or someone changing gender.

Florida-based attorney Grace Gomez, who works with LGBT asylum seekers to the United States, feels that the guide is a positive measure overall and one that places needed attention on the issue, but in an interview in the *Washington Blade* she emphasizes the fact that this is not a law, simply new guidelines and that it

> ## Countries with Legalized Same-Sex Marriage in 2012
>
> Argentina (2010)
>
> Belgium (2003, the second country in the world after the Netherlands to legalize same-sex marriage)
>
> Canada (2005)
>
> Denmark (2012, though it should be noted that Denmark began as early as 1989 allowing same-sex couples to have a "registered partnership," which provided many of the same rights as marriage)
>
> Iceland (2012)
>
> the Netherlands (2001, the first country in the world to legalize same-sex marriage)
>
> Norway (2009)
>
> Portugal (2010)
>
> South Africa (2006)
>
> Spain (2005)
>
> Sweden (2009)
>
> In addition, in Aruba, Curaçau, Israel, Mexico, Saint Maarten, and Uruguay, same-sex marriage is recognized but not performed.

hardly begins to address the needs of LGBTQ persons around the world. She said it is "a Band-Aid on a gushing wound."[18]

Only about 150 to 200 persons seek asylum in this country each year due to persecution for being LGBTQ. Due to the fact that many African and Middle Eastern countries known for persecuting LGBTQ persons are simply too far away, most asylum seekers come from nearby countries, such as Jamaica. Travel costs can be prohibitive, and it can also be difficult to get out of the country.

Role Models

France—Maman et Papa

As in the study comparing children with lesbian mothers in the Netherlands and the United States in chapter 2, many countries have come further than the United States in promoting rights for LGBTQ families.

In France, while that country had not yet in 2012 legalized same-sex marriage (it does have same-sex and heterosexual civil unions), a debate raged under then newly elected president François Hollande about doing away with the words *father* and *mother* on official documents, simply replacing them with *parents*. In an article in *Huffington Post*, France's justice minister Christiane Taubira was quoted as saying that the new French government was primarily preoccupied with the interest of the children, which is what made it review how it treats families.[19]

Tomboy, a French Slice-of-Life

In her 2011 movie *Tomboy*, French film director Céline Sciamma puts a lovely and very intimate face to a young person's gender exploration.[20]

Laure is eleven years old when she moves with her mom and dad and her six-year-old sister to a new suburb where she doesn't know anybody. Laure's attentive and loving family has always embraced her as the tomboy she is—she wears her hair short, loves to rough-house, and dresses like a boy—but they do not fully understand Laure's needs and longings.

When Laure meets some new would-be friends and they ask her name, she spontaneously tells them that her name is Michael. And that is that. In his new group of friends, Laure *is* Michael. Ingeniously, Michael constructs a penis from Play-Doh, works on a more "masculine" posture and voice, and eventually begins looking more and more like a boy. One of the girls in the group has a crush on Michael and kisses him.

But things get complicated, and despite the warm and generally accepting surroundings, the noose starts to tighten around Michael's neck. His friends come to the apartment and ring the doorbell, asking for Michael, causing stress and confusion. Only Michael's amazing little sister takes it all in stride and accepts without prejudice what is put before her. Then there is the sign-up for school, where Michael's friends can't find his name on any of the class lists.

In the end, it is Michael's otherwise loving mother who outs him and reveals his gender to his friends, or rather, the gender that has been determined for him, not the one he chose. Michael's mother is angry because she believes that Laure (as she still thinks of Michael) lied to her new friends (again, from the mother's point of view), but we also sense a strong fear in her knee-jerk anger when she realizes that she is facing something she doesn't understand, something that makes her deeply uncomfortable. As Laure's mother, she worries about the consequences for Laure of choosing a new gender, and she fears that Laure will not fit in.

In an interview in the Swedish newspaper *Dagens Nyheter*, *Tomboy* director Céline Sciamma says she believes that gender roles have gotten more prescribed, stricter, in the past years, not the other way around as one might assume.

"It's actually pretty strange," she said.

> While at the same time so much is moving forward in today's society, there are still things that are so incredibly much more reactionary than they used to be. When I grew up in the seventies it was not strange at all to have short hair. A lot of girls did. It was even fashionable. Today, the norm is for girls to have long, fluffy hair.
>
> When we tried to find girls for the movie, many of them thought it was a huge problem that they had to cut their hair to be in the movie. And when we, for example, tried to find blue or black clothes in girl sizes for the movie it was virtually impossible to find them in the stores.[21]

It is impossible to watch *Tomboy* without feeling compassion (and trepidation) for this strong child, and without desperately hoping that Laure/Michael will be allowed her/his explorations without being outed, ridiculed, or made into a victim.

Sweden—a Gender-Neutral Pronoun Debate

Though certainly not the first or the only in this category, a picture book with a genderless main character published in Sweden in 2012 stirred up some controversy, not only in Sweden but in this country as well.

The book *Kivi & Monsterhund* (*Kivi & Monster Dog*) was written by Jesper Lundqvist and illustrated by Bettina Johansson. In it, Kivi, a gender-neutral child, longs for a dog. When a dog appears—a large, smelly beast—Kivi adopts it. It is impossible to tell Kivi's gender from the pictures in the book, and throughout the story Kivi is referred to using the Swedish gender-neutral word *hen*, not the usual Swedish pronouns *hon* (she) or *han* (he). The word *hen* has existed in Sweden since at least 1966, perhaps longer, but despite many attempts to revive it over the years, it is rarely seen in media or heard in public. The gender-neutral language debate, while not new in Sweden (nor here), was revived by the publication of *Kivi*.

Swedish sociologist Elise Claeson weighed in on the gender-neutral language debate. She said in an interview in Dagens Nyheter that she believes that the gender-neutral word *hen* confuses children. It is normal and natural for little girls to go through a princess phase and for little boys to have their equivalent period (a period she does not specify) where children discover their very distinct sexuality, she said. According to Claeson, we are intended to be men and women and denying this, she says, curiously, makes the world less "romantic."[22]

The Swedish minister for equality, Nyamko Sabuni, however, welcomes the debate. "I respect those who want to test this new method," she said in an article in the Swedish newspaper *Svenska Dagbladet*. "I follow those who use this word and we hope it can be a fresh new way to achieve equality."[23]

Yet one must not assume that everybody who rejects the word *hen* is intolerant of gender identity issues or against gender equality, or that all proponents of gender equality embrace it. Ylva Johansson is the political equality spokesperson for the Swedish Social Democratic Party, a party with a strong history of being at the forefront of LGBTQ equality issues. As a rule, Johansson welcomes all attempts to break gender norms. "And I have nothing against the word 'hen' she said in an interview. But I want to warn against putting too much emphasis on one word. . . . What we need is legislation and political initiatives." Johansson does not use the word *hen* in her daily life, but she is not averse to using it. She just feels that it is important that people get to determine for themselves what they want to be called.[24]

While gender-neutral pronouns had already begun popping up around the world, the Swedish debate still caused quite a stir. Perhaps the time was right. In America the book about Kivi received attention in a number of print and online magazines, including the *Economist* and *The Week* magazine. The author himself,

Kaley's Family

Kaley, age twenty-one, grew up with two moms and a younger brother in the Southeast. She is a women, gender, and sexuality studies major at college. "I feel completely at home with my major," she said. "It's something that's natural to me. I have lived a lot of it."

Kaley's two moms adopted her from Peru when she was only six months old. They had an opportunity to talk to Kaley's birth mother through a translator, and Kaley has been told that she has her birth mother's dimple. Her birth mother would not tell them who Kaley's father was. And she said she wanted Kaley's moms to raise Kaley because she wanted her to have a better life than she could offer.

When Kaley and her moms returned from Peru and arrived at the airport in their home town, their entire Lutheran church was in the airport waiting for them with signs that said, "Welcome Home, Kaley." And that is the church that Kaley grew up in. "There were lots of little kids with two moms or dads," Kaley said. "It's a welcoming place and I feel completely at home. They have all watched me grow up. They are great people and a great community." In fact, the church is also very involved in social action issues and now houses homeless gay youth on its ground floor.

Even though Kaley comes from a supportive church, she has trouble with the part of religion that insists that marriage can only be between one man and one woman. She feels it is very difficult for people to come out when they live in an environment like that—as some of her friends do. She also finds it difficult to deal with the homophobia that comes from that. "It hurts when people are so hateful and angry. I don't understand why they hate us so much," she said.

Kaley considers herself lucky that she was sent to magnet schools growing up. She did not have to deal with any of the bullying issues in the public school system. Instead she went to art schools where having two moms was simply no biggie. Still, her moms practiced assertiveness with her. They would set up different scenarios for her and ask her what she would do in different situations. She also learned how to present the fact that she had two moms in a way that left little room for objection. Some kids were even envious and said they wished they had two moms, too. The truth was that Kaley was one of few people who still had two parents who were together. Many of her friends' parents were divorced.

Kaley remembers being annoyed by constantly getting the question about what she calls her two moms. And once a friend of hers looked at her moms and said, "You're her mom, and you're her mom, but who is the *real* mom?" One of Kaley's moms answered, "I'm real, pinch me."

Growing up with two moms, Kaley remembers feeling strange when she would visit a friend in a home with a very dominant male figure. Not because he was male but because her moms were so equal in how they did things. "Really heteronormative people still freak me out sometimes," Kaley said.

Kaley's family participated in pride events, and when they saw other families like theirs they referred to them as "family."

Now, as a young adult, Kaley considers herself radically queer, something she has come to little by little. "I'm not necessarily a moderate," she said, indicating her views on things like women's rights and social issues like housing for queer youth. Her college major and the queer conference at her school helped open her eyes, she said. As a camp counselor for COLAGE's Family Week, she adopted and embraced the term *queer spawn* for people like herself, children of queer parents. "I fell in love with it," she said. Kaley also fell in love with COLAGE, and when she finishes college she would love to work for a nonprofit like COLAGE. She wants to adopt children, maybe even siblings that are hard to find families for, knowing how really important it is to adopt children in need of families.

Maybe she will even be a teacher when she grows up, she said. Because she feels that what needs to change in society is public consciousness—"educating children is a part of that," she said. "And I love kids."[25]

Jesper Lundqvist, did not expect such strong emotions or such a rampant debate around his book. He wanted to write a book for *children* as opposed to for *boys* and *girls*, he said, and his main motivation was to get away from stereotypes. This, he said, is why he used the word *hen*. Like Ylva Johansson, however, Lundqvist does not believe that just one word can create equality. He also believes that people have misunderstood the debate. "Some people believe it is about eliminating he or

> ## Sweden–the Good and the Bad
>
> While Sweden has been groundbreaking in many areas of LGBTQ rights—it was, for example, the first country to allow people to officially change gender (1972)—it also has its dark history when it comes to treatment of LGBTQ persons. By the end of the 1970s, homosexual Swedes were, like those in many other countries, tired of having homosexuality classified as a mental disorder. Swedish author Fredrik Quistbergh wrote in a 2012 blog about how Swedish homosexual men and women organized a protest where they called in sick to work. When asked by their insurance providers what was wrong, they claimed "homosexuality." This got some attention, but it took a mass occupation of the main office of the National Board of Health and Welfare to really get Swedish politicians to listen and change the classification.[26]

she, but it's not like that," he said. "It's more about having another tool in your toolbox and being able to choose."[27]

On February 13, 2013, Swedish Minister for Integration and Gender Equality Maria Arnholm used the word *hen* in a parliamentary interpellation debate for the first time in Swedish (perhaps even world) history. She was replying to the question about what the government intended to do to give newly arrived asylum seekers access to adult education. Her reply was, "The goal is for every individual to receive the support *hen* [ze] needs in order to be able to learn Swedish as quickly as possible."[28]

The English language has a number of gender-neutral pronouns that people have tried for decades, rather unsuccessfully, to incorporate into mainstream language. The most common one is *ze*, which is used instead of he or she, and *hir*, which is used as the possessive for his or her.

Kaley, age twenty-one, said that she only recently discovered the need for LGBTQ families' involvement with the rest of the world. "In one of my first women's studies classes there was someone from Jamaica," she said. "We got to hear what it was like there [for LGBTQ persons] and how hard it is. Hearing that really opened my eyes to what it's like in other places. It changed my mind about the importance to know about people in other places. . . . It's important to understand what other people are going through."[29]

Indeed, there is much to learn from other countries, and there are many countries that need our support and help. Learning more about LGBTQ issues in other countries will help all of us.

Notes

1. International Lesbian, Gay, Bisexual, Trans and Intersex Association's (ILGA) website, www.ilga.org. Information about the United Nations human rights issues, http://www.ohchr.org/EN/NewsEvents/Pages/BornFreeAndEqual.aspx (accessed September 24, 2012).
2. (ILGA) website, www.ohchr.org/EN/NewsEvents/Pages/BornFreeAndEqual.aspx (accessed September 26, 2012). Information about the United Nations human rights issues.
3. Michael Schwirtz, "Anti-Gay Law Stirs Fears in Russia," *New York Times*, February 29, 2012, www.nytimes.com/2012/03/01/world/asia/anti-gay-law-stirs-fears-in-russia.html?_r=0 (accessed September 24, 2012).
4. Reuters, "Madonna Sued over Gay Rights Stance by Russian Campaigners," *Guardian*, August 17, 2012, http://www.guardian.co.uk/music/2012/aug/17/madonna-sued-gay-rights-russia (accessed September 24, 2012).
5. Schwirtz, "Anti-Gay Law Stirs Fears in Russia."
6. Scott Lively, "The Death Penalty in Uganda," Defend the Family, June 2, 2011, www.defendthefamily.com/pfrc/newsarchives.php?id=4480922 (accessed June 2, 2011).
7. Lively, "The Death Penalty in Uganda."
8. Marana Van Zeller, "Scott Lively, Father of Uganda's 'Pro-Family' Movement: VanGuard Extended Interview," *VanGuard, Current TV*, May 26, 2011, http://video.tvguide.com/Vanguard/Scott+Lively,+Father+of+Uganda%27s+--22Pro-Family--22+Movement--3a+Vanguard+Extended+Interview/5370099 (accessed September 14, 2012).
9. Bridget Murphy, "Scott Lively, U.S. Pastor, Wages Uganda Anti-Gay Effort, Lawsuit Alleges," *HuffPost Gay Voices* (blog), March 14, 2012, www.huffingtonpost.com/2012/03/14/scott-lively-us-pastor-anti-gay-uganda-_n_1345539.html (accessed September 14, 1012).
10. "Uganda to Officially Pass the 'Kill the Gays' Bill," ILGA, November 13, 2012, ilga.org/ilga/en/article/nODELBU1OA (accessed November 13, 2012), and Henry Wasswa, "Uganda's 'Kill the Gays' Bill Spreads Fear," Aljazeera, January 3, 2013, www.aljazeera.com/indepth/features/2013/01/2013121392698654.html (accessed February 22, 2013).
11. Alexis Okeowo, "Gay and Proud in Uganda," *New Yorker*, August 6, 2012, www.newyorker.com/online/blogs/newsdesk/2012/08/gay-and-proud-in-uganda.html#slide_ss_0=1 (accessed September 26, 2012).
12. melnathan, comment on article by Alexis Okeowo, "Gay and Proud in Uganda," www.newyorker.com/online/blogs/newsdesk/2012/08/gay-and-proud-in-uganda.html#slide_ss_0=1 (accessed September 26, 2012).
13. Associated Press in Douala,"Cameroon Jails 'Gay' Man for Texting 'I'm in Love with You' to Male Friend," *Guardian*, December 17, 2012, www.guardian.co.uk/world/2012/dec/17/cameroon-antigay-legislation-mbede-text (accessed February 23, 2013).
14. "State Sponsored Homophobia, a World Survey of Laws Prohibiting Same Sex Activity Between Consenting Adults," ILGA, May 2008, http://ilga.org/historic/Statehomophobia/ILGA_State_Sponsored_Homophobia_2008.pdf (accessed May 10, 2013).
15. "Pan Africa ILGA Calls for Cameroon Government to Cease Persecution of LGBT Persons," September 25, 2012, http://ilga.org/ilga/en/article/nK2g3Sj1jf (accessed September 26, 2012).
16. "Pan Africa ILGA Calls for Cameroon Government to Cease Persecution of LGBT Persons," ILGA, September 25, 2012, ilga.org/ilga/en/article/nK2g3Sj1jf (accessed September 26, 2012).

17. Paul Canning, "LGBT Asylum in US Just Got a Little Easier," Care2 Make a Difference, March 13, 2012, www.care2.com/causes/lgbt-asylum-in-us-just-got-a-little-easier.html (accessed September 28, 2012).
18. Chris Johnson, "U.S. Issues New Guidance for LGBT Asylum Claims," *Washington Blade*, January 26, 2012, www.washingtonblade.com/2012/01/26/u-s-issues-new-guidance-for-lgbt-asylum-claims/ (accessed September 28, 2012).
19. "France Proposes Banning Words 'Mother' and 'Father' as Part of Gay Marriage Legislation," *HuffPost Gay Voices* (blog), September 25, 2012, www.huffingtonpost.com/2012/09/25/france-mother-father-gay-parents-law-_n_1912606.html (accessed September 28, 2012).
20. Céline Sciamma, dir., *Tomboy* (Beverly Hills, Calif.: Dada Films, 2011).
21. Helena Lindblad, "Psykologisk lek med könsroller" (Psychological Games with Gender Roles, my translation), *Dagens Nyheter*, March 30, 2012, www.dn.se/kultur-noje/film-tv/psykologisk-lek-med-konsroller (accessed March 30, 2012). Section translated by me.
22. Katarina Lagerwall, "Kritiker: Hen gör barn förvirrade" ("Critique: *Hen* Confuses Children," my translation), *Dagens Nyheter*, February 14, 2012, www.dn.se/nyheter/sverige/kritiker-hen-gor-barn-forvirrade (accessed February 14, 2012).
23. Lova Olsson, "Ylva Johansson: Nytt ord skapar inte jämställdhet" ("New Word Does Not Create Gender Equality," my translation), *Svenska Dagbladet*, March 6, 2012, http://blog.svd.se/politikdirekt/2012/03/ylva-johansson-nytt-ord-skapar-inte-jamstalldhet/ (accessed November 13, 2012).
24. Olsson, "Ylva Johansson."
25. Kaley, Skype interview by author, October 30, 2012.
26. Fredrik Quistbergh, "Jag känner mig lite homosexuell idag" ("I Feel a Little Homosexual Today," my translation), www.quistbergh.se/view/514 (accessed June 27, 2012).
27. Adrianna Pavlica, "Så började debatten om hen" ("This Is How the *Hen* Debate Began," my translation), *Göteborgsposten*, February 29, 2012, www.gp.se/nyheter/sverige/1.874481-sa-borjade-debatten-om-hen (accessed November 13, 2012).
28. Lova Olsson, "Arnholm lanserar hen i riksdagen" ("Arnholm Introduces *Hen* in Parliament," my translation), *Svenska Dagbladet*, February 13, 2013, www.svd.se/nyheter/inrikes/arnholm-lanserar-hen-i-riksdagen_7911126.svd (accessed February 23, 2013).
29. Kaley, Skype interview by author.

CELEBRATING FAMILY AND COMMUNITY

··

Gay Pride—Parades and Celebrations

What is gay pride?
A parade?
A state of mind?
Pride in what?—Kivi Neimi, in an article in *LA Progressive*[1]

We all know that there is really no point in having a "Straight Pride" parade, so gay pride clearly has something to do with being a minority, about not being seen or heard. The LGBTQ community is split regarding Gay Pride and about what Gay Pride parades and celebrations should and should not convey about LGBTQ to the rest of the world. Some feel that Gay Pride should embrace and even showcase the wide array of sexual and gender expression that reflect its community, while others feel that the more atypical subgroups of LGBTQ, like drag queens for example, should be downplayed in order to not play into straight America's stereotypes of LGBTQ persons as "freaks."

In 2011 journalist Japhy Grant wrote about this issue in a comment on independent television network KCET's *SoCal Focus* blog. "From the outside looking in," he wrote,

> the [West Hollywood Pride] parade seems like a fun bacchanalia and celebration of sexual freedom; a perfect rite of late spring, but within the LGBT community, the arrival of Pride month, with its parades and parties, triggers arguments and hand-wringing.
>
> For many, gay pride is a bitter reminder of everything that is wrong with the gay community. All those mirrored speedos, feather eyelashes and pierced nipples, they would argue, are doing nothing to change the stereotypes straight America has of gays and lesbians. There's a sense, not

wholly unearned, that the crowds who come to West Hollywood's Pride Parade are coming to see the freaks. For a community exhausted of being marginalized, Pride becomes another thing they have to defend.[2]

Yet, this is just one view of Pride. While Thomas, age fourteen, does not often participate in Gay Pride celebrations, he has done it a few times, and he does feel that Pride parades and celebrations play an important role for LGBTQ families. "You're with your own kind," he said. "People that are open. I don't know how to explain it. It's a feeling of community. It makes you feel good."[3]

Despite beginning his article with some question marks, Grant believes this as well. LGBTQ persons have had to hide from the public eye for so long, he writes, and have been so marginalized and ostracized that cleaning up Pride parade, making it a more straight-friendly affair, would be a "slap in the face" of those who have come before and who have struggled for their rights to be who they are. Which is why Pride parade, Grant argues in the end, should embrace differences and not try to marginalize them, as LGBTQ persons have been marginalized throughout history.

"Something to keep in mind," Grant wrote, "next time you find yourself applauding a paper mache pirate ship filled with shirtless men wearing nothing but eyepatches and g-strings."[4]

Casey, age seventeen, loves Pride Parade. She believes it is an important way for LGBTQ people to come together. "We walk in Pride parade every year," she said. "We have a huge one [in our town]. It's really cool. It's a festival. It's Pride Week. They put up flags everywhere. It's enormous. One of the biggest in the country. The festival brings attention to LGBTQ issues. We get to feel that we're okay. . . . Everybody is happy to be with people they know are safe." And to Casey, Pride parade isn't just about the people actually marching *in* the parade. The parade is also really important for the effect it has on onlookers. "I think it helps people who are not directly involved or affected to see how important [being together] is to GLBT people. [LGBTQ rights] is not an issue you can ignore. It's ten percent of the people."[5]

Casey adds that there is a dark side of the parades as well: the people who show up and protest, holding signs telling her that her family is evil. It never fails to make her uncomfortable and sad. As unwelcome as it might be, however, Casey emphasizes that these people, too, have the right to voice their opinion.[6]

Huge, crowded events are not for everyone, however, and there certainly are other ways to affirm your family. To Zach Wahls, celebrating his family had little to do with waving banners and being with large groups of people. Growing up, he didn't participate in Pride festivals or parades. He was happiest at home with his family, he wrote in an e-mail interview. "I definitely felt the most secure when I was either at home, in church, or with the Boy Scouts. Seems like an odd trio, perhaps, for the son of a lesbian couple, but those are the places where I had both the most security and most friends."[7]

Positive Media—*HuffPost Gay Voices*

In August of 2012, *Huffington Post Gay Voices* introduced Family Friday on its website, inviting LGBTQ families to share family photos online. Family Friday was invented in response to a few online attacks on LGBTQ families the previous week, among them a tweet by American Family Association's Bryan Fischer, an outspoken proponent for antigay legislation, that went viral. Fischer referred to an essay by Robert Oscar Lopez, a self-identified bisexual man who grew up with a lesbian mother but who, as an adult, became an outspoken proponent for antigay legislation. Lopez wrote in his essay about the emotional distress that he says growing up with a lesbian mother caused him. Lopez's essay quickly became fodder for antigay legislation proponents who used it to argue that it is harmful for children to grow up with same-sex parents. Referring to Lopez's essay, Fischer tweeted, "Why we need an Underground Railroad to deliver innocent children from same-sex households."[8]

This tweet helped mobilize same-sex proponents. In launching its new venture, *HuffPost Gay Voices* writers stated, "Let's celebrate the beautiful and diverse kinds of families we have. In celebrating them, we're helping to reinforce what we already know: *Our families are legitimate and beautiful* [their emphasis.]" According to comments on *HuffPost Gay Voices*' homepage, it is obvious that this initiative is a welcome one among LGBTQ families. Comments vary from "I can't believe people honestly think those children care about the gender of their parents," and "Fabulous pictures, fun and loving families. How dare anyone claim otherwise," to "This is just AWESOME!!!," and "Very nice article HuffPo, let's keep some positive thoughts front and center! Beautiful families and everyone looks so happy."

We all want to see our families reflected around us and, especially for those who cannot take this for granted, an initiative like Family Friday is a positive and welcome celebration of all families.[9]

Literature

Another way to celebrate diverse families is through literature. *Rainbow Rumpus* is an important online resource providing stories for younger children with LGBTQ parents. Its teen initiative, *Rainbow Riot*, features nuanced literature for older teen readers. It also showcases art, poetry, and literature for and by its teen readers.

Jonathan and Patrick's Family

Jonathan, age fourteen, and Patrick, age seventeen, live with their two moms and their schnauzer-poodle pup, Max. Patrick is an avid reader and writer and is politically active. Jonathan loves music—he plays the French horn and the piano—and computers. During a year of homeschooling he dedicated a great deal of time to learning computer programming. Jonathan calls his parents Mom and Mama, while Patrick said, tongue-in-cheek, like a true teenager, that he often calls them both Mom, just to get a rise out of them. When they both answer he says, "No, other Mom."

The boys feel they live in an accepting community. Yes, people say things like, "That's so gay," Jonathan said. But he believes that "it's just a euphemism that actually has nothing to do with GLBT. The words are used but they are not used in a context. They are not really used toward people. It's just a saying."

While Jonathan follows political issues from a distance, mostly through his parents, Patrick is engaged in his high school Gay-Straight Alliance (GSA), which is very active. And at the time of our 2012 interview he was working on a project with OutFront Minnesota, an LGBT rights organization, to make schools safer for LGBTQ persons and their families. For his project, Patrick aimed to come up with a mathematical model to predict suicide in young persons, using variables such as socioeconomic status, racial demographics, religion, political affiliation, strength of conviction, number of people in the household, income, and poverty level.

Jonathan believes that conditions for LGBTQ families are improving, but like other Minnesotan LGBTQ families, he was concerned about the marriage amendment being voted on in the fall of 2012. (While same-sex marriage was still not legal in Minnesota after the 2012 election, the Minnesota marriage amendment was voted down in a historic popular rejection of attempts at prohibiting same-sex marriage.)

"Taxes are hell [for LGBTQ families]," Patrick said. He also referred to the 515 rights emphasized in Project 515 that are denied to LGBTQ persons in Minnesota (see the Resources section of this book for more information about OutFront Minnesota). "You can't get a [family] fishing license, you have no visitation rights in hospitals, you have no right to authorize an autopsy," he said, rights that other couples take for granted.

Jonathan likes to participate in events with other LGBTQ families such as walking in Pride/PFLAG (Parents, Families and Friends of Lesbians and Gays) parades. "It helps us meet people," he said. "And it's usually pretty fun." When he grows up, Jonathan wants to do something that involves computers and/or music—French horn, piano, and composing. Patrick wants to be a fiction writer.[10]

Rainbow Rumpus and *Rainbow Riot* do not preach to or patronize its readers. They simply portray a more diverse picture of family than what we tend to see in on- or off-line media.

Participating in Cultural Events

It wasn't until JamieAnn became a part of a theater production affirming gender nonconforming persons that she was able to fully accept some parts of herself, such as the body art that she acquired during some very difficult closeted years in her life. The theater put on a production of gender conversations of which JamieAnn was a part, and in order to set the stage, to meet their audience "naked," the participating actors stripped off all their clothes—well, almost all. JamieAnn found herself in front of the audience in her entire tattooed glory (body art covers her body from her neck to her calves). The actors were also asked to tell the audience what made them feel the most naked. JamieAnn's answer: being outed as a trans when she was not prepared for it, something that happens constantly, she said to her audience, almost every day.

Being a part of the theater production was affirming for JamieAnn in other ways as well. Once, her co-actors walked in while she was putting on her makeup but was not yet wearing her wig. By that time the wig had become an important identifier for her, something that "helps me move forward with confidence," she said. She explained, "It's not hair for me. It's something more. I never show up without my wig." But during the theater production, the other staff was suddenly all around her and when she, a bit flustered, commented on the fact that she was not wearing a wig, they had not even noticed, and dismissed it as something inconsequential. "You wear a wig?" they asked with a shrug. "You're just JamieAnn to us."[11]

> ## A Canadian Pageant
>
> In the spring of 2012, Jenna Talackova, a twenty-three-year-old Canadian woman, was disqualified from the Miss Universe Canada pageant for having been born male. Talackova, who knew from the age of four that she was definitely not Walter—the name she had been given at birth—but a girl, began her gender transition at fourteen and completed it at nineteen. Donald Trump, the pageant's co-owner, did not want to allow Talackova in the pageant, citing the fact that she was born male. Talackova's lawyer, Gloria Allred, eventually forced Trump to change the pageant rules and allow Talackova to participate. While Talackova did not win the contest, this was, Allred said, a civil rights victory. Talackova herself, while referring to what some people believe is the demeaning side of beauty pageants, said, "The power that you get for having the crown—you can inspire so many people. So if I have to walk in a bikini for that, I will."[12]

Church

Spiritual matters are very important to many people and families, and a church home can be a great place to celebrate family. Casey, age seventeen, and Zach Wahls both emphasized how much their accepting church home meant to them growing up and how important it was to feel that they had an accepting spiritual community. Casey talked about her moms participating in something called Freedom to Love, Freedom to Marry, which is a renewed partner commitment celebration at their church, when Casey was only ten years old. She remembers the event as meaningful and ceremonious. The newspaper was there and her family was on the front page. It became a validation and an important affirmation of her family.

Connecting through Symbols

Various social groups have their own symbols and special language often understood by no one outside the group. This is especially true for groups that, for one reason or another, need to stay under the radar. LGBTQ persons have a long history of rituals and symbols originally understood only by other LGBTQ persons and their families. Today, however, as more LGBTQ persons come out, the symbols are getting increasingly more mainstream, like the rainbow flag, something we all recognize as a bright symbol of coexistence.

CELEBRATING FAMILY AND COMMUNITY **175**

A Few Religious Institutions Known to Be Welcoming to LGBTQ Families

While many individual and unaffiliated religious institutions have minis-ters, priests, or other religious leaders and congregations that go out of their way to be welcoming to LGBTQ families, some denominations are better known for making it church policy to be welcoming to all persons and families. Following are a few examples, though the list is far from exhaustive:

Episcopalian Church (www.episcopalchurch.org)—Affiliated with the less liberal Anglican Church, the Episcopalian Church, with its more than two million members, became the largest congregation in the United States to bless same-sex unions in 2012. The new church resolution, called *The Witnessing and Blessing of a Lifelong Covenant*, nonetheless needs permission from the bishop of the parish each time it is used.[13]

The Evangelical Lutheran Church in America (ELCA) (www.elca.org)—In 2009, the ELCA Churchwide Assembly passed a policy that allows for gay clergy to be in committed same-sex relationships. The policy also allows for same-sex bless-ings and for same-sex marriage in states where it is legal. ELCA congregations that are publicly welcoming of believers of all sexual orientations and gender identities are called Reconciling in Christ congregations. ReconcilingWorks: Lutherans for Full Participation is an overarching group of Lutherans working toward full inclusion of LGBTQ persons.

Friends General Conference (www.quaker.org)—Quaker congregations tend to be very autonomous. While the more orthodox of its congregations condemn same-sex relations as sinful, it is probably safe to say that most Friends meetings in the United States today are not only welcoming but are great allies to LGBTQ persons. Some meetings perform same-sex weddings, although it varies widely.

Reform Judaism (www.reformjudaism.org)—According to its website, "The great contribution of Reform Judaism is that it has enabled the Jewish people to introduce innovation while preserving tradition, to embrace diversity while asserting commonality, to affirm beliefs without rejecting those who doubt, and to bring faith to sacred texts without sacrificing critical scholarship." In other words, Reform Judaism strongly emphasizes inclusivity: of women, of persons who want to convert to Judaism, and of LGBTQ persons.

Unitarian Universalist Association (UUA) (www.uua.org)—The Unitarian Universalist Church has supported and performed same-sex unions since 1984, and a number of its largest churches are led by LGBTQ persons. The UUA however, goes far beyond same-sex marriage in including LGBTQ persons and families. Its Welcoming Congregation Program (of which 64 percent of its churches in the United States and 97 percent of its churches in Canada are a part) works toward educating congregations in intentionally becoming welcoming and inclusive toward LGBTQ persons and families.

United Church of Christ (UCC) (www.ucc.org)—The church website declares, "We believe that all of the baptized 'belong body and soul to our Lord and Savior Jesus Christ.' No matter who—no matter what—no matter where we are on life's journey—*notwithstanding race, gender, sexual orientation, class or creed* [my emphasis]—we all belong to God and to one worldwide community of faith." The United Church of Christ voted for same-sex marriage equality in 2005.

The churches listed here have all developed written policies regarding inclusivity. As JamieAnn discovered when she tried to find a church home, having a welcoming congregation is not enough. Nor is it enough to have a written policy. Both need to be in place, and both need to be followed in order for all people to feel welcome in a congregation.

Jessica Carreras, a writer for *PrideSource*, discusses rituals and symbols of LGBTQ persons in recent history, such as men wearing a red tie or a green carnation to indicate to other gay men that they were gay. In the 1970s, Carreras wrote, the Ann Arbor Gay and Lesbian Federation would display the symbol of a butterfly to let people know they were having a picnic.

The rainbow flag—originally with eight bright stripes, now with six—can be seen everywhere from car bumpers to Pride parades and festivals. Carreras explains each stripe: "Red stands for life, orange is healing, yellow is the sun, green is nature, blue stands for harmony and purple the soul."[14]

LGBTQ activist Laura Sorensen, interviewed in Carreras's article, believes that today's LGBTQ persons and families have found new symbols and new ways to express and embrace who they are. "While youth have embraced popular

In recent history, someone might have worn a carnation to signal that he was gay.

symbols—especially the rainbow—almost to code themselves as gay or queer, I think that they're really doing it also through their fashion. They're finding really expressive ways, really stylized dressing and things like that that serve as a notice to other teenagers that they might find a friend or an ally."[15]

COLAGE—Again

In the movie *Family Time* on COLAGE's homepage, Stefan Lynch, one of the founders of COLAGE, talks about the incredible need for children with LGBTQ parents to find others like them, and how COLAGE came to be. "We had these stories that as soon as there was any kind of space for them just burst out of us," Lynch said in the movie.[16]

Hope Manley, another cofounder and the daughter of a gay father who died from AIDS, talks of the great relief of finding people she could be herself with. "The isolation, I think, that I was coming out of, and that other young people that had gay parents at that time were coming out of, I think it's almost hard to imagine anymore. But walking into that room with people who had the same family background and who had lived with the same secret, who understood, was, you know, it was monumental."[17]

Lynch said that coming out, being together, celebrating who they were—the children of gay, lesbian, or transgender parents—changed their lives and affirmed them. "This is a huge part of who we are in the world," he said. "This is the kind of energy and specialness that you only get once or twice in a lifetime."[18]

Beth Teper, a former director for COLAGE and also the daughter of LGBTQ parents, said that getting together with other COLAGErs "has given me pride in myself, my family, and my community."[19]

COLAGE is the only organization of its kind and a very important, perhaps the most important, resource for children with LGBTQ parents.

The Pendulum—Are Things Getting Better or Worse?

Like most other churches, the United Methodist Church struggles with LGBTQ issues. Even though the Methodist Church is generally known for being LGBTQ friendly, at its General Conference on May 2, 2012, the church reestablished that same-sex relationships are "incompatible with Christian teachings."[20] Cindy Hanson believes that when her father, a Methodist minister, came out in the 1960s, gay

Finding other teens with families like yours can feel like a great relief.

was not yet so much on the radar and the church probably did not have a policy in place for what to do with gay ministers. Her father even had his live-in boyfriend with him in the parsonage for a while. But after he broke the news to his congregation, he was moved to another church in the area, then apparently was offered yet another church in a small town in northern Wisconsin. At that point he quit the church altogether and became a counselor for troubled teens. So while Cindy's father was indeed treated poorly, he was not fired, and it appears as though the church administrators were more bewildered by the situation than anything.[21]

The example of Cindy's father illustrates the LGBTQ pendulum. Things don't necessarily progress in the direction we want them to, or rather, it sometimes feels like we move one step forward and two steps back.

Sarah Schulman, author of the book *Ties That Bind*, offers an interesting view on LGBTQ rights and history. While many see a pronounced advancement in LGBTQ issues today, Schulman makes a very strong case for why things are actually worse now than they were sixty years ago. It is very different, Schulman argues, to deny the rights of people you don't know and don't see. It was more theoretical then, more ignorant. It is very different, however, to look into the face of a gay person you know (and there are probably few people in the United States today who do not know a single person who identifies as LGBTQ), one who is out and who demands the same rights that everybody else has, and tell him or her "No" to his or her face.[22]

While Schulman believes that things are worse, not better, Casey, age seventeen, sees all kinds of signs of improvement for her family and for other LGBTQ persons around her. She believes it is definitely easier for LGBTQ families now than it was twenty or thirty years ago. For one thing, she said, the AIDS stigma is gone. "People are freaking out much less about that," she said. In addition, she believes it helps that there are a whole bunch of kids like herself, children of the gayby boom (which refers to the sudden and considerable increase in children with LGBTQ parents) growing up now. And a whole generation of gayby boomers behind her. The sheer numbers are bound to help, she says. She also feels that some politicians have gone so far in the antigay direction that they are exposing themselves, and people can see how crazy they are. Most of the people in her high school class know that Casey has two moms, she said, and most of them, though not all, are fine with it. When they watched a Rick Santorum speech in one of her classes and Santorum talked about LGBTQ persons in a negative manner, many of Casey's classmates were incensed. In many ways, by being with the same group of students since kindergarten, Casey feels that the students around her have been educated on LGBTQ issues just by her being there. She is, however, concerned for trans persons and believes that even in the LGBTQ community they might feel isolated. "We lump all these people together who are not in the same situation," she said. "But I feel like we should have each other's backs." Nonetheless,

Casey feels that things are going in the right direction—toward more acceptance of families like hers.[23]

Thomas, age fourteen, who grew up with two moms in the Midwest and is gay himself, feels much like Casey, though he expresses it perhaps a bit more harshly. "We just need to let some of the older generations die off and everything will come around," he said. "The social taboos are in the older generation. The majority of people my age either support [LGBTQ issues] or don't care enough to be against them. The country will come around in the next ten years and those who don't have the benefits now can take pride in being pioneers."[24]

Time

While all these ways of celebrating family—festivals, parades, spiritual and religious ceremonies, organizations, and media—can help make all families feel included, there is another important component to affirming your family: time!

JamieAnn, a TransWoman, brings up two important aspects of time, first the time spent together with family.[25] When JamieAnn first came out as trans, she was lucky to live close to her children and grandchildren. She could introduce her female self slowly to them. She could dress more and more like a woman, and her children and grandchildren could slowly get used to her until she could present (live in her new gender) full time.

While time together is important, it is the other kind of time, the one that has a lot to do with patience, that JamieAnn emphasizes for LGBTQ families. When she first came out, she knew it would take time before her family could fully accept her changes. "If I had expected to be immediately embraced, and for my family to show all kinds of love and affection . . . everything would have fallen on its face," she said.

Many children with gay and lesbian parents don't have to go through this process though, JamieAnn said. Many are born into their families and there is nothing strange about that whatsoever. But "this situation with trans is a pretty dramatic change that happens. . . . It doesn't always work smoothly," she said. And here is where that other aspect of time comes in—simply, the *passage* of time. JamieAnn tried to linger unobtrusively around her adult children and teenage grandchildren as much as she could, allowing them time to see the change in her, but she also allowed time to pass, time for her family to adjust. "I knew we were all going to be okay," she said, "when [the grandchildren] knew that JamieAnn would be at their house and they still brought friends home after school."

Now JamieAnn and her grandchildren advocate together for LGBTQ causes. All those things feel important, she said, but even more important is "the everyday stuff, the shared family experience." From spending time together, she said, "kids grow and become accepting."

"If things don't work right away [for your family]," JamieAnn said, "don't give up. If you're patient and set a good example, you'll all be alright."

Conclusion

While it is admirable to see both sides of a *political* issue, it is time to recognize LGBTQ rights as a *human rights* issue, and there really are no gray areas in this field—there is only right and wrong. In a democracy such as ours, LGBTQ persons and families must enjoy the same rights as other citizens and, until they do, we should all work toward this goal.

Notes

1. Kivi Neimi, "Gay Pride," *LA Progressive*, July 1, 2012, www.laprogressive.com/top-10 -stories-of-2011/#sthash.nEJQL08X.dpbs (accessed August 2012).
2. Japhy Grant, "What Exactly Is Gay Pride Anyway?" KCET, *SoCal Focus* (blog), May 31, 2011, www.kcet.org/updaily/socal_focus/commentary/what-exactly-is-gay-pride-anyway-33924 .html (accessed October 5, 2012).
3. Thomas, in-person interview by author, June 6, 2012.
4. Grant, "What Exactly Is Gay Pride Anyway?"
5. Casey, in-person interview by author, April 27, 2012.
6. Casey, in-person interview by author.
7. Zach Wahls, e-mail interview by author, September 12, 2012.
8. "Bryan Fischer Calls for 'Underground Railroad' Kidnapping to Save Gay Parents' Children," *HuffPost Gay Voices* (blog), August 8, 2012, www.huffingtonpost.com/2012/08/08/ bryan-fischer-underground-railroad-gay-parents-kidnapping-_n_1757378.html (accessed October 3, 2012).
9. "Introducing Gay Voices' Family Friday: Share and Celebrate Your Families with Us," *HuffPost Gay Voices* (blog), August 17, 2012, www.huffingtonpost.com/2012/08/17/ lgbtfamilies_n_1797740.html#slide=1394462 (accessed October 3, 2012).
10. Jonathan and Patrick, in-person interview by author, May 30, 2012.
11. JamieAnn, Skype interview by author, August 15, 2012.
12. Paula Newton, "Transgender Miss Universe Canada Contestant Falls Short of Title," *CNN Entertainment*, May 21, 2012, www.cnn.com/2012/05/19/showbiz/canada-miss-universe -transgender/index.html (accessed November 14, 2012).
13. Becky Bratu, "Episcopal Church Becomes Biggest US Church to Bless Gay Unions," *NBC News*, July 10, 2012, usnews.nbcnews.com/_news/2012/07/10/12666645-episcopal-church -becomes-biggest-us-church-to-bless-gay-unions?lite (accessed September 11, 2012).
14. Jessica Carreras, "A 'Rainbow' of Possibilities, LGBT Symbols—What Are They? What Do They Mean? Does the Community Still Need Them?" *PrideSource*, June 4, 2009, www.pride source.com/article.html?article=35356 (accessed October 3, 2012).
15. Carreras, "A 'Rainbow' of Possibilities."
16. Quoted in Jen Gilomen, dir., *Family Time* (Seattle, Wash.: COLAGE).
17. Quoted in Gilomen, *Family Time*.

18. Quoted in Gilomen, *Family Time.*
19. Quoted in Gilomen, *Family Time.*
20. "Methodists Vote to Keep Stand against Same-Sex Relationships," *USA Today*, May 3, 2012, usatoday30.usatoday.com/news/religion/story/2012-05-03/methodist-homosexuality-vote/54737970/1 (accessed June 26, 2012).
21. Cindy, telephone interview by author, May 23, 2012.
22. Sarah Schulman, *Ties That Bind: Familial Homophobia and Its Consequences* (New York: The New Press, 2009), 5.
23. Casey, in-person interview by author.
24. Thomas, in-person interview by author.
25. The rest of this section is based on JamieAnn, Skype interview by author, August 15, 2012.

Glossary: Words Matter

Ah, words. They can be so lovely, so poetic, so precise, and so . . . problematic. As I have mentioned in my introduction, as well as in the book, it is important to be sensitive to what people want to be called. The word that people choose for themselves is the word that should be used for that individual, none other. This glossary is an attempt at explaining proper usage of LGBTQ-related words, but keep in mind that it is an approximation at best.

Also, because of the nature of LGBTQ issues today, many of these terms have been or are currently used in a derogatory manner, which means that their usage changes constantly. As much as possible, we should stay alert to the LGBTQ community's own usage of the terms. It is essential for human interaction that we try to respect one another and avoid hurting each other. Words matter.

Ally (or **straight ally**)—person who supports and stands up for the rights of a minority group of which he or she is not a part

Altruist—someone who devotedly does things for others

Artificial insemination—see preferred term, donor insemination

Biological sex—the physical *package* you are born with based on hormones and physical attributes such as penis and vagina. It is estimated that 1.7 percent of all people are born with some of both male and female "attributes" and are thus not quite as easily separated on the gender scale as we tend to believe.

Biphobia—aversion to bisexual people

Bisexual—the sexual orientation of someone with sexual and emotional attractions toward males and females

Cis gender—where internal gender identity matches the one assigned a person at birth

Coming out—declaring a formerly hidden identity, such as being a gay man or a lesbian, transgender, or transsexual

Culturally queer—usually means someone who is heterosexual and cis gender but who feels closely aligned with the LGBTQ community

DOMA—Defense of Marriage Act; a 1996 U.S. Federal Court ruling defining marriage as an act between a man and a woman only

Donor insemination—the preferred term for the process in which a man's sperm is placed in a woman's vagina in order for her to get pregnant; children of

LBGTQ persons tend to prefer the term *donor insemination* (to *artificial insemination*) because it does not imply that they were born from an artificial process

Drag—can refer to drag king, when someone performs in masculine attire (often exaggerated), or drag queen, when someone performs in feminine attire (often exaggerated); drag does not refer to sexuality, sex, or gender

FTM—female-to-male transgender/transsexual person

Gay—male who is sexually and emotionally attracted to other men, also often used for any LGBTQ person

Gay couple—male same-sex couple

Gaybies—word sometimes used by children of LGBTQ parents to describe themselves (also queerspawn)

Gayby boom—increase in number of babies adopted by and born to LGBTQ parents after the AIDS crises in the 1980s

Gender—refers to where a person's inner identity as male or female fits on the male-female spectrum. In our gender binary system, it usually refers to the sex assigned a child on a birth certificate.

Gender binary—way of looking at the world in an either-or way, that is, someone is either male or female and there is nothing in between

Gender-neutral pronouns—pronouns that don't refer to a person as he or she, for example, *ze* for he or she, and *hir* for him or her

Gender nonconforming—the identity of a person who does not follow traditional gender roles

Genderqueer—refers to a person who rejects the traditional societal gender binary system and either makes up his or her own gender rules or rejects gender expectations altogether

GSA—Gay-Straight Alliance

Heteronormative—the belief that being heterosexual is the norm; *see also* heterosexism

Heterosexism—the belief that being heterosexual is the norm and superior to being gay, lesbian, or bisexual

Heterosexual (or **straight**)—a person attracted to persons of the opposite sex. While nonhomosexual persons are often referred to as "straight," there is a value judgment connected to this word. The opposite of "straight" is "crooked." Nonheterosexual persons are not crooked, which is why I prefer the word *heterosexual.*

Homophobia—irrational negative feelings toward homosexual persons, often aimed at all LGBTQ persons

Homosexual—someone who is emotionally and sexually attracted to members of the same sex

In the closet—hiding one's true identity for others, specifically hiding the fact that one is gay or lesbian

Lesbian—noun referring to a woman who feels same-sex attraction for other women; it can also be an adjective referring to same-sex attraction between women

LGB (or **GLB**), **LGBT**, **LGBTQ**, **LGBTQI**, **LGBTQIDK**—variations of ways to, as a group, refer to lesbian, gay, bisexual, transgender, and questioning/queer, intersex persons; sometimes IDK is added to the letter combination referring to I Don't Know

MTF—male-to-female transgender/transsexual person

Passing—refers to a transgender or transsexual person being perceived as the gender he or she identifies with, not the one on his or her original birth certificate

PFLAG—Parents, Families and Friends of Lesbians and Gays; a nonprofit support group for LGBTQ persons

PFOX—Parents and Friends of Ex-Gays and Gays; an organization that believes that you can leave unwanted same-sex attractions behind and be "not gay." PFOX is not to be confused with PFLAG (Parents, Families and Friends of Lesbians and Gays), an organization founded to support LGBTQ persons.

Pinkwashing—word that was presumably first used by breast cancer activists to refer to companies that act as though they care about breast cancer (by, for example, selling pink ribbon products) while promoting products that cause cancer. It is now often used to refer to conservative or even homophobic interests hijacking LGBTQ rights issues to further their own causes even though they have no intention of backing LGBTQ rights.

Present—verb referring to the gender someone is dressing to be

Queer—traditionally used to refer negatively to someone who does not follow gender or sexual orientation societal norms; now also used by LGBTQ communities in a positive way to embrace gender and sexual orientation nonconforming persons

Queerspawn—word sometimes used by children of LGBTQ parents to describe themselves (also gaybies)

Questioning—identity of someone who is unsure of his or her gender role and/or sexual orientation or whose gender and/or sexual orientation might be evolving

Transgender—wider term used to describe someone who transcends the gender roles we tend to assign people. Transgender does not imply sexual preference; it simply refers to gender identification.

Transphobia—the irrational antipathy or hatred toward transgender and transsexual persons

Transsexual (or **Transexual**)—refers to a person who identifies with the opposite sex from what he or she was identified as on his or her birth certificate. A transsexual person might identify simply as male or female and not consider him or herself a part of the LGBTQ spectrum.

Resources

It would be impossible to list all relevant and helpful organizations that already exist, and in addition, new resources spring up every day. What I have tried to do is list some resources that I found helpful while writing this book and that people I interviewed have told me about. It is my hope that after reading this book, you will want to start doing your own research. This list is intended as a springboard, a place to get you started on your journey. Organizations and resources that I find particularly helpful and/or enjoyable for children and young adults with LGBTQ parents have been starred.

Organizations and Websites

American Civil Liberties Union (ACLU), www.aclu.org, has the subtitle "Because Freedom Can't Protect Itself" on its website. The ACLU works toward fiercely protecting people's First Amendment rights, such as the freedom of speech, association, and assembly. It guards your right to equal protection under the law, your right to due process, and your right to privacy. All of these are rights constantly challenged for LGBTQ persons and their families.

**COLAGE, www.colage.org, is, according to its website "a national movement of children, youth, and adults with one or more lesbian, gay, bisexual, transgender and/or queer (LGBTQ) parent/s. We build community and work toward social justice through youth empowerment, leadership development, education, and advocacy." COLAGE was founded in 1990. It has more than forty chapters across the country and is a wonderful resource to check out with many activities for children of LGBTQ parents. It is, in fact, the only organization of its kind in this country.

Dear Abby, www.uexpress.com/dearabby/, has long been known as a friend to the LGBTQ community and LGBTQ-related causes. LGBTQ questions sent to her column are usually answered in an informed and intelligent manner.

Family Equality Council (formerly Family Pride), www.familyequality.org, works toward equality for families with LGBTQ heads of household, through policy changes and education, and provides community for LGBTQ families.

Gay and Lesbian Alliance against Defamation (GLAAD), www.glaad.org, uses media to bring LGBTQ stories to the forefront of American culture and attention to places in which media defames LGBTQ persons.

**Gay, Lesbian and Straight Education Network (GLSEN), www.glsen.org, "strives to assure that each member of every school community is valued and respected regardless of sexual orientation or gender identity/expression." GLSEN works to educate school administrators and staff on LGBTQ issues and help them develop curriculum that ensures the safety of all students. GLSEN also has an excellent book page, www.glsen.org/booklink, which features LGBTQ-related books.

**Gay-Straight Alliance (GSA), www.glsen.org, is an umbrella structure of individual clubs or organizations at local schools working to create a safe and welcoming atmosphere for all students, particularly those identifying as LGBTQ. GSAs are some of the fastest growing clubs in this country and can be found in all fifty states, though not yet, unfortunately, in all schools. The first GSA was started by a straight student wanting to show support for bullied LGBTQ students. You can register new GSAs on the GLSEN website, which also has great GSA resource materials.

Gender Education and Advocacy (GEA), www.gender.org, is a Georgia-based advocacy group for people who suffer from gender-based oppression. It educates on gender issues and showcases child custody court cases where a parent's changing his or her gender called into question his or her ability to be a good parent.

GLBTQ High School is just that, a (virtual high) school where you can enroll if you identify as GLBTQ. This school is a safe place for GLBTQ students and it also provides a GLBTQ community for students who may not feel they have that in their local high school.

Human Rights Campaign (HRC), www.hrc.org, works for LGBTQ equal rights, recognizing that these are essential for a fair society. It is the largest of all LGBTQ rights organizations in North America with more than a million members. Its logo, the yellow equal sign in a blue square, is often seen on car bumpers.

International Lesbian, Gay, Bisexual, Trans and Intersex Association (ILGA), www.ilga.org, is an overarching international organization working for LGBTQ rights that connects LGBTQ persons and their families with other families like them at an international level. In addition, it is an excellent resource for anyone who wants to find out what other countries are doing regarding particular LGBTQ issues.

Lambda Legal, www.lambdalegal.org, is, according to its website, "a national organization committed to achieving full recognition of the civil rights of lesbians, gay men, bisexuals, transgender people, and those with HIV through impact litigation, education and public policy work." In other words, Lambda is an organization working within the legal system for LGBTQ rights.

The Matthew Shepard Foundation: Embracing Diversity, www.matthewshepard .org, was founded by Matthew Shepard's parents in response to their son's brutal murder in 1998, a murder that brought to light the horrific hate crimes committed against LGBTQ youth around the country. The Matthew Shepard Foundation has become a safe community for LGBTQ youth, but also an organization that raises awareness of the struggles of LGBTQ youth in particular.

The Movement Advancement Project (MAP), www.lgbtmap.org, is an overarching organization focusing on research, insight, and analysis in mapping LGBT organizations, providing research and tools for activism and policy change.

National Center for Transgender Equality (NCTE), www.transequality.org, is a social justice organization with a mission to advance the rights of transgender persons. It alerts people to media outlets that are harmful to transgender persons, discusses political issues such as voter ID laws making it difficult for transgender persons to vote, and provides a safe, social-networking community for transgender persons and their allies.

National Gay and Lesbian Task Force, www.thetaskforce.org, calls itself "the uncompromising national voice for full LGBT equality" and works to eliminate inequality through grassroots lobbying and connecting communities.

Out and Equal Workplace Advocates, www.outandequal.org, works toward ending discrimination in the workplace for LGBTQ persons through education and outreach.

OutFront Minnesota, www.outfront.org, as the name indicates, is specific to Minnesota and works toward creating equality for LGBTQ families in Minnesota. Its resources, however, can be used by people in other states as well. OutFront Minnesota was one of the organizations that successfully worked to defeat the 2012 Marriage Amendment in Minnesota.

★★Parents, Families and Friends of Lesbians and Gays (PFLAG), www.pflag .org—or more correctly, a forerunner to this organization—was started by a disgruntled mother of a gay son in 1972 after her son was severely beaten in public and the police did not help him. PFLAG has widespread online presence where you can learn anything from how to influence politics in favor of LGBTQ issues to how to start your own PFLAG chapter. In addition to the COLAGE website, this is one of the most helpful sites to children with LGBTQ parents.

**Rainbow Rumpus (and its teen version, *Rainbow Riot*), www.rainbowrumpus .org, is an online magazine for children and young adults with LGBTQ parents. It empowers and affirms young people and their families with stories, poetry, and art. It is a great resource for fiction and art for LGBTQ families.

Southern Poverty Law Center (SPLC), www.splcenter.org, was founded by two civil rights lawyers in the 1970s. It is a not-for-profit organization "dedicated to fighting hate and bigotry" that I have come across many, many times during the writing of this book. It is the publisher of the free (to teachers) *Teaching Tolerance* magazine and works tirelessly for a healthier society by tracking hate groups and exposing their activities to the public.

TransParentcy, www.transparentcy.org, is a Portland, Oregon–based organization, founded in 2001, advocating for transgender parents. It provides great and varied resources—legal, emotional, academic, and much more—for transgender parents and their families.

**The Trevor Project, www.thetrevorproject.org, is a national organization focusing primarily on suicide prevention of LGBTQ youth. It operates a toll-free emergency number, staffed around the clock for youth in crises. The Trevor Project now hosts TrevorChat, Dear Trevor, and TrevorSpace, all means through which LGBTQ youth can find a safe online community. The Project's suicide prevention helpline number is (866) 488-7386.

Truth Wins Out (TWO), www.truthwinsout.org, works diligently to present the truth about homosexuality; that it is a "deeply personal identity" and not a deviant behavior. It believes that as long as people have the flawed beliefs that it is possible to change a homosexual into a heterosexual, they will not support LGBTQ issues. TWO uses undercover reporting to expose anti-LGBTQ organizations such as the ex-gay movement and Exodus International.

Movies

The Adventures of Priscilla, Queen of the Desert (1994) will feel dated to today's audience, perhaps a bit slow and even a bit stereotypical, but the story of the adventures of three drag queens[1] traveling across the Australian Outback in a rickety tour bus made history in its own way (in addition, it's pretty funny). It became known for portraying drag queens in a loving and positive way and was one of the first films of its kind.

Beautiful Boxer (2004) is based on a true story about a young boy growing up in a poor family in Thailand. He always felt like a girl, and at a young age began to realize that this is indeed what he wanted to be. Quite accidentally, however, he also learned that he was a gifted boxer, something that didn't work so well with his newfound knowledge about himself. He trained and got better and better at boxing but felt tortured that he couldn't just be the woman he needed to be. His mother supported him from the very beginning, both in his boxing and in his gender exploration; his father more hesitatingly. His close friends also accepted him for who he was, but he did, at times, get bullied for being different. Eventually, his two identities collided. He became a well-known kick boxer in Thailand and he began wearing makeup in the boxing ring. While still boxing, he began his transformation to becoming a woman. While a bit quirky, this movie is filled with love, passion, and compassion.

Beginners (2010) is a great movie about an adult son coming to terms with his father (1) dying and (2) coming out as gay.

Bullied (2010) is the story about Jamie Nabozny and his fight against bullies and the school district of Ashland, Wisconsin, which failed to protect him. The movie was sponsored and distributed by Teaching Tolerance, the Southern Poverty Law Center.

Chasing the Devil: Inside the Ex-Gay Movement (2012) is a documentary exposing the ex-gay movement, sad but very well done and well worth watching.

**Our House: A Very Real Documentary about Kids of Gay and Lesbian Parents* (2000), directed by Meema Spadola, has an intensely accurate subtitle; the movie feels very real indeed. These are not your TV families with lots of money, clean carpets, and resources; these are regular families, struggling with regular issues, giving a very naked portrait of what it can mean to grow up with LGBTQ parents.

The Perfect Family (2012) was directed by Ann Renton after a screenplay by Claire V. Riley and Paula Goldberg. While this movie does not concern children with LGBTQ parents but rather, parents of LGBTQ children, it is well worth watching. Kathleen Turner plays a distraught Catholic mother of a lesbian daughter, outraged that her daughter is not only lesbian but that she is getting married and is even having a child. Turner's character, Eileen Cleary, is torn between her Catholic faith/church, which she feels is behind everything good in her life, and, well, love.

Stonewall Uprising: The American Experience (2010) is an excellent and informative PBS documentary about the Stonewall uprising in 1969. You may watch it on line at www.pgs.org.

Tomboy (2011) is an incredibly moving film by French filmmaker Céline Sciamma, describing a young child's search for gender. The movie is so loaded with love, provided by the child's six-year-old sister, that we can handle the pain of the child trying to find her way in a world that is very hard on people who are seen as different.

Trevor (1994) is a short movie about a teenage boy who falls in love with a popular boy in his school. His crush is discovered and Trevor is humiliated. He decides to end his life, but his new self emerges and Trevor learns to find comfort in who he is becoming. *Trevor* is a sweet coming-of-age story.

Books and Pamphlets

Ball, Carlos A. *From the Closet to the Courtroom: Five LGBT Rights Lawsuits That Have Changed Our Nation* (Boston, Mass.: Beacon Press, 2010). This book goes into great detail about what the author believes to be the five most significant lawsuits in terms of changing the trend of LGBT rights in this country.

**Boylan, Jennifer Finney. *She's Not There: A Life in Two Genders* (New York: Random House, 2003). Of all the books on this list, this might be the most enjoyable and even educational read. Boylan writes movingly but with an enormous sense of humor and insight about her journey from man to woman. Already a well-published author, writing comes easily to Boylan, and she goes into great emotional depth about what her leaving one gender and entering another means to her and her family.

Curoe, Carol, and Curoe, Robert. *Are There Closets in Heaven? A Catholic Father and Lesbian Daughter Share Their Story* (Minneapolis, Minn.: Syren Book Company, 2007). This memoir is told in two voices by a lesbian woman and her father, both warmly Catholic, about the daughter's coming out as a lesbian. While the story is not written from the angle of a teenager in an LGBTQ family, it does discuss relevant issues: the repercussions of coming out on family, your work environment, and your friends, as well as the impact your church can have, for better and for worse. When she first came out, Curoe's family members, while loving and prepared to accept her the way she was, struggled immensely, partly because they felt the Catholic Church condemned homosexuals and partly because they were worried about the safety of their daughter and the reception the news would have in their small Iowa community. In short, almost all the issues were related to *What will they think?* Robert Curoe, Carol Curoe's father, grappled with his Catholic faith and tried hard to reconcile what he believed with who his daughter was.

★★Fakhrid-Deen, Tina, with COLAGE. *Let's Get This Straight: The Ultimate Handbook for Youth with LGBTQ Parents* (Berkeley, Calif.: Seal Press, 2010). This is one of the best books I've seen for youth with LGBTQ parents. Fakhrid-Deen, who is the daughter of a lesbian mother, wrote this book from her own experiences and those of teens she came across working for COLAGE and later as a high school teacher. Her incredibly thorough book talks about topics such as family structure, divorce, religion, school, bullying, our own internal homophobia, and much more.

Goldberg, Abbie. *Lesbian and Gay Parents and Their Children: Research on the Family Life Cycle* (Washington, D.C.: American Psychological Association, 2010). This is a densely researched academic book that considers all aspects of LGBTQ parenting, including particular issues that come with divorce, the times we live in, job loss, job gain, different ages of the children, socioeconomic background, and much more. It is not a quick, easy read, but it is thorough and interesting, and for those who wish to delve deeper, it is a great resource.

Green, Richard. *Sexual Science and the Law* (Cambridge, Mass.: Harvard University Press, 1992). While a bit dated in an area where things are happening with lightning speed, this book is nonetheless an interesting read regarding LGBTQ issues. Green, who taught law psychiatry and human sexuality at the UCLA law school and is a much-sought-after expert witness in court cases involving LGBTQ issues, very thoroughly describes subjects like transsexualism, early child custody cases involving LGBTQ parents, sex education, and much, much more.

★★Howey, Noelle, and Samuels, Ellen, eds. *Out of the Ordinary: Essays on Growing Up with Gay, Lesbian, and Transgender Parents* (New York: St. Martin's Press, 2000). Despite its publication date, this book is far from dated. These essays are written from the heart and with great introspection by the now adult children of LGBTQ parents.

★★Kokie, E. M. *Personal Effects* (Somerville, Mass.: Candlewick Press, 2012). While this young adult novel is very relevant to LGBTQ families (not the least in which it brilliantly illustrates the devastating effects that Don't Ask, Don't Tell had on military families), the romance, the teen angst, and the emotional roller coaster make it vastly more than an issue-driven novel. It is a young adult novel at its very best.

Oz, Amos. *How to Cure a Fanatic* (Princeton, N.J.: Princeton University Press, 2010). This tiny volume can be read in one sitting. Oz, an Israeli author and journalist, has tackled something as big as the Palestinian-Israeli conflict to show how fanaticism plays out in the world and how it can be overcome with hard work. In Sweden, the Order of the Teaspoon, an organization created to promote tolerance, was based on Oz's book *How to Cure a Fanatic*.

Schulman, Sarah. *Ties That Bind: Familial Homophobia and Its Consequences* (New York: The New Press, 2009). Schulman shows in her book how family and governmental oppression of LGBTQ persons influence LGBTQ families to oppress each other.

★★Wahls, Zach, with Littlefield, Bruce. *My Two Moms: Lessons of Love, Strength, and What Makes a Family* (New York: Gotham Books, 2012). One might suspect, in light of Wahls's testimony in Iowa in 2011, that his book would be fiercely steeped in the defense of gay marriage or his right to using the same label "family" as others, but it is not so. The fact that Wahls has two moms feels incidental in his book. Wahls is comfortably normalizing his strong family. While yes, of course, discussing his parents' marriage and the reaction of the world around him, he is very clear about one thing: he does not define himself as the son of a lesbian couple, or if he does, it comes far down on his list of characteristics. What has defined him more is his mother Terry's battle with multiple sclerosis when Wahls was in high school and the courage of both of his mothers facing this debilitating illness. Wahls is also an Eagle Scout and a devout Unitarian Universalist whose faith has been very influential to him and his family.

★★Winfield, Cynthia L. *Gender Identity: The Ultimate Teen Guide* (Lanham, Md.: Scarecrow Press, 2007). As the title indicates, Winfield's thorough and very accessible book discusses the many aspects of sex and gender. This book will help expand your worldview.

Note

1. Drag queens, of course, may or may not identify as transsexual or transgender.

Index

Abundant Life Bible Institute, 124
ACLU. *See* American Civil Liberties Union
activism, 61, 76, 135–36, 140–42, 148–49, 189
adopted, 15, 65, 164
AIDS, 60, 81, 99–100, 177, 179, 184
American Civil Liberties Union, 61, 187
American Family Association, 171
anger, 31–32, 87, 101, 131, 161
Anoka-Hennepin School District, 90–93
Arendt, Hannah, 57
artificial insemination. *See* donor insemination
Ashland School District, 92–93, 191

Bachmann, Michele, 1, 90, 125–26, 147
Ball, Carlos A., 14, 61, 64, 92, 192
Bible, 116–18, 125–26
binary: gender, 40–41, 54, 184; sexual, 24
biological sex, 39, 183
Bono, Chastity. *See* Bono, Chaz
Bono, Chaz, 99–100
bottom surgery. *See* genital reconstructive surgery
Boy Scouts, 20, 127, 130–32, 170
Boylan, Jennifer Finney, 29, 39, 43, 54, 192

Cameroon, 153, 157–58
Canfield-Lenfest, Monica, 11, 29, 40, 42, 46, 54
Catholic Church, 120, 148, 158, 191–93
Chick-fil-A, 129–30
cis gender, 54, 144, 183
civil rights, 64, 74, 91, 148, 174, 189–90
civil unions, 60–61, 160

closet/closeted, 3, 30, 33, 43, 60, 62, 100, 103, 173, 184
COLAGE, 11, 14–15, 40, 71, 75–76, 112–13, 135, 138, 164, 177–78, 187, 190, 193
coming out, 29–33, 43, 46, 50–53, 74, 84, 99–104, 110–11, 115, 120–21, 125, 135, 143–44, 148–49, 159, 163, 174, 177–78, 180, 183, 191–93
Congregational Church, 118
conversion therapy, 124
Cooper, Anderson, 99, 102–4
court cases, 14, 29, 35, 61, 64, 92–93
culturally queer, 183
Curoe, Carol and Robert, 27, 32, 120, 135, 148, 192–93

Day of Silence, 81, 109
Dear Abby, 107–8, 187
Defense of Marriage Act (DOMA), 59, 61–62, 127, 183
Diagnostic and Statistical Manual of Mental Disorders (DSM), 13
DOMA. *See* Defense of Marriage Act
domestic partnership, 26, 60–61
donor insemination, 71–72, 75, 77, 183–84
donor siblings, 75
Don't Ask, Don't Tell, 62, 65, 80, 129, 194
drag, 184; king, 184; queen, 100, 169, 184, 191, 194
DSM. See Diagnostic and Statistical Manual of Mental Disorders

egg donation, 69
ELCA. *See* Evangelical Lutheran Church in America

emergency, 96, 190
Episcopalian Church, 175
Evangelical Lutheran Church in America, 175
ex-gay, 13, 124–25, 158, 190–91
extended family, 27

Family Research Council, 61, 127
female-to-male (FTM), 42, 44, 184
first gay marriage, 62
fogging, 95
forms, 65, 77, 85, 150
FTM. *See* female-to-male

Gay, Lesbian and Straight Education Network, 80, 95, 149–51, 188
gay pride, 153–54, 157, 169, 170
gay rights, 14, 61, 93, 126, 136, 149, 154–56, 158
Gay-Straight Alliance, 81, 92, 106, 109, 148, 172, 184, 188
gayby boom, 179, 184
gender-neutral pronouns, 150, 162, 165, 184
gender nonconforming, 47, 49
gender privilege, 54
gender queer, 52–53
genital reconstructive surgery, 78. *See also* sexual reassignment surgery
Girl Scouts, 130–31
GLAAD, 108, 131, 188
Glee, 99, 101–2, 110
GLSEN. *See* Gay, Lesbian and Straight Education Network
Goldberg, Abbie E., 3, 10, 22, 24, 31, 35, 48, 79, 84, 95, 150, 193
Green, Richard, 21–22, 29, 35, 48, 193
GSA. *See* Gay-Straight Alliance

healthcare, 65, 80
hermaphrodite, 9
heterosexism, 184
homecoming, 150

homophobia, 12, 15, 23–24, 31, 86, 88, 92, 100, 102, 105, 108, 163, 184, 193–94
Human Rights Campaign, 81, 105, 188

identification card, 78
ILGA. *See* International Lesbian, Gay, Bisexual, Trans and Intersex Association
immigration, 136, 158
initialism, 3, 7, 9
International Lesbian, Gay, Bisexual, Trans and Intersex Association (ILGA), 153, 158
intersex, 9, 153, 158, 185, 188
It Gets Better, 96

Jamaica, 160, 165

Ku Klux Klan Act, 93
*Kung*älv Model, 94

Lambda Legal, 81, 93, 189
lie/lying, 5, 13, 17
Lively, Scott, 117, 156

male-to-female (MTF), 44–45, 130–31, 185
Manford, Jeanne, 12, 80
Manford, Morty, 12
marriage: amendment, 53, 172, 189; ban, 126; license, 59, 62
Modern Family, 99, 101
Mormon Church, 115, 120
MTF. *See* male-to-female

Nabozny, James, 14, 92–93, 191
National Gay and Lesbian Task Force, 10, 47, 189
National Organization for Marriage, 14, 15
National School Climate Survey, 86
the Netherlands, 23–25, 67, 84, 110, 153, 159–60

Olweus Bullying Prevention Program, 85, 90, 94
omnisexual, 8
ovum donation, 69

pageant, 174
pansexual, 8, 51
Parents, Families and Friends of Lesbians and Gays (PFLAG), 12, 80, 107–8, 142, 146, 148–49, 173, 185, 189–90
persecution, 129, 157–60
PFLAG. *See* Parents, Families and Friends of Lesbians and Gays
polysexual, 8
presenting, 50, 52, 143, 180, 185
Project 515, 172
public restrooms, 78

Quaker, 175
queer, vii, 8–9, 11, 15, 52–53, 76, 81, 95, 151, 164
queerspawn/queer spawn, 9, 76, 164, 184–85
questioning, 8–9, 11, 185

Rainbow Riot, 106, 171, 173, 190
Rainbow Rumpus, 104–6, 171, 173, 190
Reform Judaism, 175–76
reparative therapy, 13
repression, 88–89
reproduction, 4, 17, 158
Russia, 153–55

safe room stickers, 109
Schulman, Sarah, 69–70, 102, 179, 194
secret/secrets, 30–31, 88, 178
sex-positive approach, 75
sexual identity, 9, 15, 24, 42, 51, 125
sexual reassignment surgery, 45
sound bite, 138–39
South Park, 108
sperm bank, 71–72, 75

sperm donor, 4, 6, 20, 30, 34, 70–75, 77, 111–12; anonymous, 71, 73, 75; known, 72; open identity, 72, 77
Spitzer, Dr. Robert, 12–13
stereotypes, 22, 100–102, 110, 143, 149, 158, 164, 169
stigma, 21, 23, 36, 179
Stonewall, 12–13, 109, 192
straight ally, vii, 94, 107–8, 126, 146–51, 175, 177, 183, 189
Sweden, 94, 110, 159, 162, 165, 194
symbols, 9, 95, 174, 176–77

Title IX, 80, 142
trans woman, 11, 29, 40, 143
transgender, vii, 3, 8–11, 15, 17, 21, 24, 29, 32, 39–40, 43, 46–49, 78–81, 104, 130–31, 141, 143, 154, 158, 178, 183–85, 187, 189–90, 193–94
transphobia, 15, 86, 105, 185
transsexual, vii, 8, 10, 17, 21, 29–30, 39, 42, 44, 46, 48, 84, 99–100, 143, 183–85, 193–94
Trevor Project, 96, 190
turkey baster, 70, 76

Uganda, 117, 155–56
Unitarian Universalist Association, 11, 89, 115, 151, 176, 194
United Church of Christ, 176
United Methodist Church, 121–22, 178
United Nations, 154–55

Wahls, Zach, 11, 19, 30, 33–34, 57–59, 90, 95, 115, 127, 131–32, 140, 142, 170, 174, 194
wig, 52–53, 107, 173
Williams Institute, 17, 67

ze, 165, 184
Zimbabwe, 153

About the Author

Eva Apelqvist is a fulltime freelance writer, translator, and author of *Swede Dreams* (2007) and *Getting Ready to Drive* (2011) for children and young adults. She grew up in Sweden and emigrated to America in her mid-twenties.